MASTERING SOFTWARE QUALITY ASSURANCE

Best Practices, Tools and Techniques for Software Developers

MURALI CHEMUTURI

Copyright © 2011 by Murali Chemuturi

ISBN 978-1-60427-032-7

Printed and bound in the U.S.A. Printed on acid-free paper
10 9 8 7 6 5 4 3 2 1

Library of Congress Cataloging-in-Publication Data

Chemuturi, Murali, 1950-
    Mastering software quality assurance : best practices, tools and techniques for
software developers / by Murali Chemuturi.
        p.   cm.
    Includes index.
    ISBN 978-1-60427-032-7 (hardcover : alk. paper)
    1. Computer software—Development. I. Title.
    QA76.76.Q35C45 2010
    005.1′4—dc22   2010019184

Direct all inquiries to J. Ross Publishing, Inc., 5765 N. Andrews Way, Fort Lauderdale,
Florida 33309.

Phone: (954) 727-9333
Fax: (561) 892-0700
Web: www.jrosspub.com

TABLE OF CONTENTS

FOREWORD

 As I sit surrounded by the majestic forests and glacial lakes in the North American state of Maine, I am reminded of how the laws of nature, planet Earth's natural processes, have carefully constructed, nurtured, and sustained this stunning example of natural engineering and process implementation.

Strict compliance with this natural process, rather than process experimentation and improvisation, has allowed these forests to grow and thrive unencumbered by the special cause of variation from destructive forces. Indeed, the natural world has suffered from attempts to circumvent this process with disastrous results, and when left to recover does so with alarming alacrity and efficiency. There is much to be learned from this natural process that can be applied to the software engineering discipline.

Granted, software engineering does not have the luxury of unlimited time and resources, and business will not wait eons for change to occur. But the application of and compliance with a basic process architecture—which includes at its foundation software quality assurance—is the key to wringing value from engineering process improvement.

A thoughtfully constructed architecture with software quality assurance serving the foundational role of mentor, messenger, and accelerator will lay a foundation for flexibility in a process designed to serve and support a wide variety of projects with different objectives. In this sense, we require a "set of standard processes," not a single standard process, that comply with our process architecture and are supported by a robust and flexible software quality assurance organization.

Like a great concert violinist who spends years embracing and developing the discipline and mechanics of his or her craft before learning his or her first concerto and venturing onto the concert stage, software engineers cannot achieve creative success without embracing an appropriate process architecture and learning to master their craft by first mastering the natural laws that guide them.

Too long has software engineering been hampered by cowboy-style coding—a behavior that appears heroic at the time, but that proves to be damaging in so many ways in the long run. It's high time someone wrote at length about the role of software quality assurance and process compliance in the software engineering field. Murali's book breaks new ground and gives us a glimpse into the promise of disciplined, productive, and efficient software engineering. It paints a picture of a brighter future for an industry that has long been suffering from cost and quality issues and will allow software engineers to reach new levels of performance and creativity.

Jeff Dalton
President and CEO, Broadsword Solutions Corporation
www.broadswordsolutions.com
SCAMPI Lead Appraiser
www.askTheCMMIAppraiser.com

PREFACE

Gerald M. Weinberg, author of the book *The Psychology of Computer Programming*, is attributed with the quote "If builders built houses the way programmers built programs, the first woodpecker to come along would destroy civilization." According to an anonymous quote, "Software and cathedrals are much the same; first we build them, then we pray." And the confidence in software developers continues to grow.

If manufacturers controlled and assured quality the way software developers do, I think many accidents and injuries, even fatalities, would be the sad result. Many, many improvements have been made in the way programs are written, but even after nearly 50 years of software development history, the approach to software quality still leaves much to be desired. While manufacturing learned from construction and construction in turn learned from manufacturing, software development stubbornly refuses to learn from either industry, especially in the matter of quality assurance of deliverables.

At the beginning of my career in the 1970s, I was employed at a manufacturing organization that produced control instrumentation for atomic reactors. In that organization, quality was sacrosanct and very rigorous. The result of such high standards of quality is that in a third-world country (as it was in the 1970s, when the reactors were built), the atomic reactors have been working without accident or mishap for the last 40 years! I attribute that record to the importance that was given to quality assurance. I narrate but one incident from that experience: On the last day of the fiscal year, the quality department held up a shipment that would have added significantly to the financial results, as it found a "tiny scratch" on the painted surface of the back side of one piece of the equipment. Even though the scratched surface would have been facing a wall, rectification was insisted upon, and the shipment was released late in the evening only after the "tiny scratch" was fixed. The paint shop guys worked furiously to repair that insignificant defect. The boss did not berate the quality department for pointing out an insignificant defect, but rather educated the handlers on the necessity of careful handling.

Contrast this with the software industry, where important software such as an operating system is shipped with so many bugs that it needs a service pack within three months of its release to make it function and another service pack a year later to fix the remaining bugs. Windows 2000 had four service packs, XP had three service packs, and a service pack for Vista has already been released. I have come across a few situations where software is delivered with known defects to be corrected as part of warranty services or product support.

When I switched over to the software development industry in the early 1980s, my first surprise was that there was no inspection or testing of the programs developed. The programmer certified the program, and if there were any issues with it, they were due to improper data or usage. The programmer would make the program better, if and when necessary. Never was it said that perhaps the program lacked quality, nor did anybody accept that inferior quality was a possibility.

Things did change later on. Peer reviews and testing emerged as standard procedure, followed soon after by independent verification and validation. But even now, I do not find the rigor of software quality assurance to be anywhere near the rigor of quality assurance that I was used to in the manufacturing industry where I was employed in the early 1970s. Most people in the software development industry abhor the terms "inspection" and "testing" and use verification and validation instead. Whereas inspection and testing imply detail and have a ring of authority to them, verification and validation somehow connote cursory actions that lack any true authority. In manufacturing, inspection is carried out by persons specialized in inspection, and testing is carried out by persons specialized in testing. In the software industry, however, the "independent" in independent verification and validation means someone other than the person who programmed the software; it does not mean a specialist.

In manufacturing, there are no agencies that certify the maturity of capability, such as the Software Engineering Institute (SEI) of Carnegie Mellon University, except for the International Organization for Standardization (ISO), which certifies for process quality. While automobiles have been manufactured for over 100 years, an automobile manufacturing capability maturity model does not exist! A quality department is *sine qua non* in the manufacturing industry even though no certification model requires it. In the software development industry, however, no model suggests that a quality department is necessary.

I know of many software development organizations that do not have a quality assurance department. Most of these organizations are ISO certified and rated at a Capability Maturity Model or Capability Maturity Model Integration maturity level 3 or higher by SEI. The software development industry seems to understand that quality assurance is nothing but testing. You can find many advertisements seeking applications for the position of quality assurance engineer—to do software testing. How this misunderstanding came about, I do not know, but nothing could be more wrong than this misconception.

There is a lot of room for improvement in quality assurance in the software development industry, and a comprehensive reference on quality assurance is needed that ties together all aspects of quality assurance, not as the software development industry does but in its true spirit. Hence this book.

Feel free to e-mail me at murali@chemuturi.com with your thoughts, questions, or criticisms. I will respond to all e-mails. I look forward to hearing your feedback.

Murali Chemuturi

ABOUT THE AUTHOR

 **Murali Chemuturi** is an information technology and software development subject matter expert, hands-on programmer, author, consultant, and trainer. In 2001, he formed Chemuturi Consultants, an information technology consulting and software development firm that helps software development organizations achieve their quality and value objectives. The firm provides training in several software engineering and project management areas such as software estimation, test effort estimation, function point analysis, and software project management, to name a few. The firm also offers a number of products to aid project managers and software development professionals, such as PMPal, a software project management tool, and EstimatorPal, FPAPal, and UCPPal, a set of software estimation tools.

Mr. Chemuturi has over 15 years of industrial experience in various engineering and manufacturing management positions, as well as more than 23 years of information technology and software development experience. His most recent position prior to forming his own firm was Vice President of Software Development at Vistaar e-Business Pvt., Ltd.

Mr. Chemuturi's undergraduate degrees and diplomas are in electrical and industrial engineering and he holds an MBA and a postgraduate diploma in computer methods and programming. He has several years of academic experience teaching a variety of computer and information technology courses such as COBOL, Fortran, BASIC, computer architecture, and database management systems.

In addition to being a widely published author in professional journals, Mr. Chemuturi is a member of the Institute of Electrical and Electronics Engineers, a senior member of the Computer Society of India, and a Fellow of the Indian Institute of Industrial Engineering

ACKNOWLEDGMENTS

When I look back, I find that there are so many people to whom I should be grateful. Be it because of their commissions or omissions, they made me a stronger and a better person and both directly and indirectly helped to make this book possible. It would be difficult to acknowledge everyone's contributions here, so to those whose names may not appear, I wish to thank you all just the same. I will have failed in my duty if I did not explicitly and gratefully acknowledge the following persons:

★ My parents, Appa Rao and Vijaya Lakshmi, the reason for my very existence. Especially my father, a rustic agrarian, who by personal example taught me the virtue of hard work and how sweet the aroma of sweat from the brow can be.

★ My family, who stood by me like a rock in difficult times. Especially my wife, Udaya Sundari, who gave me the confidence and the belief that "I can." And my two sons, Dr. Nagendra and Vijay, who provided me the motive to excel.

★ My two uncles, Raju and Ramana, who by personal example taught me what integrity and excellence mean.

★ Drew Gierman, Publisher & Vice President of Sales at J. Ross Publishing, especially for his belief in the content of this book, for his generous allocation of time, and for leading me by the hand through every step of making this book a reality.

★ Steve Buda, Sandy Pearlman, and the staff of J. Ross Publishing, all of whom were involved in bringing this book to the public.

★ Ms. Sandra Rychel of Montreal, Canada, who pored over every word of this book to ensure that each is the right one. But for her editing genius, this book would not have been as readable as it is now.

To all of you, I humbly bow my head in respect and salute you in acknowledgment of your contribution.

Murali Chemuturi

*Free value-added materials available from
the Download Resource Center at www.jrosspub.com*

At J. Ross Publishing we are committed to providing today's professional with practical, hands-on tools that enhance the learning experience and give readers an opportunity to apply what they have learned. That is why we offer free ancillary materials available for download on this book and all participating Web Added Value™ publications. These online resources may include interactive versions of material that appears in the book or supplemental templates, worksheets, models, plans, case studies, proposals, spreadsheets and assessment tools, among other things. Whenever you see the WAV™ symbol in any of our publications, it means bonus materials accompany the book and are available from the Web Added Value Download Resource Center at www.jrosspub.com.

Downloads available for *Mastering Software Quality Assurance: Best Practices, Tools and Techniques for Software Developers* consist of a comprehensive tool for assistance in software testing (TestPal), a tool for increasing personal effectiveness (PET), and templates illustrated within the text that are adaptable to your own needs.

QUALITY ASSURANCE BASICS

CONNOTATIONS OF THE WORD *QUALITY*

We often see the word *quality* used as a stand-alone term, without any adjectives attached to it. People do not normally use the term *good quality* to express their satisfaction with the products or services they use. To say that a certain product is a *quality product* implies that the product is of good quality. On the other hand, people certainly use the term *bad quality* to express their dissatisfaction with the products or services they use. Therefore, the adjective *good* is implicitly attached to the word *quality* in the minds of most people. Thus, the word *quality* connotes *good quality* to most people, including technical professionals.

Before attempting a more elaborate definition of quality, let us consider the various connotations the word invokes, as it means different things in different sections of society:

★ For a customer or end user of a product, quality connotes defect-free functioning, reliability, ease of use, acceptable levels of fault tolerance during use, and safety from injury to people or property.

★ For a customer or end user of a service, quality connotes reliability of performance, ease of obtaining service, expert service, pleasant service, and protection from consequential damage.

★ For a producer of goods, quality connotes conformance of the product to specifications, which may be defined by a government body, an industry association or standards body, or by the producer's own organization.

★ For a provider of services, quality connotes meeting deadlines and delivery of service that conforms to customer specifications and standards which may have been set by a government body, an industry association or standards body, or by the provider's own organization.

★ For government bodies, quality connotes safety and protection of consumers from fraud.

★ For an industry association or standards body, quality connotes safeguarding the industry's reputation, protecting the industry from fraud and lawsuits, and addressing the concerns of consumers, government bodies, and the industry itself.

Given the above distinctions in the meaning of quality, it is clear that the word has multiple connotations attached to it.

WHAT IS QUALITY?

Before proceeding further, we first need to define the word *quality* in a manner that addresses all the connotations noted above. The International Organization for Standardization (ISO 9000, second edition, 2000) defines quality as the degree to which a set of inherent characteristics fulfills requirements. Quality can be used with such adjectives as poor, good, or excellent. *Inherent*, as opposed to *assigned*, means existing inside something, as a permanent characteristic.

This definition contains three key terms: requirements, characteristics, and degree. *Requirements* can be stated by a customer in a made-to-order scenario or by product specifications in a commercial off-the-shelf product scenario. *Characteristics* refers to the capability of the deliverable or, in other words, the robustness (fitness) of the product. The word *degree* implies that quality is a continuum, beginning with zero and moving toward, perhaps, infinity. This inference, however, is ambiguous and leads to the wrong perception. What is the level at which quality is called "poor" or "good" or "excellent"? More importantly, who is authorized to define the terms "poor," "good," and "excellent"?

Another popular definition of quality, as defined by Joseph Moses Juran, is *fitness for use,* with *fitness* and *use* being crucial to proper understanding of quality. Unless we define these two key words, the definition of quality is incomplete. Consumer interpretations and provider interpretations of these two terms often are at loggerheads.

SPECIFICATIONS

Because *fitness* and *use* are crucial terms, they cannot be left open to interpretation. Organizations often define these two terms in their specifications for a product or service they provide. Let us look closely at the attributes of specifications:

★ Specifications may be explicit or implicit. *Explicit* means that the provider selects the specifications and makes them available to customers. *Implicit* means that the specifications are not defined but are understood to be necessary; examples include safety, security, and fault tolerance requirements.
★ Specifications may be defined by either the provider or an external body, such as a government organization, an industry association, or a standards body. They are made available to customers, and they are adhered to by the provider.

Oftentimes, providers resort to unethical definitions of specifications and provide services or products that can be detrimental to customers and perhaps to the industry. This has resulted in industry organizations coming together to form associations, such as manufacturers associations and service provider associations, which define specifications for their particular industry's products or services. Governments also step in and form standards bodies, which define specifications for various products and services. Defense departments of various countries often define specifications for the diverse range of products to be used by their armed forces. These specifications stipulate a minimum set of standards to be adhered to by providers of products or services, so that fitness for use is defined and ensured.

Such formally defined specifications become *industry standards* and are released by industry associations to the general public for a nominal fee that covers the cost of production and distribution of these standards. Examples of bodies that release standards on a regular basis include the American National Standards Institute, British Standards Institute, Joint Services Specifications, Deutsches Institut für Normung, ISO, International Electrotechnical Commission, International Telecommunications Union, National Electrical Manufacturers Association, and Institute of Electrical and Electronics Engineers. In recognition of their contributions to quality and general consumer well-being, a day has been set aside every year to celebrate such organizations: World Standards Day is October 14.

Standards specify, at a minimum, the following:

1. Attributes of the components that make up a product, which may include the material used and the dimensions and methods of testing the product
2. The intended use of the product or service
3. The limitations of the product that need to be conveyed to customers
4. The process by which the components are made
5. The security and safety parameters that need to be built in

Understanding that specifications are at the heart of quality, we can now define the term in a more cogent manner. Moreover, it is important that quality be defined from the standpoint of the provider, as it is the provider that builds quality into products or services, and it is at the provider's location where quality is ensured.

DEFINITION OF QUALITY FROM THE STANDPOINT OF THE PROVIDER

> **Quality** *is an attribute of a product or service provided to consumers that conforms in toto to or exceeds the best of the available specifications for that product or service. It includes making those specifications available to the end user of the product or service.*
>
> *The specifications that form the basis of the product or service provided may have been defined by a government body, an industry as-*

sociation, or a standards body. Where such a definition is not available, the provider may define the specifications.

This definition of quality mandates that the provider:

★ Define specifications if they are not already defined by a higher body, such as a government body, an industry association, or a standards organization
★ Adhere to the best of the available definition of specifications
★ Ensure conformance is 100% or better—no less
★ Make available to the customer the specifications to which conformance is ensured

The result of a product or service that meets the above definition of quality is that the customer is able to effectively use the product for the length of its life or enjoy the service fully. This result further mandates that the provider is responsible for providing any support that is required by the customer for the enjoyment or utilization of the product or service throughout its life.

Any product or service that meets the requirements of this definition is rated a "quality product/service," and any product or service that does not meet the requirements of this definition is rated "poor quality."

QUALITY AND RELIABILITY

Quality and reliability are intertwined and are inseparable, but what does *reliability* mean?

Reliability of a product is its capability to function at the defined level of performance for the duration of its life.

Two phrases are critical in this definition:

1. **Defined level of performance**—Performance level is defined in the specifications for the product or service. It should be 100% or more of the specifications and no less. Continuous use is also a specification. For example, a car may be capable of being driven at 100 miles per hour, but how long can a car withstand being driven continuously at that speed? Normally, performance is defined at two levels: *normal performance* and *peak performance*.

2. **Duration of its life**—Duration needs to be specified for normal performance as well as peak performance. A product has two lives:

   ★ *First life or initial life*—Initial life, before any repairs become necessary, normally is specified as the warranty or guarantee period. After expiration of this life, regular maintenance may be required to maintain performance at the level specified for the product.

   ★ *Operating life*—The period of time after the warranty expires, assuming maintenance is performed. After expiration of this life, it may not be economical to maintain the product to operate at the specified level of performance.

In other words, *quality* involves delivering the specified functionality under the specified conditions, and *reliability* involves delivering the specified functionality at a specified level of performance over the duration of the product life, even with slight deviations in the specified conditions.

While initial life is specified by manufacturers as the warranty period, the life after the warranty period usually is not specified. If it is, it is specified with such stipulations as "subject to the condition that the product is maintained and serviced by our own expert technicians" or something similar. If product maintenance is entrusted to the manufacturer or its authorized maintenance shop, the manufacturer specifies two norms: mean time between failures and mean time to repair.

Mean time between failures is the average period between two successive failures, assuming that proper maintenance is performed every time and maintenance conforms to the manufacturer's stipulations. It is expressed in the number of running hours for the product. Mean time to repair is the average time it takes to restore the product to its original functionality by carrying out the necessary repairs. It is expressed in the number of clock hours it takes to repair the product. Reliability is gauged by these two measures.

In terms of software, an observation often made is that software has no moving parts that cause the product to deteriorate through wear and tear. Once a software product functions at its defined level of quality and functionality, there should be no need for maintenance. Therefore, the term reliability should not be applicable to software. However, this reasoning is true only if the configuration on which the software product runs remains unaltered. If the hardware and software configurations are unchanged, no repairs should be necessary, rendering the attribute of reliability inapplicable. These days, however, many other factors play a role in how stable the hardware and software configuration remains. The following are a few common situations that can alter the configuration of hardware and software:

1. New operating systems enter the market every three years.
2. New Web browsers or updates to current browsers are released regularly.
3. New viruses and spyware are unleashed on unsuspecting Internet users.
4. Computers often are flooded with a host of new tools, ranging from office suites to antivirus software to downloadable utilities.
5. Changes are introduced to tiers (middleware) in multitier architecture software products.
6. Software products may make use of shared libraries that are part of the system software supplied along with the operating system. It is likely that these shared libraries are updated or modified.
7. Software products may make use of third-party code libraries to perform special functions such as rules processing, database independence, etc. These third-party code libraries may be updated or modified.
8. Installing and uninstalling utilities on a system may result in changes to or removal of the shared libraries used by a software product.

All of these activities change the configuration of the system on which a software product is running, and this is where the question of software reliability comes into play. A software product is said to be reliable if it can withstand minor patches to the operating system and to the middleware.

As software quality professionals cannot predict what future upgrades will be made to the system software (be it the operating system, database, browser, or middleware), they cannot specify the reliability of software in running hours. They also may not be able to specify the mean time between failures of a software product in running hours, because a software product does not fail due to use over a number of hours. It can, however, fail due to a change in the system configuration. Such is the case with mean time to repair, because the repair is not to restore the software to as near the original condition as possible but rather to remove the impact of some change in the system configuration.

Nonetheless, software quality professionals recognize that the term *reliability* is applicable to the domain of software. Some hints for building reliable software are offered in this book.

EVOLUTION OF THE CONCEPTS OF QUALITY

Although quality is an age-old word, its understanding at the organizational level has evolved in recent times, especially since World War II. Initially, it was thought that only the artisan could achieve a "quality" product state. However, as the Industrial Revolution moved manufacturing out of artisans' shops and into factories, with multiple artisans working on a single product, the supervisor became pivotal in achieving a quality product. If a part was missing or a bolt was loose, it was the supervisor's fault for not noticing it. As pressure on the supervisor to ensure quality increased, actual supervision took a back seat, which affected productivity and production.

It finally dawned on management that appointment of an independent inspector was needed to ensure that every part was mounted properly and every bolt was tightened. Thus came about the profession of inspection, along with the development of a host of inspection tools, techniques, and methods. Inspection became a research area in itself. Examples of tools developed specifically for inspection that are now standard in manufacturing milieus include "go/no-go" gauges and inspection jigs.

Inspection, as a link in the manufacturing chain (see Figure 1.1), served well for some time, but became inadequate as the functionality of products became more varied. Ensuring that every part is properly mounted and that every bolt is properly tightened was soon found to be inadequate to ensure proper functioning of products. This was especially true for electrical products like motors and machines, as such products required functionality testing in addition to overall inspection. It was realized that inspection alone was not enough to ensure the quality of products and that products leaving the factory should be tested for their functionality as well.

Around the same time, subcontracting of the manufacture of parts to specialized manufacturers began to take place, starting in the auto industry. This brought in a new issue: ensuring the quality of inputs. Thus, inward inspection (inspection of parts received from suppliers and subcontractors) and testing also arose. Batch and job manufacturing also began to emerge around the same time, resulting in a new concept: *quality control* (see Figure 1.2). A host of new lit-

Figure 1.1. Inspection

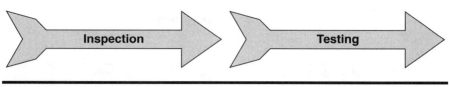

Figure 1.2. Quality control

erature on methods of quality control came into being, including sampling inspection, statistical quality control, control charts, and so on.

Up to this point, the emphasis in terms of quality was on ensuring the quality of manufacturing. As competition increased among manufacturers and as organizations began to provide similar—and perhaps better—products, it was discovered that products can fail because of design defects, even if the manufacturing quality was tightly controlled. One example that comes to mind is two brands of two-wheel scooters: Vespa and Lambretta. Both were similar in terms of horsepower and in the specification of being able to accommodate two people, yet they were different in design. The Vespa used a shaft-based power transmission, while the Lambretta used a chain-based power transmission. Lambretta ultimately closed down, while Vespa is still in business today. The lack of popularity of the Lambretta scooter was not due to an issue of manufacturing quality. Rather, it was an issue of design, and therefore an issue that affected the very survival of the organization itself. The quality of a product design, which depends on the specifications set for that product, is equally, if not more, crucial to the success of the product as is the control of quality during the manufacturing stage.

In order to achieve better design, it became necessary for manufacturers to establish design guidelines, drawing upon the experience and knowledge of organizations in a particular industry, as well as feedback from the field (customer complaints, maintenance personnel observations, and studying competitors' products). This resulted in the development of standards and guidelines to ensure quality of design and specifications. Design reviews followed to ensure quality in product design.

While this aspect of product design surely belonged in the arena of quality, it was beyond the capacity of an organization's quality control department. This development gave rise to the concept of *quality assurance* (as depicted in Figure 1.3), an integral part of manufacturing that includes inspection, testing, and standards for design.

There is a misconception in the software development industry that quality assurance means testing. I am not sure how this misconception came about. Testing is testing; quality assurance encompasses inspection (verification), test-

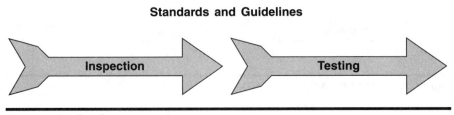

Figure 1.3. Quality assurance

ing, and standards. In the glossary of the Capability Maturity Model Integration (CMMI®) model document for development (version 1.2, 2006), quality assurance is defined as "a planned and systematic means for assuring management that the defined standards, practices, procedures, and methods of the process are applied."

One occurrence of note that had a significant impact on the evolution of the concepts of quality was the transformation Japanese manufacturing organizations underwent. Japanese manufacturers rose from their reputation as suppliers of cheap, poor-quality goods to become suppliers of high-quality products. It was a phenomenal transformation, and studies conducted on Japanese manufacturing methods were widely publicized. Some of these methods include *quality control circles, zero defects*, and *right first time.*

One of the Japanese techniques widely adopted by manufacturers across the world is quality control circles, or simply *quality circles*, as they popularly became known. A quality circle is a voluntary association of workers from the same facility who meet to discuss quality-related issues in their facility and come up with possible solutions to improve quality. If their discussions point out a defect, together they come up with a solution, trying it out on a pilot basis and presenting the results to management. If management is satisfied with the proposal, it is implemented, and the members of the quality circle that came up with the suggestion are rewarded.

It was reported that the Japanese manufacturing industry benefited greatly from these quality circles, and these benefits were felt all over the world in the form of improved goods from Japan, a nation now known for its high-quality products. While the concept of quality circles was welcomed by other economies, its implementation did not produce such spectacular results elsewhere. India in particular wholeheartedly adopted this concept and spent a considerable amount of resources to implement it, but did not achieve any tangible or auditable, positive, and commensurate results.

However, what the transformation in the quality of Japanese products did result in was the awareness that quality is not just the responsibility of the quality department alone; it is an organizational issue. If quality is neglected, the very survival of the organization may be at stake. This realization led to the development of the concept of total quality management, which requires the entire organization be involved in achieving quality—not just in terms of deliverables, but in every activity of the organization. The organization is seen as a culture— a culture based on quality—that views quality as a critical ingredient in all of its activities.

The development of technology created a new dimension to help achieve quality: robots. Japan again took the lead and extensively deployed robots in its factories. Since the chance of human error was removed from a significant number of operations, the probability of defects was eliminated. Thus, the need for inspection became marginal, although testing remained important. It simply was not possible to inspect everything. Take, for example, a gearbox assembly. Once assembled, the inside cannot be inspected unless the gearbox is opened, but if it is opened, it has to be reassembled. This gave rise to the concept of *process quality*, which embeds the concept of quality into the manufacturing process itself.

QUALITY GURUS

No book on quality can be complete without noting the contributions of the pioneers in quality: William Edwards Deming, Joseph Moses Juran, and Philip Bayard Crosby. Very brief sketches of these gurus are given in the following sections.

William Edwards Deming

Dr. William Edwards Deming is considered by most people to be the father of modern philosophy on quality. Deming was a consultant to Japan in the early 1950s and helped Japanese companies attain worldwide success. The Japanese government recognized his contribution and honored him with the Order of the Sacred Treasure, Second Class in 1960.

In the 1970s, Deming's philosophy was summarized by his Japanese disciples as follows:

★ When organizations concentrate on quality, quality tends to rise over a period of time, and costs tend to fall.
★ If organizations focused on costs, costs would rise and quality would decline over a period of time.

In short, quality improves productivity. This philosophy was proven by Japanese companies, and they are among the world's best today.

In 1981, after it incurred a loss of $3 billion, Ford Motor Company recruited Deming as a consultant. By 1986, Ford became the most profitable of the American automobile manufacturers. The turnaround was credited to Deming. He proposed a new way of looking at management, offering 14 key principles for business success in his book *Out of the Crisis,* published in 1986. These principles, now known as the famous "Deming's 14 Points," can be summarized as follows:

1. **Constancy of purpose**—Create constancy of purpose toward improvement of product and service. The purpose is important, and it needs to be constant over a period of time.
2. **Adopt the new philosophy**—Conditions change, and the philosophy ought to be aligned with the current conditions.
3. **Statistical inferencing**—Deming advocated the use of statistical techniques for quality control in place of 100% inspection of mass-produced components.
4. **Price**—When making buying decisions, Deming suggested doing away with the practice of awarding contracts on the basis of lowest price. This rationale gave rise to the present-day two-bid (technical bid and financial bid) system for selecting vendors.
5. **Improve continuously**—Find problems and solve them.
6. **On-the-job training**—Deming advocated that organizations provide learning opportunities on the job, as well as guided learning.
7. **Supervision**—Deming advocated *leadership* in place of supervision in organizations.
8. **Fear**—Deming strongly felt that fear should not be used as a motivator in organizations. He suggested driving fear out of organizations so that everyone can work effectively.
9. **Barriers**—Deming scorned watertight walls between departments in organizations. He recommended that people work together so that they can learn from each other.
10. **Methods**—Deming recommended development and provision of right methods of working to obtain results. He was against exhortations and slogans. He stated that targets, without using the right methods to achieve them, are meaningless. He clarified that most of the causes of low quality and low productivity are beyond the people who perform the work.

11. **Eliminate quotas**—Perhaps Deming recognized the unlimited potential of human beings to improve productivity. He therefore argued that numerical quotas should be eliminated. He suggested management by objectives and leadership in order to improve output.

12. **Pride**—Deming argued that workers feel proud of their work-related achievements, and they should not be robbed of this pride by annual performance appraisals. He suggested the removal of any barriers that could stand between workers and their pride in their workmanship.

13. **Retraining and education**—Deming strongly advocated educating employees as a means of increasing their awareness and improving their sense of responsibility and ownership.

14. **Management**—Deming suggested a structured management to drive the above 13 points in the organization, to achieve the desired transformation in the organization.

Deming short-listed the four stumbling blocks to transforming a business into a vibrant organization caused by management:

1. Neglecting long-range planning
2. Relying on technology to solve problems
3. Seeking proven methods rather than developing new solutions
4. Hiding behind the excuse "our problems are different"

Deming advocated a four-step cycle for transformation to a successful business:

1. **Plan**—Plan for the action.
2. **Do**—Carry out and implement the plan.
3. **Check**—Check the results of the action and draw inferences.
4. **Act**—Modify the plan as necessary.

Deming's 14 principles and *plan-do-check-act* cycle are used outside the manufacturing area, in various fields, with success.

Joseph Moses Juran

Dr. Joseph Juran led an active working life for about 70 years, and his *Quality Control Handbook* (first edition, 1951) is still a reference for quality professionals today. Juran started his career at the Hawthorne Works of Western Electric and rose to the position of chief industrial engineer at its headquarters. Later, Juran became chairman of the department of administrative engineering at New York University, where he taught for quite a few years. He was also a consultant and the author of several books.

Juran was an active member of the American Management Association, on behalf of which he delivered many lectures internationally. His management philosophies are now embedded in American and Japanese management philosophy. He developed a quality trilogy, which can be summarized as follows:

1. **Quality planning**—Begin by identifying customers and their needs, and then develop a product that meets those needs. Optimize the product so as to meet the organization's needs as well as the customers' needs. That is, quality starts with specifications and design.
2. **Quality improvement**—Define a process that can produce the product, and then optimize the process. That is, quality depends on the process.
3. **Quality control**—Test and prove that the process can successfully produce the product, and then implement the proven process in operations.

The Union of Japanese Scientists and Engineers invited Juran to Japan to teach the principles of quality management after World War II. His lectures were published as a book titled *Managerial Breakthrough* (1964). He was awarded the Order of the Sacred Treasure, Second Class by the emperor of Japan. Juran also founded the Juran Institute, a consulting company through which he could propagate his ideas and work; it is one of the leading consultancies in quality management.

He was the first to incorporate human aspects into quality management, which helped to shape the concept of total quality management. Joseph Juran also is credited with the popular definition of quality: *fitness for use.*

Philip Bayard Crosby

Philip Crosby was a businessman and author who contributed to general management theory and quality management practices. He began his career at ITT Corporation and then opened his own consultancy under the banner Philip Crosby Associates, Inc., which now operates in eight countries. His books *Quality Is Free* (1979) and *Quality without Tears* (1984) are still popular today.

Crosby defined quality as conformance to certain specifications set forth by management and not to some vague concept of "goodness." The specifications are not arbitrary either; they must be set according to customer needs and wants. Crosby promoted the popular phrase "do it right the first time," or DIRFT, and the concept of *zero defects*. He compiled four principles of quality:

1. The definition of quality is conformance to requirements, not to the concepts of goodness or elegance.
2. The system of quality is prevention, which is preferable to quality inspections.
3. The performance standard for quality is zero defects, not "that's close enough."
4. The measurement of quality is the price of nonconformance (poor quality), not indices. This is the precursor to the concept of the cost of poor quality.

Crosby defined a 14-step process for management to follow in order to achieve and improve quality:

1. Be committed to quality, and ensure that this commitment is clear to everyone in the organization.
2. Create quality improvement teams, with representatives from all departments.
3. Measure the process to determine the current and potential quality issues.
4. Compute the cost of quality (or poor quality).
5. Raise quality awareness in all employees.
6. Take visible action to correct quality issues.
7. Monitor the progress of quality improvement, and establish mechanisms to monitor the zero defects concept.
8. Train supervisors in quality improvement.
9. Hold "zero defects" days.
10. Encourage employees to create their own quality improvement goals (this is perhaps the precursor to the Software Engineering Institute's Personal Software Process).
11. Encourage employee communication with management about obstacles to quality.
12. Recognize the efforts of participants (workers) in achieving and improving quality.
13. Create quality councils.
14. Do it all over again. Quality improvement is endless.

Crosby listed five key characteristics of a successful organization:

1. People routinely do things "right the first time."
2. Change is anticipated and is used to the organization's advantage.
3. Growth is consistent and profitable.
4. New products and services are developed when necessary.
5. Everyone is happy to work in the organization.

Here are some of Crosby's most popular quotes:

1. "Quality has to be caused, not controlled."
2. "Quality is the result of a carefully constructed cultural environment. It has to be the fabric of the organization, not part of the fabric."
3. "Very few of the great leaders ever get through their careers without failing, sometimes dramatically."
4. "You have to lead people gently toward what they already know is right."
5. "Change should be a friend. It should happen by plan, not by accident."
6. "In a true zero defects approach, there are no unimportant items."

Philip Crosby believed that management has the primary responsibility for ensuring quality in the organization.

TOTAL QUALITY MANAGEMENT

The most popular quality concept in the manufacturing industry today is total quality management (TQM). Almost all professionally managed manufacturing companies have implemented TQM and practice it diligently. The software development industry, knowingly or unknowingly, leapfrogged into TQM through process quality certifications such as ISO and CMMI®. ISO defines TQM as "a management approach for an organization, centered on quality, based on the participation of all its members, and aiming at long-term success through customer satisfaction and benefits to all members of the organization and to society."

TQM is an organization-wide quality initiative, which means it involves the entire organization in the management of quality. One major aim of TQM is to reduce process variation within the organization. In Japan, TQM includes four steps:

1. **Kaizen**—Focus on continuous process improvement, to make every process in the organization visible, repeatable, and measurable.
2. **Atarimae hinshitsu**—Belief that products will function as they are designed to function.
3. **Kansei**—Study the way a user uses the product, to facilitate improvement of the product.
4. **Miryoketuki hinshitsu**—Belief that products should have aesthetic value along with usability. For example, a car needs to look attractive in addition to its capability to transport people.

TQM advocates quality standards in all aspects of organizational functioning, as well as the philosophy of "do it right the first time." It also recommends elimination of waste in all its forms. As it stands today, TQM is adopted to some degree in organizations that have quality assurance at their heart, with inspection, testing, and standards implemented thoroughly and consistently.

Although the concept of quality was developed in manufacturing organizations, all of the concepts discussed above are relevant to software development organizations as well.

ARE WE GIVING ADEQUATE IMPORTANCE TO QUALITY IN ORGANIZATIONS?

The term "we" is used here to mean providers of software development services, because although consumers can demand better quality, they have no control over it. They can raise their voices against poor quality and perhaps abstain from purchasing poor-quality goods and services, but it is providers that can supply goods and services of better quality.

The quality function in an organization is akin to the audit function in the finance department of an organization. What is the negative impact of not having an audit function? Management may steal money from the organization. Recognizing this possibility, governments made it mandatory that an external auditor, one approved by a statutory body or certified by a professional association of public or chartered accountants, audit a company's books of accounts and certify that the finances are managed honestly. These external auditors are expected to ensure integrity in an organization's accounting process. When we see an organization's audited financial report, we believe that it is an honest statement of the financial position of that organization. The external auditor is viewed as a watchdog over management, to safeguard the interests of the organization's owners (that is, the shareholders).

While the practice of external auditing of an organization's books, either yearly or quarterly, is mandatory in most countries, it is not mandatory for an organization to include the quality function as one of the departments that regularly undergoes external quality audits. This may be surprising, but the fact of the matter is that many organizations do not have a robust quality department. Some organizations do have a quality department, but in name only; the department does not have any real authority to prevent defective products from reaching customers. Few organizations have a robust quality department that is empowered to exercise authority in stopping shipments to customers if necessary.

Why is this? Is it because shareholders' money needs to be protected, but not the interests of consumers, who are putting trust in a product or service, risking money, safety, and perhaps health? Does this mean that the quality of goods or services is unimportant? Does this imply that the adage "buyer beware" is an adequate safeguard against poor quality?

Software now runs almost everything in this world, from financial systems to airplanes to weapon systems and many more applications. The purpose of some software has strategic importance, and perhaps the purpose of other software is trivial. What is the level of importance being accorded to quality by software development organizations?

Most governments are focused on money more than the quality aspects of products or services being offered by organizations. But what is the purpose of safeguarding the accounting process of an organization that is producing poor-quality goods or services and is heading toward failure?

While mandatory declarations of financial results make it feasible to compute a host of financial ratios (metrics?) that allow us to ascertain the financial health of an organization, there is no way we can compute the quality metrics necessary for us to assess the quality health of an organization. Most organizations never declare what their defect density is. Worse still, most organizations do not even have the wherewithal to derive such metrics. A significant number of organizations, especially in the software development field, do not have a head for their quality department.

When we learn that an organization has been appraised by the Software Engineering Institute using CMMI® or that an organization has obtained certification from ISO, we feel confident about the organization's commitment to quality. Surprisingly, these certifying bodies do not insist that an organization have a quality department, let alone a competent quality department chief. Their methods of certification do not include ensuring that internal quality controls are in place and are doing their job diligently, as is the case in the field of finance.

Generally speaking, the quality function is one of the most neglected organs of an organization. Of course, there are exceptions, but for most organizations, quality is a headache, and when there is a conflict, management can—and almost always does—rule against the quality department. Yet management cannot rule against an audit in the field of finance. While it only seems logical to have a similar system in place for the quality function in any industry, including software development, the reality is quite the reverse. Although it is possible for the head of an organization's internal audit department to become the head of the finance department and for the head of finance to become the CEO, it is a very rare occurrence for the head of the quality department to become CEO of the organization.

Activists like Ralph Nader have forced industries to focus on quality. Initially, all guarantees and warranties were against "manufacturing defects," but activism and lawsuits forced industry to expand guarantees and warranties to cover all defects, including design defects.

Unfortunately, however, such activism is absent in the area of software development, and as a result, quality is given scant respect in this industry. Perhaps about 10% of software development organizations may be able to declare their auditable defect density.

Most software development organizations do not have full-fledged, full-time, and fully staffed quality departments. This does not mean to say that products are released without any inspection or testing. Although such activities are carried out by the technical department, most software development companies do not designate a set of their qualified professionals to tend to the task of the quality function, as is the normal practice in the manufacturing industry. The main function of the quality department in software development organizations, where there is one, is to interface with the certifying agencies and ensure that certification is obtained or maintained. The quality department also guides and assists the technical departments in keeping and updating records that are necessary to maintain certification. Championing the organizational quality comes second to certificates.

The most popular process model in the software development industry, CMMI® of the Software Engineering Institute of Carnegie Mellon University, does not mandate a full-time quality department. The second most popular issuer of certificates, ISO 9000, which mandates a quality policy and a quality management system for the organization, also does not mandate a quality department. It is as if they are saying, "As long as you manage quality, it is okay.

We are not concerned how you do it." This goes against the very grain of the process quality they evangelize.

Processes are important, and who champions those processes should be considered equally important. The above models seem to take umbrage at TQM, in which the CEO is the quality champion. True, the total productive maintenance concept also nominates the CEO as the chief production manager. The marketing concept designates the CEO as the chief marketing manager. The CEO may be responsible for every function in the organization, but each department needs a separate head. That way, each department receives due attention besides allowing the CEO to focus equal attention on all functions.

Under the marketing concept, the marketing department has a head in addition to the CEO. Under total productive maintenance, the organization has a production manager and perhaps a maintenance manager as well, besides the CEO. It is only the quality department that does not seem to need a professional and knowledgeable department head in many organizations. The general feeling within industry is that the quality department can be managed by the technical head on a part-time basis. Surprising, isn't it?

ORGANIZATIONAL GOALS AND QUALITY GOALS

Every organization has goals, mostly financial in nature. The most common organizational goals can be classified as follows:

★ Strategic (survival, growth)
★ Financial (revenue, profit)
★ Marketing (reach, share, customer support)
★ Product (innovation, quality, reliability, delivery)
★ Human resources (staff retention, growth, succession)

Of the above classes, the ones that attract the attention of senior management are strategic and financial goals. Market forces compel senior management to focus its attention on marketing and product goals, as these have a significant impact on the strategic goals. The remaining goals are delegated to the next line of management to focus on and achieve. Quality goals, which are normally part of product goals, are further relegated downward. It is rather rare to see quality goals distinguished as a separate set of goals. Financial charts frequently are displayed behind the desk of the CEO (and in the lobby of the corporate headquarters) in most organizations, but it is uncommon to find a CEO who has quality charts anywhere in his or her office (or in the lobby, for that matter).

Should the CEO be focusing on quality goals? Is it not the function of the development manager to ensure the quality demanded by the customer? The TQM philosophy states that the CEO needs to be the chief quality manager of the organization. Without the focus and support of the CEO, the quality function becomes an appendage of the technical department.

Quality goals can either be generic for all software development organizations or specific to an organization. Quality goals can include the following:

★ Achieve and surpass industry benchmarks for product quality
★ Achieve and surpass industry benchmarks for product reliability
★ For productivity goals of quality assurance activities specifically, reduce time spent on inspection, testing, and other related quality assurance activities, by process improvement and usage of better tools
★ Reduce the cost of quality assurance, meaning the amount of money expended on quality assurance activities, without any reduction in quality levels
★ Quality improvement goals specific to an organization, such as
    ☆ Reduction in defect density
    ☆ Reduction in defect injection rate
    ☆ Improvement in sigma level

The first and second goals focus on quality at the product level, while the rest focus on quality at the organizational level. Also, quality goals dovetail into product goals. Therefore, quality goals ought to be shared by the technical department responsible for delivery and the quality department responsible for monitoring organizational quality. Since the CEO is responsible for achieving the organizational goals with respect to all functions, with the actual responsibilities delegated to lower level managers, achievement of quality goals needs to be delegated as well. But is the technical manager in charge of delivery the right choice for delegating the achievement of quality goals? The technical manager's primary responsibility is to deliver—and deliver on time; quality of deliverables is a close second. When the possibility of having to delay delivery to fix a quality issue arises, most often delivery takes precedence. Therefore, it is necessary to have a quality champion in the organization, whose primary responsibility is achieving the organization's quality goals. That entity is the quality department.

IS A QUALITY DEPARTMENT IN SOFTWARE DEVELOPMENT ORGANIZATIONS REALLY NEEDED?

I had occasion to discuss this very topic with the CEO of a medium-sized software development organization, which is preparing itself for CMMI® appraisal. I was trying to impress on him the need for a fully staffed quality department with a full-time and knowledgeable quality head. He asked me, "Why do we need a quality department? We are performing peer reviews and independent tests rigorously. What additional value can a quality department add? I do not wish to increase overhead without any benefit to the organization." He went on to add that instituting a quality department would directly undermine the commitment of the technical department to quality, in that the technical department would believe that management no longer has confidence in its ability to build in quality. I explained in as much detail as he allowed me, which I offer below, what a quality department can achieve.

Here is why software development organizations need a quality department that is fully staffed with competent professionals and with a full-time, competent quality head:

1. The quality viewpoint would be provided unhindered by delivery objectives at any time.
2. Continuous implementation of quality assurance activities would be ensured, without exception.
3. By continuously monitoring the quality achievements of the organization, a quality department would be able to:
   a. Prevent deterioration of organizational quality before any real damage is caused
   b. Drive the organization to higher levels of quality and, thus, toward excellence
4. Process performance would be measured and analyzed to determine if it is achieving its organizational objectives, as well as to make it feasible to effect necessary improvements to ensure that the processes perform as designed.
5. Organizational quality achievements would be benchmarked with peer organizations, and industry benchmarks would be applied to the organizational processes, thus raising the bar of quality levels.
6. There would be an in-house expert on matters of quality and analysis, who would continuously hone the organization's leading edge on quality expertise.

7. Expert support and training on how to achieve quality objectives would be provided to technical teams.
8. A repository for quality data generated by the organization would be made available to those who need it.
9. Defect analysis would be carried out and elimination of the top causes of defects would be facilitated, pushing the organization toward achieving "right first time."
10. Continuity of the organization's initiatives for quality improvement would be championed.
11. A "watchdog," "in-house customer representative," and "eyes and ears" of management in matters of product and deliverable quality of the organization would exist, raising its voice when quality trends show a downturn.

Thus, the quality department has a vital role to play in the organization. Yet a full-fledged quality department in software development organizations is still not common practice.

THE PRESENT SCENARIO IN SOFTWARE DEVELOPMENT ORGANIZATIONS

The software development industry has not imported the quality philosophy, techniques, and tools from the manufacturing industry. While independent teams of inspectors and testers are the norm in the manufacturing industry, the software development industry uses project team members to conduct inspections and testing. Some organizations do have an independent testing department to conduct system testing and coordinate acceptance testing, but this is not a norm across the industry.

Insistence on certification by outsourcing organizations such as the U.S. Department of Defense forced software development organizations to seek certifications and maturity level ratings from authorized agencies. Now it is becoming normal to see the quality department in a software development organization coordinate the certification activities under the umbrella of process quality rather than champion product quality.

Every software development organization's brochure contains a statement about its commitment to quality, but this statement is not supported by a strong quality department within the organization. When you question such a company, it asserts that it puts less emphasis on quality conformance activities and places more emphasis on activities that build quality into the product, such as training staff, providing tools, defining processes, conducting audits, and so on. Such companies make it sound as if everybody in the organization is quality conscious and that quality is everybody's responsibility. Yet the fact remains that quality is an unwanted child in the organization, because "everybody's responsibility" generally means that no one can be held accountable.

To sum up, the present scenario in software development organizations is characterized by the following assertions:

1. All companies firmly state their commitment to quality. Most organizations do have one or more certifications/maturity ratings.
2. Very few organizations have a full-fledged quality department, staffed by competent professionals and led by a knowledgeable quality professional. Most companies either have a quality department in name only or not at all.
3. Where there is a quality department in name only, its role is relegated to interfacing with certifying agencies rather than championing organizational quality.
4. Quality assurance is understood as being equal to testing in most software development organizations.
5. Most software development organizations do not have auditable measurement data for their quality capability. Most do not even attempt it.
6. Most software development organizations do not have objective quality goals.
7. Most software development organizations place the quality function under the technical department, whose primary responsibility is delivery.
8. Most software development organizations do not have independent inspection and testing teams; the development teams perform these activities.

This is the quality scenario in the software development industry. Clearly, there is a lot of room for improvement. The focus of this book is how to achieve quality at the product level and how to monitor and improve quality at the organizational level.

FOUR DIMENSIONS
OF QUALITY

CHAPTER OVERVIEW

★ Four dimensions essential to achieve quality: specifications, design, construction, and conformance
★ How to build in quality in each of the four dimensions
★ How to ensure quality in each of the four dimensions

BACKGROUND

Quality has four dimensions (as depicted in Figure 2.1):

1. Specification quality
2. Design quality
3. Development (software construction) quality
4. Conformance quality

Specifications are the starting point in the journey of providing a product or service, followed by design and then development. Conformance quality is ensuring how well that quality is built into the deliverable at every stage. These dimensions are discussed in detail in this chapter.

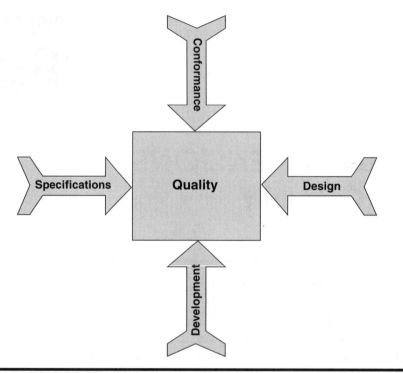

Figure 2.1. Four dimensions of quality

SPECIFICATION QUALITY

Specification quality refers to how well the specifications are defined for the product or service being provided. Specifications have no predecessor activity, and all other activities succeed specifications. Thus, if the specifications are weak, design will be weak, resulting in the development and manufacture of an inferior or incorrect product, and the effort spent on ensuring that quality is built in will have been wasted. Therefore, it is of paramount importance that specifications are comprehensive and well defined and that they take into account all possible aspects that have a bearing on the quality of the product.

Specifications normally should include the following six aspects:

1. **Functionality aspects**—Specify what functions are to be achieved by the product or service.
2. **Capacity aspects**—Specify the load the product can carry (such as 250 passengers on a plane or 100 concurrent users for a Web application) or the number of persons to whom a service can cater.

3. **Intended use aspects**—Specify the need or needs the product or service satisfies.
4. **Reliability aspects**—Specify how long the product can be enjoyed before it needs maintenance, or the surety of delivering the service and the conformance to the user requirements.
5. **Safety aspects**—Specify the threshold levels for ensuring safety to persons and property from use of the product or service.
6. **Security aspects**—Specify any threats for which the product or service needs to be prepared.

How do we make sure that we have comprehensive and correct specifications? The first aspect of ensuring that specifications are drawn up right is to engage qualified persons, such as business analysts or systems analysts, to carry out the job. These professionals must be properly trained to carry out requirements engineering. The second aspect is to either develop in-house standards or adopt the standards of a professional association or a standards body that the analysts are to follow. These standards set minimum levels in drawing up specifications.

Initially, specifications should be developed for a product in the usual way. In an internal or external customer-driven project scenario, user requirements are collected. In a commercial off-the-shelf product scenario, requirements are gathered from a market survey exercise.

Once requirements have been collected, they need to be developed. This involves separating the requirements into functional requirements, usability requirements, safety and security requirements, reliability requirements, and so on. These requirements also must be checked against organizational standards for usability, safety, and security, and any missing requirements need to be filled in. Then, each class of requirements is analyzed for comprehensiveness against either the backdrop of an existing product or a past project. If neither is available, functional experts should scrutinize and fill in the missing requirements. If access to experts is not available, then a team inside the organization is formed to carry out a brainstorming exercise to ensure that the specifications are comprehensive in all the classes. In a commercial off-the-shelf product scenario, a second market survey to tap the potential users can be conducted to improve the specifications.

DESIGN QUALITY

Design quality refers to how well the product or service to be delivered is designed. The objectives for design are to fulfill the specifications defined for the product or service being provided. Design determines the shape and strengths of the product or service. Therefore, if the design is weak, the product or service will fail, even if the specifications are very well defined. Although design is a creative activity, it can be split into two phases: conceptual design and engineering. *Conceptual design* selects the approach to a solution from the myriad approaches available. *Engineering* uses the approach selected and works out the details to realize the solution. Conceptual design is the creative part of the process, and engineering is the details part.

Let's use the design of a bridge as an example to illustrate the difference between conceptual design and engineering. A bridge can be either a simply supported bridge or a suspension bridge. A simply supported bridge has a number of equally spaced pillars (columns) that support the bridge and the traffic that flows on it. A suspension bridge has a pillar at each end, with cables drawn from these two pillars to support the bridge. For this class of bridge, there are many alternatives for the suspension material, location of the pillars, design of the pillars, design of the suspension cables, and so on. Conceptual design decides these aspects. Engineering design works out details such as the dimensions for each component, selection of materials, methods of jointing, and so on.

In terms of software, conceptual design refers to software architecture, navigation, number of tiers, approaches to flexibility, portability, maintainability, and so on. Engineering design refers to database design, program specifications, screen design, report design, etc. Software design normally contains the following elements:

1. Functionality design
2. Software architecture
3. Navigation
4. Database design
5. Development platform
6. Deployment platform
7. User interface design
8. Report design
9. Security
10. Fault tolerance
11. Capacity
12. Reliability
13. Maintainability
14. Efficiency and concurrence
15. Coupling and cohesion

16. Program specifications
17. Test design

How do we ensure that the right designs are selected and implemented? As with specification quality, before software design is attempted, it is essential that qualified people, trained in the art and science of software design, are in place. Either software design standards are developed in-house or, alternatively, they are adopted from a professional association or a standards body. These standards assist designers to achieve the best design possible.

It is normal to conduct a brainstorming session at the beginning of a software design project, to select one optimum design alternative and to decide on the overall design aspects, such as the number of tiers, technology platform, software coupling and cohesion, etc. A brainstorming session helps designers arrive at the best possible solution for the project at hand. A prototype of the design may be created and evaluated, which is normal practice specifically in the case of commercial off-the-shelf product development.

The final design is then evaluated against the organizational standards to ensure that the design will work for the project. The design is subjected to reviews from peers, experts, and managers as required before carrying out the detailed design of the entire product.

DEVELOPMENT (SOFTWARE CONSTRUCTION) QUALITY

In certain fields, there is no way quality can be tested without destroying the product itself. For example, the thickness and adherence of paint on a surface cannot be ensured without destroying the paint itself. Various shafts used in automobiles are forged and heat treated to make them stronger, and there is practically no way to test them to ensure that the desired qualities are built in without destroying the shafts. In such cases, in-process inspection is performed to ensure that the process is adhered to diligently and a few samples are subjected to destructive testing.

Fortunately, when it comes to software, nothing needs to be destroyed during testing, and corrections can be made without any material loss, but testing takes much longer to perform in the software development field than it does in manufacturing. Inspection and testing take only a fraction of the time it takes to fabricate a part or a product in manufacturing, but software testing can sometimes take more time and effort than it takes to develop the software. It is commonly agreed that 100% testing is not practical in the software development field. Therefore, the way in which software is developed assumes greater importance.

Normally, the following activities form part of developing software:

1. Create the database and table structures
2. Develop dynamically linked libraries for common routines
3. Develop screens
4. Develop reports
5. Develop unit test plans
6. Develop associated process routines for all other aspects, such as security, efficiency, fault tolerance, etc.

Good-quality construction is achieved by adhering to the coding guidelines of the programming language being used. Normally there is a separate coding guideline for every programming language used in an organization. It is customary to define the coding guidelines before beginning to write programs in a language. Coding guidelines contain naming conventions, code formatting, efficiency guidelines, and defect prevention guidelines that help developers write reliable and defect-free code. Of course, it is very important to have qualified people trained in software development. Construction follows software design, and it should always conform to the design document. In this way, good quality in construction can be achieved. Sample coding guidelines are given in Appendix I.

CONFORMANCE QUALITY

Conformance quality deals with how well an organization ensures that quality is built into a product through the above three dimensions. It is one thing to do a quality job, but it is quite another to unearth any defects lurking in the work product and ensure that a good-quality product is indeed built. Essentially, conformance quality examines how well quality control is carried out in the organization.

How do we determine how well an organization conducts the activities that ensure that quality is indeed built into a deliverable? One way to ascertain the efficacy of quality assurance activities is to use a set of quality metrics. These metrics include the defect removal efficiency of each of the quality control activities, product quality, and the defect density. Another way to ascertain the efficacy of quality assurance activities is to compare industry benchmark data for quality metrics with the organizational metrics. Appendix G covers quality metrics and measurements in greater detail.

This book discusses how to build quality into a deliverable and ensure that quality is built into the first three dimensions mentioned (software specifications, design, and construction), as well as ensure the quality of conformance itself through quality measurement and metrics.

ENSURING QUALITY IN SPECIFICATIONS

This is the first activity in building either a product or a service. Needless to say, it is a creative activity. In the software industry, specifications are referred to as user requirements. That is, end users of a software product perceive them as the requirements for the proposed product. The following are possible scenarios for obtaining user requirements:

1. A business analyst conducts a feasibility study, writes up a report, and draws up the user requirements. The analyst:
   a. Meets with all the end users and notes their requirements and concerns
   b. Meets with the function heads and notes their requirements and concerns
   c. Meets with management personnel and notes their requirements and concerns
   d. Consolidates the requirements and presents them to select end users, function heads, and management personnel and receives their feedback, if any
   e. Implements the feedback and finalizes specifications
2. A ready set of user requirements is presented as part of a request for proposal
3. A request for proposal points to a similar product and requests replication with client-specific customization

Regardless of the scenario, once the specifications are ready, quality assurance steps in. The role of quality assurance in this area is to ensure that the specifications are exhaustive and cover all areas, including functionality, capacity, reliability, safety, security, intended use, etc.

The tools for building quality into specifications are as follows:

1. **Process documentation**—Details the methodology for gathering, developing, analyzing, and finalizing the specifications
2. **Standards and guidelines, formats, and templates**—Specify the minimum set of specifications that needs to be built in
3. **Checklists**—Help analysts to ensure comprehensiveness of the specifications

Using these tools, analysts can develop specifications that are comprehensive and are clear in order to carry out the next activity (which is design) and that ensure quality is built into specifications.

The tools that can be used to carry out quality assurance to ensure quality of specifications are expert reviews and peer reviews. The methodology for carrying out an expert review is detailed in Chapter 5.

ENSURING QUALITY IN DESIGN

Put simply, the process of design is converting product specifications (or user requirements) into design documents that can be used by programmers to develop the source code required for the product being built. Normally, software design is a two-step process:

1. **Conceptual design**—Referred to as high-level design, functional design specification, software requirements specification, and software architecture design. In this step, the overall architecture of the software product, including the number of tiers, modules, approaches to achieving the functionality, database design, robustness, reliability, and security, are determined and documented. This document is used by the designers to carry out the engineering design.
2. **Engineering design**—Referred to as low-level design, detailed design specification, software design description, and software program design. In this step, detailed specifications are drawn up for each program unit, screen, report, table, etc., and programmers use this document to develop source code.

The tools for building quality into design include the following:

1. **Process documentation**—Details the methodology for design alternatives to be considered, criteria for selecting the alternative for the project, and finalizing the conceptual design.

2. **Standards and guidelines, formats, and templates**—Specify the possible software architectures along with their attendant advantages and disadvantages, the methodology for short-listing of design alternatives, and so on.

3. **Checklists**—Help designers to ensure that design is carried out comprehensively and appropriately.

Using these tools, designers can develop designs that are comprehensive, are clear in order to carry out the next activity (which is software construction), and ensure that quality is built into designs.

The tools that are available for ensuring quality of design are expert reviews, peer reviews of each design specification, and managerial reviews of the overall design. The methodology for conducting reviews is detailed in Chapter 5.

ENSURING QUALITY IN DEVELOPMENT (SOFTWARE CONSTRUCTION)

Development is the act of building the software product in conformance with the design. In this stage, the source code is developed and is linked with the pre-existing code libraries, to complete the code required for the product. This code is converted into executable code that can run on the hardware selected. This is also the stage in which the database is designed and built, so that data can be loaded and used by the software.

How is quality built into a product during the development stage? It is built in by adhering to the organizational standards for code quality as well as the coding guidelines for the development language being used. Uncontrolled changes can wreak havoc with code quality. Therefore, change management and configuration management assume importance for ensuring code quality.

There are two techniques to ensure that quality is built into a product: reviews (walkthroughs) and testing. These are detailed in Chapters 5 and 6.

ENSURING CONFORMANCE QUALITY

Ensuring that conformance quality is at desirable levels in the organization is achieved through quality measurements and metrics. Defect removal efficiency of verification and validation activities, defect injection rate, and defect density are all used for this purpose. In addition, projects are benchmarked at the organizational level and trend analysis is performed. These methods are detailed in Appendix G. Audits also are conducted to ensure that projects conform to various applicable standards for building quality into all activities, including specifications and design. In addition, organizational data is benchmarked against industry benchmarks, and corrective or preventive actions are taken to ensure that organizational conformance is indeed on a par with the industry.

Conformance quality is built in through process definition and continuous improvement for all software development activities as well as quality assurance. Conformance quality is ensured through metrics and measurement.

Table 2.1 summarizes the techniques available for ensuring quality in each of the four dimensions of quality.

Table 2.1. Conformance techniques for four dimensions of quality

Quality dimension	How to build in quality	Techniques for ensuring quality
Quality of specifications	Specification development process documentation; standards and guidelines, formats, and templates for defining specifications; and checklists	Expert reviews, peer reviews, and brainstorming
Quality of design	Software design process documentation; standards and guidelines, formats, and templates for software design; and checklists	Expert reviews, peer reviews, managerial reviews, and brainstorming
Quality of development	Coding guidelines, configuration management, and change management	Peer reviews and software testing
Conformance quality	Diligent application of all quality assurance activities in the organization, process definition, and improvement	Audits, measurement and metrics for quality assurance activities, and benchmarking of organizational metrics against industry metrics

3

SOFTWARE PRODUCT QUALITY

CHAPTER OVERVIEW

★ How to achieve quality from the standpoint of core functionality and ancillary functionality
★ How to achieve quality in the code
★ Errors, defects, and faults in software
★ How to achieve software program quality
★ How to measure the quality of a software product using a composite metric

---

FUNCTIONALITY STANDPOINT

Software product quality has multiple attributes. In this chapter, we will examine these attributes, starting with the highest in importance. The basic and most important attribute of a software product—or any other product, for that matter—is that it delivers its specified functionality accurately. A product has two types of functionality: core functionality and ancillary functionality.

Core Functionality

Core functionality refers to the main functionalities the product is designed to fulfill, without which the product is useless. For example, the core functionality of a car is to transport people from one place to another. If a car cannot do that, it is not useful, no matter how attractive or comfortable it may be.

In terms of a software product, consider, for example, a material management system whose core functionality is procurement management and warehouse management. The exhaustiveness of its core functionality determines its class among the available products in the market that fulfill the same core functionality. In the case of material management software, it can be a single-user version, a multiuser version that is limited to a single location, or a Web-based application that serves geographically disparate locations. While the core functionality is similar in all these applications, the quality is different.

Another angle from which to look at the exhaustiveness of core functionality of a software product is the data volume it can handle. A material management application that is designed to handle 100,000 items in a warehouse and another application that is designed to handle a million items have different levels of quality.

Still another aspect of core functionality is functional flexibility. A material management application that is designed for a specific industry, such as engineering, for example, should be usable in every type of engineering industry, be it the fabrication, machining, electrical, or electronics industry. If such is the case, then the software has functional flexibility.

Core functionality is primarily an aspect of specifications and design. Benchmarking a software product against other competing products and performing market surveys to ascertain customer perceptions of gaps in current products are both useful sources of information to increase the core functionality of a product under development. The quality of core functionality is ensured through expert reviews, peer reviews, positive testing, and functional testing.

Ancillary Functionality

Ancillary functionality is functionality that is supplemental to the core functionality. Even if ancillary functionality is absent, the product is still useful. Air-conditioning in a car is an ancillary functionality; a car is still useful even if it does not have air-conditioning. Again using the example of material management software, allowing executives access to stock information, procurement status, etc. is an ancillary functionality.

It is the ancillary functionalities that increase the value of a software product. Ancillary functionalities are further classified into the following subcategories:

1. **Safety and security functionalities**—These provide safety and security to the people using the product as well as to the product itself.

The body of a car, for example, protects passengers from injury caused by flying objects. The windshield protects passengers from the weather and provides the driver clear visibility. The speedometer provides velocity information to allow the driver to maintain an acceptable speed. In material management software, preventing unauthorized access and restricting modification rights based on the role of the user are two examples of safety and security functionalities. These functionalities are achieved through specifications and software design. The quality of these functionalities is ensured through security testing.

2. **Usability functionalities**—These allow the product to be used more comfortably or more conveniently. The automatic starter in a car was a great improvement over cranking the engine. A steering wheel is more convenient than using handlebars to drive a car. The fuel gauge protects the driver from getting stranded due to unknowingly running out of gas. All these features facilitate more convenient use of the product. In material management software, an online help function, automatic transfer of information from the materials department to the finance department, and customizable screen colors are all examples of usability functionalities. Another excellent example of a usability functionality that aids users is the alert that comes up on the screen to indicate that the caps lock key is on. Usability functionalities are achieved through usability guidelines, design guidelines, and software architecture guidelines. The quality of these functionalities is ensured through reviews and usability testing.

3. **Fault tolerance functionalities**—Slight misuse or unintended use should not damage the product. A minor accident should not render a car unusable. Similarly, software should tolerate unintended use or misuse to a reasonable degree. Unintended use of software can occur in a variety of ways, and software should be able to protect itself against these misuses and maintain its integrity. Fault tolerance functionalities are achieved through design standards, user interface design guidelines, and data validations. The quality of these functionalities is ensured through negative testing.

4. **Feel-good functionalities**—These functionalities make users feel more comfortable when using the product. Air-conditioning and a sound system in a car fall under this category. These functionalities are referred to as "bells and whistles" in the software industry. Animation and special graphics are examples of this functionality. Another is an error message indicated by a beeping sound. Feel-good functionalities

are achieved through aesthetics guidelines. The quality of these functionalities is ensured through expert and managerial reviews.

5. **Esteem functionalities**—These functionalities enhance the appearance of the product. In a car, the angles and contours in the shape of the body, custom paint, a removable roof, and automatic windows are all esteem functionalities. In a software product, jazzy screens with animation are an esteem function. Esteem functionalities are achieved through user interface design guidelines and brainstorming. The quality of these functionalities is ensured through positive testing.

6. **One-upmanship (competitive edge) functionalities**—These functionalities help software developers upstage their competition. A television set in a car is a one-upmanship functionality, as is a phone with Internet capability. In materials management, allowing vendors to see the status of their proposals over the Internet is an example of one-upmanship functionality. One-upmanship functionalities are achieved through managerial guidance. The quality of these functionalities is ensured through normal testing.

The basic attribute needed for a product to claim the quality tag is that it must perform the functions it is designed to. If the functions are performed correctly and the results delivered are accurate, the product has basic quality, which is of the highest importance if the product is said to have quality at all. Using the example of a car once more, if a car is expected to be able to transport four people 500 miles at a stretch without stopping and it meets this expectation, then the basic attribute to claim the quality tag is fulfilled by that car.

The quality of functionality is achieved through the dimension of specifications, discussed in Chapter 2. The quality of functionality is ensured through positive testing of the product once it is built. Table 3.1 summarizes software product quality from a functionality standpoint.

WHITE BOX (GLASS BOX) STANDPOINT

In order to achieve product quality, a software product is built to include the following characteristics:

1. **Maintainability**—The product is developed in such a way that it is maintainable, meaning that functionality can easily be added, removed, or modified. To achieve maintainability, the code must be

Table 3.1. Software product quality from a functionality standpoint

Functionality	How to achieve	How to ensure quality
Core functionality	Software specifications and software design, standards and guidelines	Functional testing, reviews
Ancillary functionality		
Safety and security functionalities	Software specifications and software design, standards and guidelines	Security testing, reviews
Usability functionalities	Usability guidelines, design guidelines, and software architecture guidelines	Reviews and usability testing
Fault tolerance functionalities	Design standards, user interface design guidelines, and data validations	Negative testing
Feel-good functionalities	Aesthetics guidelines	Managerial review
Esteem functionalities	User interface design guidelines and brainstorming	Positive testing
One-upmanship functionalities	Managerial guidance	Normal testing

readable and understandable by programmers other than the original author. This is made possible by the original coder defining and adhering to the coding guidelines. The following specific precautions make code maintainability possible:

★ Use standard naming conventions so that subsequent programmers can differentiate between program variables, constants, table fields, etc.

★ Format the code in the standard manner so that it is easily readable and the beginning and end of multiline statements are clear.

★ Use inline documentation statements extensively to help subsequent programmers understand the logic.

★ Use simple constructs instead of complex constructs.

2. **Portability**—Portability allows a software product to be shifted from one platform to another. To achieve this feature, standard constructs of the programming language should be used, and machine-specific

constructs should be avoided. This means that minimal modifications are needed when the software product is ported to another platform that supports the same programming language. This aspect needs to be included in the language-specific coding guidelines.

3. **Flexibility**—Flexibility is another key feature a product must have if it is to be called a "quality product." Flexibility makes it feasible to use the product even if some of the values change, or it allows the product to be used in a slightly different environment than originally intended. For example, if the tax rate changes, the code should not need to be changed in order to implement the new tax rate. As another example, if inventory management software for the manufacturing industry can be utilized in the pharmaceutical industry without a code change, then the software is considered to be flexible. Flexibility is achieved by avoiding both hard coding of constants and parameterizing the product as much as possible. This aspect would normally be part of the coding guidelines.

4. **Efficiency**—Efficiency means minimizing the consumption of system resources and execution time. Software consumes random access memory and central processing unit time while it is in operation. Minimization is achieved by careful declaration of variables (avoiding declaration of unused variables, reusing declared variables, etc.), closing files or tables when their use is finished, and not tying up the central processing unit with slow peripherals such as printers (which happens if printing directly from the program instead of spooling print jobs). Efficiency is achieved by following the efficiency guidelines portion of the coding guidelines.

5. **Modularity**—Modularity refers to building the software product using stand-alone or near stand-alone modules in such a way that functionality is not duplicated, so that when a module is changed, the change does not impact other modules of the software. Modularity is achieved by following software architecture guidelines and software design guidelines.

6. **Reusability**—Reusability refers to development of source code in such a way that it can be used again and again in other products. This is achieved by developing code as classes or as independent components to the extent possible. Reusability is achieved by following reusability coding guidelines.

7. **Readability**—Developed code ought to be readable, and readability is the first requisite for maintainability. It is achieved by proper formatting of the code, allowing recognition of the beginning and end

Table 3.2. Summary of product quality features from a white box standpoint

Feature	How to achieve the feature
Maintainability	Coding guidelines
Portability	Standard constructs and coding guidelines
Flexibility	Coding guidelines and avoid hard coding and parameterizing
Efficiency	Efficiency guidelines
Modularity	Software architecture guidelines and software design guidelines
Reusability	Reusability coding guidelines
Readability	Formatting guidelines
Testability	Software design guidelines

of composite multiline statements. Readability is achieved by following the formatting guidelines portion of the coding guidelines.

8. **Testability**—A software product is testable when every one of its units can be tested independently. Code should not be written in such a way that a set of preceding software units must be run in order to test a software unit. Each software unit on its own ought to be testable with its test data. Testability makes it easier to fix defects during development, because testing and fixing defects one unit at a time is simpler than testing a set of units and trying to locate the origin of a defect from among all the units. Testability is achieved by following software design guidelines.

Table 3.2 summarizes product quality features from a white box standpoint.

PRESENCE OF DEFECTS IN THE PRODUCT

It is generally accepted across industries—including the software industry—that some defects do remain in products even after extensive quality assurance activities have been performed. Even so, every organization strives to eliminate all defects, which quality assurance activities are designed to accomplish. Residual defects in a product often are the result of gaps in specifications, product design, or development or due to inadequate testing.

Before proceeding, the following terms need to be understood properly within the context of software development:

★ **Error or bug**—Both words mean the same thing. "Bug" is a collo-quial term used by software developers, and the process of removing errors is termed "debugging." An error is an incorrect step in a program, an improper data definition (its type and size), or an in-correct result produced by a step in a program. An error is intro-duced into a product during the construction stage of software development and has escaped the net of quality assurance activities performed on the product.

★ **Defect**—A defect is a pre-existing condition in a finished product. It can be due to an error or the operating environment in which the software is being used. A defect can originate in any of the three stages (specifications, design, or development) and can escape qual-ity assurance activities.

★ **Fault**—A fault occurs when the operation of the software encounters a defect. Errors and defects lurk in software until the portion (or function) where the error or defect resides is accessed by a user. A fault may result in failure if fault tolerance is not built into the system.

★ **Fault tolerance**—Fault tolerance is the set of mechanisms built into a product that provide a corrective action or an alternative action so that failure does not result. In software products, fault tolerance refers to the provision of an alternative course of action that facili-tates continued usage of the other functionalities of the software that are not defective.

★ **Failure**—Failure is the result of a product encountering a fault when in operation where a fault tolerance feature is not present. Failure prevents the smooth changeover to another functionality. It stops operation of the product, and the only way to resume is to restart the operation from the beginning. Failure is repeated every time the same set of conditions recurs until the fault causing the error is eliminated from the product.

As stated earlier, it is not feasible to build a product that is 100% defect-free. Thus, the question is: Which defects are permissible and which are not? To help answer this question, defects can be divided into three classes:

1. **Critical defects**—Critical defects cause failures. They remain in the product until corrective action is taken to eliminate them and the product is updated. These defects must be fixed immediately.

2. **Major defects**—Major defects are fault conditions for which a fault tolerance feature is built into the product. While these defects do not interfere with the use of other functionalities, they remain until they are resolved. However, major defects are not showstoppers; they do not need to be fixed immediately, but they should be corrected at the earliest possible time.

3. **Minor defects**—Minor defects are mere nuisances. They do not cause failures, and no alternative action is necessary. Functionality can be used without any interruption, but they are defects just the same. Examples of minor defects include:

   ★ Spelling error or wrong spelling on a screen (A spelling error is incorrect in any country, but a wrong spelling is incorrect only in some countries. For example, "color" is incorrect in countries that use British spelling, but it is correct in countries that use U.S. spelling.)

   ★ Misalignment of data on a report

   ★ Text not fully visible in a text box or a combo box

   ★ Need to scroll a screen both vertically and horizontally

   ★ Poor color contrast on a screen

A "quality product" can have no critical defects. Such defects give users a highly negative impression of the product. The consequence of a critical defect is that end users are not able to use the functionality until the defect is fixed, which holds up the customers' operations. Therefore, critical defects are strictly forbidden if a product is to be tagged a "quality product." Critical defects can be uncovered through software reviews, negative testing, and stress testing, in addition to the usual types of testing to which a product is subjected.

A minor defect makes a product a laughingstock. It is visible for everyone to see, point out, and make fun of. A minor defect also is the club with which a product developer's quality tag can be beaten. The presence of a minor defect indicates the laxity with which the quality assurance activities are carried out in the organization. Minor defects are easy to trap and eliminate, and it is best that software developers take the time to eliminate them if they want to claim the quality tag for their product. Minor defects can be uncovered using a careful system of software verification and checklists during reviews.

A major defect provides an alternative course of action which camouflages the defect from the user's view. Furthermore, the user understands that a specific set of circumstances produces the fault. Since failure does not result from the defect, the user can continue with the operation and usually is willing to wait for the defect to be fixed. Thus, a major defect is harmless insofar as claims to a product's quality tag. Major defects lurk inside a product, and it is very difficult to uncover and eliminate all of them. They surface only under a specific set of operating conditions. It is not practical to produce every possible combination of operating conditions during software testing. That is why major defects continue to lurk inside products.

Thus, software developers can confidently claim that a product is defect-free as long as there are no critical or minor defects present in the product. The presence of a few major defects does not affect the status of the quality tag. All the same, though, a product of true quality should not contain any defects, as all defects will eventually be discovered by users. One or two defects may not perturb a user, but too many will certainly cause users to question the product's quality tag.

PROGRAM QUALITY

A program is the smallest unit of software. During recent changes in software development, programs underwent a metamorphosis. Programs from the 1970s look vastly different than those of today. Today's programs are now referred to as routines, methods, classes, objects, components, agents, and macros, among other names. People may be sensitive about what a program is called, but the fact remains that all these names are ways of referring to software programs.

Building a quality product begins with the smallest unit of a software product, and that is a program. The attributes of a good program are the same as those of a quality software product (maintainability, flexibility, portability, etc.). These attributes can be built into the program using general coding guidelines for all programming and coding guidelines for each programming language used in an organization. Appendix I provides general coding guidelines as a reference. In addition to the information found there, the following suggestions also are helpful in developing good software programs.

As far as possible, do not combine multiple functionalities into one program. Keep one function for one program. Sometimes that one function can result in a longer program, but multiple functionalities should not be combined just because a program is very short. This makes software maintenance easier.

Keep programs short in length. In the days of third-generation-language programming, structured programming was the norm, with one main calling routine and multiple called subroutines. Now, however, with event orientation in program execution, some amount of structured programming is built into the programming language itself. Therefore, it makes more sense to keep each event response program short. What is a short program? There is no universally defined optimum length for a short program, but the industry rule of thumb is that 50 to 100 lines is a manageable program. Extreme conditions might call for longer programs, but as much as possible, keep each routine to a maximum of 100 lines of code.

Make extensive use of callable subroutines (subprograms) instead of writing longer programs.

Make all programs and subroutines general purpose by passing parameters to them. This also facilitates reuse of the code in other projects.

Always try to make reuse of proven code wherever possible instead of writing fresh code from scratch. Proven code has been tested to confirm that all quality aspects have been built in.

Build as many dynamically linked libraries as possible instead of building the functionality into programs. Dynamically linked libraries enter random access memory (RAM) on an as-needed basis. This saves RAM and avoids large amounts of virtual memory being used.

Avoid hard coding (defining constants inside the program itself) completely except in the case of flags and counters for finite loops. If there are many constants, use a parameter file that is read at the start of the program or as needed, and import the values into the program during execution.

Use only flat files for storing the parameters of the program. If the parameter data is in a table, some values might need to be hard coded to connect to the database and open the table.

Always keep only one entry point and one exit point for the program. Multiple exits in particular can leave some tables, files, or connections open, which can cause problems.

Do not open files, tables, or database connections at the beginning of the program; open them just before use. Remember that opening these occupies a minimum of one block each of RAM (the size of a block changes from system to system, but the normal size is one kilobyte). In these days of multiuser and multitasking operating systems, RAM gets filled very fast and the system starts to use virtual memory from disk. Using large amounts of virtual memory can result in thrashing (exchanging too many pages from RAM to disk and vice versa), which causes the computer to slow down.

When opening files or tables or connecting to databases, ensure they are closed again as soon as the function of reading or updating is completed. Do not leave these files and database connections to be closed automatically by the act of closing the programs.

When declaring variables, use as many local variables (local to the routine in which they are used) as possible. Global (static) variables stay on even though the routine is closed, and they occupy RAM needlessly until the product closes.

Declare one variable per line. Why? Many languages permit declaring multiple variables per line. Remember that once the program is promoted to production, most organizations do not permit the deletion of lines of code. The existing line is commented out and a new line is inserted in its place. An explanatory commenting line is added to make this change. If it becomes necessary to delete one variable from a list of variables that are declared on the same line, that line needs to be commented out and a new line inserted with all other variables except the deleted one. This process of commenting and inserting lines is prone to error. All opportunities for error need to be eliminated.

Avoid "goto" control structure unless absolutely essential. This structure takes the flow control away from the programmer and could lead to multiple program exits. Always use subroutines that return control to the calling routine.

When defining naming conventions, do not use names longer than 15 characters, even though most languages permit use of longer names for variables. Longer names are the leading cause of syntax errors in programs because frequently spelling errors are made when typing. Almost every word can be abbreviated to two or three characters. Use abbreviated words instead of full words to build the names of variables. A 15-character variable name can represent four words, where each is abbreviated to three characters with three separators between the words. How often does a variable name require more than four words?

As far as possible, do not direct output from the program directly to the printer unless it is printing a receipt across a counter. Large outputs in particular should be directed to a print file. Spooling utilities provided by the operating system are much better at controlling the printer than programs developed by software developers. Spooling utilities take care of events such as paper outage, paper jam, printer offline, printer not powered up, ink/toner exhausted, etc. without hanging the computer. Unless the printing is to be done immediately, it is better to save the report and use other programs that are better at executing the printing function. When printing from the program, be sure to include an exhaustive error handling routine.

One of the leading causes of poor-quality software is leaving error handling to the operating system or the development platform. Each can manage many errors, but they cause software to close abruptly, resulting in loss of data or data integrity or requiring the program to restart. To ensure smooth operation, all errors must be trapped, and an appropriate message that is meaningful to end users must be displayed in addition to an alternative permitted course of action. The following errors should be handled inside the program itself:

★ **Connecting to databases**—Check for success of connection.
★ **Opening a flat file**—Check for success in opening the file.
★ **Opening a table**—Check for success in opening the table.
★ **Writing information to a file or a table**—Check for success of the operation.
★ **Arithmetic division**—It is essential to check that the denominator is not zero before any arithmetic division operation is performed. If it is, a nonrecoverable error will result.
★ **Arithmetic multiplication**—It is essential to check that the receiving variable has adequate width to accommodate the result without truncation.
★ **Connecting to any device**—Check for success of connection.

Many programming languages provide brief statements that can be used by expert programmers to improve the productivity of programming work. These statements are good and generally work very well. However, sometimes these brief statements make it very difficult to trace and debug an error, especially when debugging an inaccurate result. Writing more lines where one complex line will do allows developers to step through every line and trace the result to pinpoint which statement is injecting the error. The gain in programming productivity would be lost by the additional debugging time. Also significant is the fact that developers cannot be sure that software maintenance will be performed by expert programmers. Programmers who are not experts might find it extremely difficult to maintain such code efficiently. In view of these considerations, it is better to write multiple lines of code rather than a single brief advanced line.

Today, most programming languages accommodate longer lines. Although each line is allowed up to 255 characters, it is impossible to see all 255 characters in a single line on a screen or on a printout. When the line is wrapped around, the line breaks are random, which makes it difficult to read and understand the code. Every programming language allows lines to be broken up by some mechanism. Use that facility, and break long lines into multiple short, convenient lines. The norm is that a line must be visible on the screen without scrolling horizontally or the line wrapping around. It is thus easier to read, understand, and maintain the code. By breaking up a long line into multiple short lines, productivity improves at the peer review and maintenance stages in addition to the debugging stage.

Break up long arithmetic statements into multiple statements. Debugging a long arithmetic statement for inaccurate results can be quite tedious. Short, multiple arithmetic statements make it easier to trace the result across each statement and nail an error.

Use simple algorithms in place of complex algorithms. The following typical scenario I once came across explains why. An arithmetic computation statement was in a program. The next statement raised the result to its square. Then the next statement computed the square root of the result, and this result was used in the next statement. Apparently, the programmer used this algorithm to avoid the result going negative (raising any number to its square makes it positive), as the language did not provide for absolute value function. Finding the square root of a number is a stack operation, which consumes more time and resources. Also, the square root might cause a precision problem, due to a long number of decimals. Instead, the programmer could have used an if-then construct and multiplied the number by minus one (−1) if the result was negative (or less than zero). For most complex problems, simple solutions do exist. Use the simpler ones in place of complex algorithms. Simple solutions improve the efficiency of software maintenance, if not the efficiency of the execution.

In some programming languages that are available across multiple systems, there are system-specific extensions that make programming easier. These system-specific constructs also can facilitate achievement of functionality that is not available in the standard language. However, using the system-specific constructs affects portability. Therefore, as far as possible, do not use system-specific constructs. Determine whether a library utility that uses the standard constructs to achieve the same functionality can be developed, and if so, use it across the software product. If it is absolutely necessary to use system-specific constructs, see if they can be put into a callable routine so that developers know which routines need special action when porting the software. Use them inside the main program if none of the above alternatives are workable.

MEASUREMENT OF PRODUCT QUALITY

The market judges the quality of a commercial off-the-shelf product, and this judgment is what determines the relative position of the product in the market. The product is subject to market forces.

For a make-to-order software product, quality is assured by the software development process and acceptance testing. Acceptance testing can never be exhaustive. Few companies measure the performance of the software process, even though it is mandated by such standards as ISO 9000 and by such models as the Capability Maturity Model Integration. Therefore, software product quality needs to be measured, especially in a make-to-order software development scenario.

Product quality does not easily lend itself to measurement, let alone to accurate measurement. The second issue is at what stage the quality of a software product should be measured. A physical product, such as a car, is subjected to extensive actual or simulated field trials before it is released to the public. Software products that are commercial off-the-shelf in nature also are subjected to field trials, but no field trials are performed for software products that are built for a single customer, except for provision of support during the warranty period. Therefore, if the quality of a software product is to be measured at all, it has to be done at the release stage.

I propose a composite metric to measure the quality of a software product, which is based on the following parameters:

1. An organizational environment that fosters product quality
2. Effectiveness of organizational quality assurance activities
3. Peer review coverage of software artifacts
4. Unit testing coverage of code
5. Exhaustiveness of software testing

In this proposed metric, each of these parameters is rated, and a composite product quality rating is calculated by assigning a weight to each parameter. How to rate each of these parameters is discussed in the next sections of this chapter.

An Organizational Environment that Fosters Product Quality

Table 3.3 gives the attributes for rating this parameter. The value for the organizational environment rating (OER) is computed using the following formula:

$$\text{OER} = (\text{Rating for quality department} \times W_{o1})$$
$$+ (\text{Rating for software process} \times W_{o2})$$
$$+ (\text{Rating for process conformance} \times W_{o3})$$
$$+ (\text{Rating for rewards and recognition} \times W_{o4})$$

The weights (W_{o1}, W_{o2}, W_{o3}, W_{o4}) are explained in Table 3.3

For the calculations in this chapter, we will use the following values:

Rating for quality department   = 4
Rating for software process   = 5
Rating for process conformance   = 3
Rating for rewards and recognition   = 3

Therefore, the value for the OER is

$$OER = (4 \times 0.3) + (5 \times 0.4) + (3 \times 0.2) + (3 \times 0.1)$$

$$= 4.1$$

Keep this value aside until the other values have been computed.

Table 3.3. Attributes for rating an organizational environment that fosters product quality

Attribute	Rating
Existence of a quality department: weight = 0.30 (W_{o1})	
Fully staffed quality department; independent testing team; quality head equal in rank and pay with delivery head; champions process and product quality	5
Fully staffed quality department; independent testing team; quality head lower in rank and pay compared to delivery head; champions process and product quality	4
Fully staffed quality department; independent testing team; quality head lower in rank and pay compared to delivery head; champions process	3
Quality department staffed to perform quality audits and to coordinate process activities; stopgap quality head; coordinates process activities; depends on project teams for independent testing	2
Quality department staffed to coordinate process activities; no qualified quality head; coordinates process; independent testing is the responsibility of project teams	1
Existence of software development processes: weight = 0.40 (W_{o2})	
Process covers all aspects of software development and quality assurance; standards and guidelines exist for all software development activities; a formal metrics and analysis mechanism exists; a formal process improvement mechanism is in place	5

Table 3.3. Attributes for rating an organizational environment that fosters product quality (continued)

Attribute	Rating
Process covers all aspects of software development and quality assurance; standards and guidelines exist for all software development activities; formal process improvement mechanism is in place	4
Process covers most aspects of software development, but does not fully cover quality assurance; standards and guidelines do not fully cover all aspects of software development; process improvement is event driven	3
Process covers some but not all aspects of software development; process improvement is not really an important aspect	2
Organization is not driven by process at all	1

Process conformance: weight = 0.20 (W_{o3})

Attribute	Rating
Process conformance audits are process driven; all audits are carried out, in conformance with an approved plan; all nonconformance reports receive serious attention by management; management review meetings are held, in conformance with approved plan without fail	5
Process conformance audits are process driven; most audits are carried out, in conformance with an approved plan; important nonconformance reports receive serious management attention; management review meetings are held regularly	4
Process conformance audits are process driven; audits are conducted regularly, but not according to an approved plan; nonconformance reports are resolved by the head of quality, the software engineering group, or by the delivery head; management review meetings are conducted by the head of quality, the software engineering group, or the delivery head	3
Process audits are process driven; audits are conducted based on organizational convenience; management review meetings are conducted based on the convenience of the person chairing the meeting; nonconformance reports are resolved mostly by the auditor	2
Process audits are conducted as and when convenient; not process driven; nonconformance reports remain open for a long time	1

Rewards and recognition: weight = 0.10 (W_{o4})

Attribute	Rating
A formal mechanism exists to recognize and reward efforts to improve quality of products, and the awards are given regularly	5
A formal mechanism does not exist, but rewards are given regularly for efforts to improve product quality	3
Recognition and rewards for efforts to improve product quality are given occasionally, but only for outstanding effort	1

Table 3.4. Derivation of EQAR

Sigma value of the organization	Rating
6 sigma (3 defects per 1 million opportunities)	5
5 sigma (3 defects per 100,000 opportunities)	4
4 sigma (3 defects per 10,000 opportunities)	3
3 sigma (3 defects per 1,000 opportunities)	2
2 sigma (3 defects per 100 opportunities)	1

Effectiveness of Organizational Quality Assurance Activities

The effectiveness of organizational quality assurance activities should result in the elimination or minimization of residual defects passed on to the customer. This effectiveness can be measured using the defect density of the product delivered, which is also called the sigma value. This aspect is covered in greater detail in Appendix G on quality metrics and measurement. Use the sigma value of the organization to derive the effectiveness of organizational quality assurance activities rating (EQAR). Table 3.4 shows the derivation of this rating. For our computational purposes, we will assume a value of 4 sigma.

Peer Review Coverage of Software Artifacts

Subjecting all software (information as well as code) artifacts to 100% peer review and 100% managerial review is a best practice. However, many organizations skip a peer review in some cases, under the assumption that a managerial review is adequate.

The percentage of artifacts covered by peer review is computed as:

$$\frac{\text{Number of software artifacts covered by peer review}}{\text{Total number of software artifacts}} \times 100$$

Using this percentage, a peer review coverage rating (PRCR) is derived as shown in Table 3.5. For our computational purposes, we will assume a value of 90% coverage.

Table 3.5. Derivation of PRCR

Percentage of review coverage	Rating
100%	5
80% and above, but less than 100%	4
70% and above, but less than 80%	3
60% and above, but less than 70%	2
Less than 60%	1

Unit Testing Coverage of Code

Here, unit testing means independent unit testing, which is carried out by a person who did not code the artifact that is being tested. Subjecting all software code artifacts to 100% independent unit testing is a best practice. However, many organizations skip unit testing in some cases, under the assumption that self unit testing (that is, unit testing by the programmer who coded the artifact) is adequate.

The percentage of artifacts covered by unit testing is computed as:

$$\frac{\text{Number of software artifacts covered by unit testing}}{\text{Total number of software artifacts}} \times 100$$

Using this percentage, a unit testing coverage rating (UTCR) is derived as shown in Table 3.6. For our computational purposes, we will assume a value of 75% coverage.

Table 3.6. Derivation of UTCR

Percentage of unit testing coverage	Rating
100%	5
80% and above, but less than 100%	4
70% and above, but less than 80%	3
60% and above, but less than 70%	2
Less than 60%	1

Exhaustiveness of Software Testing

Exhaustiveness of software testing on a software product includes two aspects: the number of tests that should have been conducted and the number of test cases that should have been executed.

In terms of the number of tests that should have been conducted, each software product, depending on its nature (number of tiers, functional domain, development and target platforms, etc.), needs to be subjected to certain types of tests. Some products, such as reservation systems, require more exhaustive testing for parallel and concurrent testing than other types of tests. Other products, such as financial systems, need to be more rigorously tested for accuracy and precision. Products such as online stores need to be tested more for their response times.

Thus, the types of tests to which a software product should be subjected depends on its nature. A more exhaustively tested software product has a better chance of being a quality product than a product that is less exhaustively tested. The types of testing to which a software product normally should be subjected are recorded in the test plan document for the project. In the case of outsourced projects, the types of tests to be carried out are specified by the customer.

This specification needs to be compared with the actual tests that are carried out. Sometimes all the required tests are not conducted. The following are some of the reasons why:

1. Due to a lack of time, all the planned or specified tests are not carried out.
2. Based on the results of peer reviews and initial tests, the decision might be that further testing is not really necessary.
3. Delivery and schedule pressures might force a decision to abandon further testing.

The percentage of tests conducted is computed using the following formula:

$$\frac{\text{Number of tests actually conducted}}{\text{Number of tests that should have been conducted}} \times 100$$

Using this percentage, a rating for exhaustiveness of tests conducted is derived as shown in Table 3.7.

Similarly, all the planned test cases might not have been executed. The percentage of test cases executed is computed using the following formula:

Table 3.7. Derivation of exhaustiveness of tests conducted rating

Percentage of tests conducted	Rating
100%	5
80% and above, but less than 100%	4
70% and above, but less than 80%	3
60% and above, but less than 70%	2
Less than 60% conducted	1

$$\frac{\text{Number of test cases actually executed}}{\text{Number of test cases that should have been executed}} \times 100$$

Using this percentage, a rating for exhaustiveness of test cases executed is derived as shown in Table 3.8.

A weight is assigned to each of these two ratings. A weight of 0.6 is assigned to exhaustiveness of tests conducted, as a test missing altogether is much more serious than missing a few test cases. A weight of 0.4 is assigned to exhaustiveness of test cases executed.

The exhaustiveness of testing rating (ETR) is computed as:

$$\text{ETR} = (\text{Exhaustiveness of tests conducted} \times \text{Weight})$$
$$+ (\text{Exhaustiveness of test cases executed} \times \text{Weight})$$

Let us assume a rating of 4 for exhaustiveness of tests conducted and a rating of 5 for exhaustiveness of test cases executed. Thus, the ETR is

Table 3.8. Derivation of exhaustiveness of test cases executed rating

Percentage of test cases executed	Rating
100%	5
80% and above, but less than 100%	4
70% and above, but less than 80%	3
60% and above, but less than 70%	2
Less than 60% conducted	1

$$\text{ETR} = (4 \times 0.6) + (5 \times 0.4)$$
$$= 2.4 + 2$$
$$= 4.4$$

The composite product quality rating can now be computed.

Composite Product Quality Rating

The first activity in computing the composite product quality rating (CPQR) is to assign appropriate weights to each of the product quality parameters. Table 3.9 shows the suggested weights.

If the organizational environment is one that fosters product quality, then all other parameters automatically get the highest importance in the organization. That is the reason for assigning the highest weight to this parameter. The EQAR is higher if the organization fosters product quality, which is dependent on peer review and unit testing. If peer review and independent unit testing are carried out effectively and exhaustively, then software testing is automatically taken care of.

The CPQR is computed using the following formula:

$$\text{CPQR} = (\text{OER} \times W_1) + (\text{EQAR} \times W_2) + (\text{PRCR} \times W_3)$$
$$+ (\text{UTCR} \times W_4) + (\text{ETR} \times W_5)$$

Table 3.9. Weights for product quality parameters

Product quality parameter	Weight
OER	0.35 (W_1)
EQAR	0.25 (W_2)
PRCR	0.15 (W_3)
UTCR	0.15 (W_4)
ETR	0.10 (W_5)
Total weight	1.00

Substituting the values computed in the above formula, the CPQR is thus:

$$CPQR = (4.1 \times 0.35) + (3 \times 0.25) + (4 \times 0.15)$$
$$+ (3 \times 0.15) + (4.4 \times 0.10)$$
$$= 1.44 + 0.75 + 0.60 + 0.45 + 0.44$$
$$= 3.68$$

The CPQR is 3.68 on a 5-point scale.

The following points should be noted:

1. As unique conditions dictate, it is possible that some organizations might see the need to add or delete some of the parameters mentioned here. They may do so.
2. Some organizations assign different levels of importance to these parameters, and therefore might prefer to assign different weights to them. They may do so.
3. While a 5-point scale is suggested, organizations can use a different scale.

Do we really need to measure the quality of the product that is developed against specified user requirements and for a specific order to do so? It is an accepted fact that there would be some residual defects, and this is measured by the sigma level of the organization that developed the software product. After all, it is the end product that we are really interested in, and not the organizational environment or other factors that are included in the measure described here.

Sure, the sigma level of the organization alone is adequate to measure the quality of the product "iff" (a term used in mathematics to mean "if and only if") the sigma level is diligently and accurately derived. Most organizations engaged in development of custom software do not have internal mechanisms to diligently collate and analyze all customer defect reports and derive the organizational sigma level. These organizations support the customer only during the warranty period, with the focus on resolving a defect rather than diligently recording and analyzing it. Normally organizations designate a project leader or an equivalent person to provide support to the customer during the warranty period, and the customer communicates with this person. Organizational-level mechanisms for deriving the organizational sigma level are more frequently absent than present. After the warranty period ends, the customer is likely to take on maintenance of the software in-house or entrust it to the original developer or a third party. The defects that are unearthed during software maintenance are never considered for inclusion in the data used to compute the organizational sigma level.

Therefore, the sigma level alone is inadequate to measure the quality of a software product produced through custom software development. In the example for which we computed the CPQR, the sigma level of the organization was 5, but the product quality turned out to be only 3.68.

It is very easy to collect the data to compute this metric. The information needed to derive the organizational environment is most likely available on the company's Web site, except perhaps for the existence of a quality department. This information cannot be classified as confidential by any stretch of the imagination and is therefore easy to obtain.

The effectiveness of organizational quality assurance activities depends on the sigma level of the company. Any organization should be glad to share this information. If an organization does not derive and maintain its sigma value, consider it to be at a 4-sigma level (that is, 3 defects in 10,000 opportunities) and proceed further.

Peer review coverage information can be obtained from the review records of the project. Unit testing coverage information can be obtained from the unit test plans and unit test logs of the project. Exhaustiveness of testing information can be obtained from the product test plans and product test logs of the project. Thus, the information needed to derive the CPQR is easy to obtain, and the methodology is fairly simple.

How should the CPQR metric be interpreted? Table 3.10 shows the maximum possible values for each of the factors that go into deriving the CPQR.

Obviously, a CPQR value that tends toward 5 is most desirable. To determine the minimum acceptable CPQR value, the minimum values that can be expected from each of these factors used in computing the CPQR in a process-driven organization need to be known.

Even if an organization does not have a quality department or a rewards and recognition system, it at least has a software development process, which contributes 0.70 ($0.40 \times 1.75 = 0.70$) toward the CPQR. If a process exists, then at least sketchy process conformance is in place, which on an average level contributes 0.35 ($0.2 \times 1.75 = 0.35$) toward the CPQR. Thus, the minimum expected from an organizational environment factor in a process-driven organization is 1.05.

Table 3.10. Maximum possible values for CPQR factors

Product quality parameter	Maximum possible value
OER	1.75
EQAR	1.25
PRCR	0.75
UTCR	0.75
ETR	0.50
Maximum possible CPQR value	5.00

A process-driven organization is at least at a 4-sigma level. The effectiveness of organizational quality assurance activities factor is therefore

$$(0.25 \times 3) = 0.75$$

The peer review coverage factor assuming a rating of 4 would be a minimum of

$$(4 \times 0.15) = 0.60$$

The unit testing coverage factor assuming a rating of 4 would be a minimum of

$$(4 \times 0.15) = 0.60$$

The exhaustiveness of testing factor assuming a rating of 4 would be a minimum of

$$(4 \times 0.10) = 0.40$$

The minimum acceptable CPQR is, therefore,

$$(1.05 + 0.75 + 0.60 + 0.60 + 0.40) = 3.4$$

Therefore, the CPQR for a software product developed in a process-driven organization can range from a minimum of 3.4 to a maximum of 5. Of these factors, organizational environment and effectiveness of organizational quality assurance activities are beyond the purview of the current project. If those values are low, it is an indication that the development organization needs to improve. If the CPQR is low, the other three values should be inspected and improved upon.

While a CPQR of 5 is desirable, a value of 4 is not bad. This metric can be computed before going in for acceptance testing. Then it is possible to insist on improvements based on the CPQR.

To conclude the discussion on product quality measurement using CPQR, I would submit that computing this metric is extremely useful, since it is accepted that 100% testing and 100% defect removal are not possible. The CPQR provides a quick, reliable, and objectively derived measure that assists the customer in judging the quality of the product being delivered and ensures that the product is as defect-free as it possibly can be.

4

ORGANIZATIONAL ENVIRONMENT THAT FOSTERS A QUALITY CULTURE

CHAPTER OVERVIEW

★ Need for an independent quality assurance department
★ Definition of the role of the quality assurance department and its position in an organization
★ Organization and staffing of the quality assurance department
★ A well-defined and institutionalized process for software development and quality assurance
★ A system of recognition and rewards
★ Commitment of senior management

QUALITY AND ORGANIZATIONAL ENVIRONMENT

When we receive something for free, we can be fairly certain it will be more trouble than it is worth. Nothing good in life is ever free, and there is no such thing as a free lunch. No statement is truer when speaking of quality. Quality does not happen by accident; we have to consciously work to achieve it. The first step in ensuring the quality of anything is to recognize that quality itself is the key to true customer satisfaction and to the very survival of an organization. Japanese companies realized this in the early 1950s, and look where they are today in terms of the quality of their products, profitability, and their position in the world market—they are among the top organizations.

Working to achieve quality first involves setting up a well-defined department for the quality function and then providing staff, planning the quality assurance (QA) activities, and diligently directing and controlling those activities. Each of these aspects should be monitored and adjusted in order to continually improve them. The key ingredients for building an organization that fosters a culture focused on building quality into its end product include the following:

1. A QA department that champions quality within the organization
2. A well-defined and institutionalized software development process that focuses on quality and includes a minimum set of QA activities that need to be performed at the project as well as organizational level, as well as a system to ensure its continual improvement
3. An explicit system of rewards and recognition for achieving excellence in quality
4. The commitment and involvement of senior management to fostering a culture of quality in the organization

Each of these ingredients is discussed in greater detail throughout this chapter.

NEED FOR AN INDEPENDENT QUALITY ASSURANCE DEPARTMENT

In the good old days of organizational management, each individual did his or her assigned job, and the CEO supervised everyone. For example, the marketing concept, total productive maintenance (TPM), and total quality management (TQM) implied that the CEO was the chief marketing manager, chief mechanic, and chief quality manager, respectively. However, such concepts, wonderful as they are, resulted in some confusion as to roles and responsibilities and provided leeway for CEOs to do away with departments considered inconvenient—specifically the QA department. It is true that the CEO is responsible for all activities in the organization, but equally true is the fact that no CEO alone can supervise and control all those activities unless the organization is very small. CEOs delegate responsibilities to next-line managers, who take ownership of the details.

While the marketing concept and TPM did not eliminate the positions of the marketing manager and the maintenance manager, TQM did assist some organizations in justifying elimination of the quality manager and in some extreme cases the QA department itself. This was especially so in the software development industry and, thus, an unfortunate misuse of a great concept. What is interesting about some of the organizations that have done this is that they are certified in both the International Organization for Standardization's ISO 9000 series of standards and the Software Engineering Institute's Capability Maturity Model (CMM®) or Capability Maturity Model Integration (CMMI®)! The CEOs of such organizations state that they personally look after the quality function and, as TQM suggests, ensure that all quality activities are embedded within the development activities themselves.

At a conceptual level, this sounds great, but at a practical, nuts-and-bolts level, the main responsibilities of a CEO are to deliver results and to show a profit. A CEO would certainly focus on marketing if the order book were empty. But would a CEO find time to focus on the quality function, which does not generate any direct and tangible revenue? Very unlikely!

The TQM philosophy does not advocate doing away with the QA department altogether; all it states, in essence, is that the QA department alone cannot ensure quality and that all personnel, beginning with the CEO, have to work to achieve quality.

Of those software development organizations that have a QA department, the department focuses almost entirely on achieving and maintaining such certifications as ISO and CMMI®. It is rare to find an organization that has a full-fledged QA department which looks after not only process quality but also product quality. Rarer still is the software development organization that has specialized staff to conduct independent verification and validation.

When CEOs take on the role of quality manager on a part-time basis, the amount of attention and focus they can give to the quality function is diluted by the daily issues of finances, personnel, customer pressure, delivery concerns, etc. In such organizations, there is no one person others can easily approach for guidance on matters pertaining to quality. Quality activities, if they are performed at all, are performed by the people developing the software.

A QA department is essential in a software development organization for the following reasons:

1. The responsibility for championing quality in the organization is vested with a specific entity.
2. Developers can obtain counsel and guidance from experts on quality matters.

3. Personnel who specialize in verification and validation can offer their expertise and knowledge in uncovering most defects, thus vastly improving quality.
4. No quality activity would be missed during product construction.
5. The benefits of organization-level analyses of measurement and improvement of quality can be realized.
6. The concepts of zero defects and right first time can be championed in the organization, minimizing the need for rework and resulting in better productivity, quality, and motivation of personnel.
7. Continual monitoring of quality achievements and carrying out trend analysis enable the organization to proactively resolve quality issues before they become serious problems.
8. It becomes possible to benchmark quality achievements against comparable organizations.
9. The QA department can evaluate and obtain tools that can improve productivity and quality for the organization.

A full-fledged QA department more than underwrites its own expenses; it can, in fact, effect a larger savings for the organization. A best practice for a software development organization that focuses on the quality of its deliverables is to have an independent, fully staffed, and robust QA department.

THE ROLE OF THE QUALITY ASSURANCE DEPARTMENT

Each organizational role has a specific purpose and a specialized niche, and it can be responsible for its own results. Consider the following examples:

★ The role of marketing is to win orders, and its performance depends on its own efforts. It is the custodian of an organization's order book and customers.
★ Finance arranges required financing and carefully monitors expenditures and revenues. It is the custodian of an organization's monetary resources.
★ Human resources secures the necessary employees for the organization. It is the custodian of an organization's personnel.

★ Delivery (sometimes called the technical department) develops the necessary software and delivers it to the customers. It is the custodian of an organization's products and technology.

The QA department is the custodian of the quality of the products built by the delivery department. Unlike the tangible assets of the departments listed above, quality is an intangible result of the QA department's work. If the quality of the deliverable is great, then the delivery department is viewed as having done a great job, but if a deliverable is of poor quality, somehow it is the QA department that is viewed as not having been adequately diligent in performing quality control activities.

The role of the QA department was once to act as a "watchdog," monitoring the quality of deliverables (see Figure 4.1). Watchdogs not only bark when something is amiss; they might bite if necessary. This is how the QA department should be. However, political correctness has changed the role of the QA department from a watchdog to the "eyes and ears" of management to gauge the state of organizational quality. "Eyes and ears" are well equipped for conveying information, but a "bark" or a "bite" is much better suited to galvanizing action—the action of rectifying nonconformance and improving quality—along with conveying information (a "bark" conveys information much more effectively than an e-mail does, even one flagged as "high importance") on behalf of management.

Eyes and ears   Watchdog

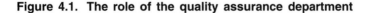

Figure 4.1. The role of the quality assurance department

That is why the role of the QA department in software development organizations should be as a watchdog, as it is in the manufacturing domain.

THE POSITION OF THE QUALITY ASSURANCE DEPARTMENT IN AN ORGANIZATION

Some organizations place the QA department under the delivery function, based on the following line of arguments:

★ All QA activities are related to delivery.
★ All QA suggestions are implemented by the delivery department.
★ If the head of the delivery department is convinced of the QA department's recommendations, all QA activities are properly implemented. It is impossible to implement QA activities and initiatives without the cooperation and willingness of the delivery department.
★ The QA department should not be allowed to force solutions that are not implementable by the delivery department. (What better way to achieve this than by placing the QA department under the control of the delivery department.)

While the above scenario is the reality in some organizations, it is not a correct arrangement. These organizations, in essence, take away the "bark" and the "bite" from the watchdog. The primary responsibility of the delivery head is to deliver product that passes acceptance testing. For the delivery head, quality is one of several secondary responsibilities, which include project acquisition, productivity, staff motivation, team morale, customer satisfaction, profit management, cost control, technology updates, etc. It is not an exaggeration to say that quality does not find a place second or third in this list of priorities.

Statistical methods, on which most quality analyses are based, are always open to misinterpretation and misuse. Changing a few data items can generate a totally different result. If the QA department is placed under the delivery function, the following scenarios can arise:

1. Quality analyses can be tailored to suit the delivery department's convenience.
2. Certain facts or trends that pose an inconvenience to the delivery department may never reach the CEO's attention.

3. If the delivery department either violates or poorly implements QA activities or initiatives, the QA manager cannot overstep the delivery head (his or her boss) to bring the matter to a higher authority without risking his or her job.
4. If the quality manager and the delivery head disagree on an aspect of QA, the quality manager has little choice but to accept the decision of the delivery head.
5. QA initiatives can be restricted by the priorities of the delivery department. (Instead, they should be dictated by organizational requirements and industry trends.)

It is therefore very shortsighted to make the QA department subordinate to the delivery department. The QA department should be on equal footing with other departments, including the delivery department, and should report directly to the CEO. A suggested placement of the QA department is shown in Figure 4.2.

When the QA department is at an equal level with the delivery department, it can raise issues it might have with the delivery department on matters relating to quality to a higher level of authority in an effort to resolve them. In the course of organizational operations, differences of opinion on nonconformance issues pointed out by the QA department are a common occurrence between the delivery department and the QA department. When the QA department operates independently, it is possible to ensure rectification of these nonconformance issues. Various quality measurements and analyses can be carried out

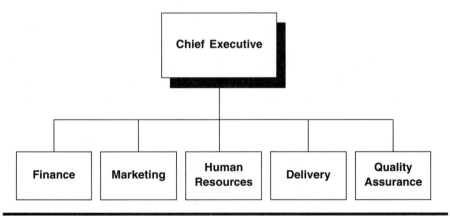

Figure 4.2. Suggested placement of the quality assurance department in a software development organization

regularly, on either an event-driven basis or a periodic basis, with the results made available to all executives concerned. This would bring about awareness of and improvements in the organizational processes.

Conflict between the delivery department and the QA department is the one negative aspect of an organization having an independent QA department, since the focus of the delivery department is expediting delivery and the focus of the QA department is uncovering inherent defects. However, such conflicts are easily manageable, first by having a well-defined process in place and, second, by escalating the matter to the next level of authority if necessary. Conflict is part and parcel of an organization's environment. For example, marketing pushes for faster delivery in order to beat the competition to the market, while the delivery department favors slower delivery to ensure the product is defect-free. Finance pushes for higher selling prices in order to increase profits, while marketing favors lower prices to win orders. Conflict between the QA department and the delivery department is simply one more example.

To achieve better organizational quality, the QA department should be independent and on a par with the delivery department.

ORGANIZATION OF THE QUALITY ASSURANCE DEPARTMENT

What functions should be entrusted to a full-fledged, independent, watchdog-style QA department in a software development organization? Most software development organizations that have a QA department entrust it with the process quality function (championing the organizational software development process), interfacing with certifying agencies, and other related activities. Some organizations consider their independent testing department to be the QA department. In order to do justice to the organizational function of assuring quality in deliverables, a comprehensive QA department should perform the following functions:

★ Software development process definition and improvement
★ Standards and guidelines development and improvement
★ Software inspections and audits
★ Software testing
★ Measurement and analysis

Each of these functions is discussed below.

Software Development Process Definition and Improvement

The software development process includes all aspects of software development and QA; standards and guidelines for all software development activities; a formal measurement, metrics, and analysis mechanism; and a formal process improvement mechanism. Additionally, it may include the processes that guide other organizational entities, as standards such as ISO 9000 mandate. This function includes the following activities:

★ Initial definition of the software development process for the organization—This entails identifying people to document the processes, providing them with the necessary facilities, coordinating QA for the artifacts developed, piloting the artifacts, and rolling out the process.

★ Definition of a process that automatically initiates process improvements based on event triggers or period triggers—This involves defining the possible event triggers for process improvement (such as external audits, periodic audits, etc.), defining the period for triggering process improvements, defining the mechanisms for receiving process improvement suggestions, consolidating all process improvement suggestions and carrying out necessary analyses, obtaining necessary approvals for implementing the process improvements, allocating personnel to effect the necessary improvements, and rolling out the revised process.

★ Rollout and implementation of the process developed in the organization—This involves piloting the process on a sample project, guiding the pilot implementation, receiving and implementing feedback (if any) from the field, obtaining necessary approvals, and rolling out the process for implementation.

★ Periodic appraisals of the efficacy of process compliance in the organization—This entails regularly carrying out either audits or process compliance appraisals to ensure that process compliance is at the desired level and to plug deficiencies if any are uncovered.

★ Analysis of the results obtained from the process compliance appraisals using process performance measurement—This entails analyzing any nonconformances uncovered to see if there is a perceptible trend that might reveal an assignable reason which can be addressed or to see if the nonconformances are due purely to chance occurrences. The results of this analysis are presented to senior management for informational purposes and for guidance.

★ Compute and periodically update organizational process capability baselines that can be used by software project managers during software project execution. Various capabilities of the organization, such as productivity for various development platforms, quality capabilities (sigma level, defect density, and defect injection rate), schedule compliance capability, customer satisfaction, etc., can be computed and published as information for the organization's stakeholders so they can use this data in their activities. The data needs to be updated periodically to reflect recent achievements.

★ Compare and contrast organizational processes with those of popular process models (such as ISO 9000 and CMMI®), and effect process improvements that are beneficial for the organization.

★ Spearhead organizational initiatives for obtaining compliance certification from ISO 9000, CMMI®, etc., and guide the organization in implementing these models in both letter and spirit.

★ Interface with the certifying agencies to organize certification audits or maturity appraisals, and ensure they are concluded successfully for the organization.

The QA department should be the organizational entity that champions organizational process initiatives.

Standards and Guidelines Development and Improvement

Standards and guidelines are part and parcel of organizational processes, but they deserve special mention for the following reasons:

★ They achieve uniformity of output from different people. This makes software maintenance easier later on.

★ They ensure a minimum level of quality in output, even from disparate individuals.

★ They save effort of people working on software development.

★ They guide new entrants to the organization in carrying out work efficiently and with less training.

★ They are the main tool to achieve higher levels of quality in the organization.

Some people complain that standards restrict the freedom of creative individuals. This is true to some extent, but when faced with the choice of either an utter lack of uniformity or restriction of freedom, the choice is clearly tilted in favor of standards and guidelines. Besides, every standard provides for exception handling with special approval, which ensures that any deviation from a standard is for the sake of improvement. In other words, there can be exceptions to standards.

The QA department also champions the definition and improvement of standards and guidelines for the organization as part of the organizational process definition and improvement described above.

Software Inspection and Audits

It is possible to assign all software inspections and phase-end audits to specialists in the QA department. Many organizations use software development personnel from within the project or from other projects to carry out these activities, but it is advantageous to have specialists perform inspections and audits. It would not be economical to keep a large staff of inspectors and auditors to conduct an organization-wide audit, but it would certainly pay to keep a minimum number of in-house specialists who conduct phase-end audits and software inspections. The same set of inspectors and auditors would form part of the audit team for organization-wide audits. This team would conduct as well as bring stability and continuity to organization-wide audits, especially when auditors from projects can change from audit to audit. This should be a key function of the QA department.

Software inspection and audit activities are described in greater detail in Chapter 5.

Software Testing

The following software testing is carried out in organizations:

1. **Unit testing**—This is the testing of every software code artifact developed, including screens, reports, table scripts, stored procedures (triggers), programs, etc. Unit testing is normally carried out by someone on the development team other than the author of the unit.

2. **Integration testing**—This type of testing checks for proper coupling of software units into modules and modules into a software product. Integration testing can be conducted by an independent testing team, although it is frequently conducted by independent peers from the project team.

3. **System testing**—This type of testing ensures that the product works without error on all target platforms where it is slated to function. System testing can be conducted by an independent testing team, although it is frequently conducted by independent peers from the project team.

4. **Acceptance testing**—This type of testing is conducted to ensure that the software product is accepted by the customer. Acceptance testing is normally coordinated by the software project manager, but it can also be coordinated by the QA department.

5. **Additional testing**—This includes negative testing, load testing, stress testing, end-to-end testing, etc. Additional testing is conducted on an as-needed basis by an independent testing team.

Very few software development organizations have an independent testing department. Most that do have one do not have adequate and qualified staff to plan and conduct most of the planned testing. Testing departments, in my observation, typically try to use testing tools to automate product testing mainly for regression testing purposes and in some cases act as an expert group to guide and assist the project teams in conducting testing effectively.

In the manufacturing industry, an independent testing team is *sine qua non;* that is, mandatory. It is unthinkable that the product designers themselves would conduct the testing to certify that the product is ready to ship. Only in the software development industry does the software engineer perform almost every step in product development—from requirements to design and from coding to testing—and declare the product fit to use. I concur with the argument that the effort, duration, and cost of testing in the manufacturing industry are much less than the effort, duration, and cost to manufacture the product, but this is not so in the software development industry. In the software development industry, sometimes the effort, duration, and cost expended for testing software products exceed these same expenses for developing the software product. There is some validity to the claim that a project does use independent peers to conduct testing, which is equivalent to testing conducted by an independent testing team, but I would say only to a limited extent. I agree that independent unit testing, which is white box testing, be carried out within the project team itself, but other types of testing, which are black box testing, can be carried out by independent testing teams.

I strongly advocate that the QA department be equipped with testing teams to conduct the following two tests at least, to ensure that the right product is built:

1. **Functional testing**—This type of testing ensures that all the expected functions are working as required or designed.
2. **Negative testing**—This type of testing ensures that adequate data validation routines, which handle erroneous input that can come from various sources, are built into the software product. Negative testing also ensures that unintended use will not crash the software product. A software crash of any kind sullies an organization's reputation, even if it is the result of unintended use, and should be prevented through proper testing.

Other types of testing can be entrusted to the testing department if an organization prefers, and I encourage this. What is important is that the QA department be equipped with a software testing wing that conducts some types of software testing and also is recognized as the expert group to guide other testers in the organization in achieving excellence in testing and thus software quality.

Software testing is discussed in greater detail in Chapter 6.

Measurement and Analysis

More often than not, measurement and analysis are a neglected area in software development organizations. Various software process improvement networks (or SPINs, which are networks of professionals in a geographical area who are engaged in software development or software quality and are trying to compile and benchmark numerous quality and productivity figures; SPINs are encouraged by the Software Engineering Institute) found that organizations simply do not have reliable/auditable data. Often, the measurement and analysis function is entrusted to the project management office, which itself is an appendage of the delivery department, and therefore does not receive adequate attention. A common occurrence in the measurement and analysis function is that the time sheets used in software development organizations to collect details of the effort spent by the staff are more oriented toward billing and salary administration than collating and analyzing valuable data.

Measurement and analysis, to be carried out properly, need reasonable expertise in the field of statistics and engineering analysis. It is rare to find such people entrusted with this work in software development organizations. While ISO 9000 and CMMI® do insist that measurement and analysis be carried out, merely starting the activity qualifies an organization for certification; the organization can then stall on this activity until the next certification audit or appraisal.

In software development organizations, management often argues that analysis shows, in auditable figures, facts it already knows, albeit instinctively. Therefore, management's question is: What is the added value of diligently performing this activity?

When it comes to quality in software development organizations, myopia is the norm rather than the exception, unfortunately. The concepts of quality, when diligently put into practice, increase productivity by eliminating rework. This results in reduced costs and higher customer satisfaction, which further results in increased revenues. Although this fact has been proved beyond reasonable doubt in Japanese companies such as Sony and Honda, it is overlooked in software development organizations. The success of Japanese companies is attributed more to their focus on quality than anything else.

When measuring organizational performance, true performance is revealed when the effect of special occurrences is removed. With true performance figures, precise plans for improvements can be drawn up and implemented. Using the measure-analyze-improve-monitor cycle, organizational performance can be moved into an ever-expanding circle of continual improvement. However, without proper measurement and analysis of organizational performance, it can never be known for certain where an organization stands or where it is heading.

Recognizing that measurement and analysis are important for an organization is one thing, but entrusting the activity to the right entity is another. The QA department is the right entity to shoulder this responsibility, because measurement and analysis are really an appendage of the quality function. Real figures of organizational performance are the tools that put the "bite" in the "bark" of the QA department, the organizational watchdog. The QA department can see the true value of measurement and analysis, whereas other departments, such as the project management office, cannot. Measurement and analysis demarcate the performance of the QA department itself to a degree.

Therefore, best practice dictates that organizations recognize measurement and analysis as a critical function and entrust this function to the QA department.

ORGANIZATION AND STAFFING OF THE QUALITY ASSURANCE DEPARTMENT

A QA department in a software development organization needs to carry out all the functions described so far in this chapter and can be organized as shown in Figure 4.3.

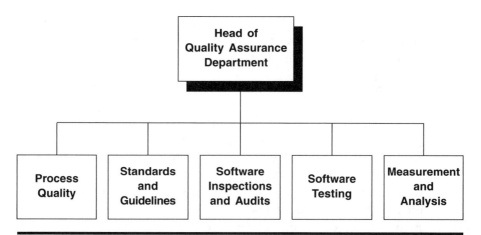

Figure 4.3. Suggested organization of the quality assurance department

How many people are required in each of these functions is a question that needs to be answered on a case-by-case basis. The following two main aspects should be considered in each case:

1. **Highest level of service**—The requester of the service does not have to wait to obtain the service.
2. **Highest utilization of personnel**—There is no idle time for the QA staff, but the requester of the service might need to wait for some time to obtain the service.

In reality, the QA department aims to balance these two objectives.

Another aspect that influences staffing is the uniformity of the workload. In real life, the workload is rarely uniform; it has its peak loads and troughs of underloading. Balance needs to be achieved between planning for the peak load period and planning for the underload period.

A manpower strategy needs to be defined as well. The strategy can be either placing all resources on call or using a strong set of in-house resources and temporarily hiring additional resources during peak workloads. In the case of temporary hiring, a decision must be made whether to hire resources in-house from the delivery department or to hire from outside. One good strategy is to rotate software developers in the QA department so that they learn the importance of the quality function firsthand.

Organizing and staffing a QA department really boils down to manpower planning, which is best performed by qualified industrial engineers. Manpower planning involves the following steps:

1. Enumerate all the activities performed by the department based on each distinct function.
2. Enumerate the number of iterations that might be required in a year for each activity.
3. Assign the time required to accomplish each enumerated activity per iteration, in person-hours.
4. Compute the amount of time required to perform all iterations for each of the enumerated activities.
5. Arrive at the total workload for each distinct function in person-hours required annually by totaling the times computed in step 4.
6. Arrive at the manpower requirements for each distinct function by dividing the corresponding workload by 2,000 (the number of person-hours per person per year).
7. Round fractions up to the next whole number. This provides spare time that can be utilized for other tasks.
8. Alternatively, round down to the next whole number. This could cause some stress on the resources in times of peak workload, or temporary hires might be needed to supplement manpower during peak workload periods.

Table 4.1 shows a sample manpower requirement computation. While this may seem to be a simple exercise, I strongly suggest employing the help of industrial engineers, who have specialized knowledge in work study and manpower planning, to plan the staffing requirements for the QA department.

A WELL-DEFINED AND INSTITUTIONALIZED SOFTWARE DEVELOPMENT PROCESS

According to a significant number of practitioners, especially software developers and delivery managers, this is the number one aspect of the parameters for fostering a quality culture in an organization. However, I rank it second. Unless there is a watchdog, the process might not be as well defined or implemented as it is made out to be. There should be "checks and balances" for all human endeavor. Without proper checks and balances, human endeavor will deteriorate over a period of time. Checks and balances (QA) are to human endeavor

Table 4.1. Manpower computation for a quality assurance department

Activity	Person-hours per iteration	Number of iterations per year	Total person-hours per year
Phase-end audit (3 per project for 25 projects per year)	4	75	300
Software inspections (3 per project for 25 projects per year)	5	75	375
Periodic audits (6 per year)	20	6	120
Process improvement coordination (4 times per year)	175	4	700
Measurement and analysis (12 times per year)	80	12	960
External audit coordination (2 times per year)	40	2	80
Assistance to projects, assuming 10 concurrent projects with 1 person for every 5 projects			4,000
Add any further activities in the manner shown above			
Total hours		3.27 or 4 persons	6,535
Total hours specialty-wise			
Audits and inspection		0.4 person or 1 person	875
Process definition and improvement		0.35 person or 1 person	700
Measurement and analysis		0.48 person or 1 person	960
Project assistance		2 persons	4,000
Total number of persons required		**minimum of 4 persons maximum of 5 persons**	

what brakes are to a car. True, brakes do not provide any motive power to the car (just as QA does not contribute to construction of the product) and they do consume gas (just as QA expends resources), but brakes save the car and its passengers from grave danger (just as QA prevents defective products from reaching customers).

All certification models mandate an organization to have a defined set of processes to refer to for guidance. A defined process brings to all human resources a common understanding of how to carry out their assignments. It also assists in bringing uniformity of output from a diverse set of individuals working on different projects in the organization. In addition, a defined process facilitates work study to improve methods of working through process improvement.

Defined means *documented*, and a *defined* process in this context means a *documented process. Well defined* means that the documentation adheres to the principles of good documentation (meaning it follows organizational, national, or international documentation guidelines), and the documents are comprehensive and exhaustive in that they cover all relevant aspects of the activity detailed by the process.

A *process* in this context is a comprehensive set of documents that defines the methods for performing a major activity in the organization. It consists of procedures, formats, templates, standards, guidelines, and checklists. Examples of a process are the project management process, verification process, validation process, and measurement and analysis process.

Institutionalization implies that the process is implemented in the organization, that all persons in the organization are trained in the process, and that they all are well versed in the process. They use the process in their daily routines without being prompted. The process has been in use for a sufficiently long duration that it has become second nature to the staff while performing their work. Organizations often claim that they have an institutionalized process within two months of implementing a process. This cannot possibly be true. After rolling out a process, it takes years for institutionalization to take hold and for staff to grasp the spirit of the process and use it in their daily activities without being prompted and without needing to refer to documents.

The CMMI® model document for development (version 1.2, August 2006) defines *institutionalization* as "the ingrained way of doing business that an organization follows routinely as part of its corporate culture." It takes time for a process to become *ingrained.* How *much* time depends on the intensity of education, the seriousness of the implementation, and the individual learning skills of the organization's human resources. A safe assumption is that a process is institutionalized after a minimum of one year from the date of implementation, provided all individuals are comprehensively trained in the process and assistance is available if needed.

Thus, a *well-defined and institutionalized process* in the context of software development organizations means:

> *an organization-wide process that is documented, where the documentation adheres to good documentation principles in a comprehensive and exhaustive manner and covers all relevant aspects of the software*

development activity and all related organizational activities, and all the staff of the organization are educated in the process. The process is fully implemented and has been in use in the organization for a sufficiently long duration that all staff are well versed in the process to the extent that it has become second nature and they can perform the process without reference to the process documentation.

The first step in institutionalizing a well-defined process is to define it comprehensively, accurately, and completely. The following are the major processes in a software development organization, in alphabetical order:

1. Configuration management process
2. Measurement and analysis process
3. Process definition and improvement process
4. Project management process
5. Quality management process
6. Software construction process
7. Validation process
8. Verification process

Other organizational processes that aid in software development activity include the following:

1. Administration processes for purchasing, facilities, etc.
2. Human resources processes for recruitment, training, retention, separation, etc.
3. Marketing processes for project acquisition, customer relationship management, revenue management, etc.
4. Finance processes for budgets, expenditure management, profit management, etc.

Each of these processes has procedures for each of the activities of which it is comprised. Chapter 8 discusses the topic of process quality further.

One point that requires special mention here is that the software development process set should contain processes for QA activities, measurement, analysis, and improvement of the process itself. The QA process should define the minimum set of QA activities mandated for each project executed in the organization. The process improvement process must define the sources of suggestions for process improvement; the methods for analyzing and short-listing candidate suggestions for implementation; and procedures for piloting the improvements, updating the process documents, obtaining the approvals, and rolling out the improved process.

EXPLICIT SYSTEM OF REWARDS AND RECOGNITION FOR ACHIEVING EXCELLENCE IN QUALITY

 All employees are expected, in theory, to perform at their peak capacity, but this expectation is limited to paper. Peak performance normally is seen at the time of initial entry into the organization and when jobs are threatened. Most other times, employee performance hovers from just above the penalty-avoidance level to the above-average level. During planning and goal setting, only average performance (normal-case scenario), not peak performance (best-case scenario), is considered.

Ergonomic and industrial engineering studies show that peak performance is not sustainable for long periods, but that it is possible to improve performance over a period of time. Professor Elton Mayo's studies at the Hawthorne Works of Western Electric have shown conclusive evidence that human performance can rise to unheard-of peaks with the right motivation. While it is not practical to list and discuss the many current theories on motivation here, it is well recognized that a properly designed rewards and recognition system does elevate the commitment of individuals, motivating them to higher levels of performance. Therefore, most organizations use a variety of rewards and recognition systems to motivate employees.

For a rewards and recognition system to be effective and result in higher levels of performance, it must feature the following characteristics:

★ It must be a formal mechanism that recognizes and rewards efforts to improve the quality of products, with the rewards handed out regularly.

★ It must be based on objective data that is obtained through systematic measurement.

★ It must set aside a formal occasion when rewards and recognition are handed out. This occasion should be periodic and held without fail on the appointed day.

★ It must allow star performers (those who always receive rewards and recognition) to be recognized separately and provide rewards for a wider group of employees. If it turns out that the same person, even with a stellar performance, earns the reward on every occasion, the system demotivates the rest of the employees. The system ought to give hope to all employees so that they aspire to receive the reward and work for it without having to compete with the "heavyweight champion."

★ It must recognize an adequate number of employees on every rewards occasion. If only one employee out of a thousand is recognized once a year, the other employees will have no hope of receiving a reward in their career with the organization. The material value of the reward can be reduced and the number of reward-earners increased so that a larger number of employees can have hope that they will achieve the coveted recognition. Hope drives people to scale higher peaks in performance. It is the recognition that matters, not the material value.

The human resources department and industrial engineers are usually able to assist an organization in designing the right system of rewards and recognition.

In recognizing quality achievements, two parameters should be taken into account: productivity and quality. I suggest using a defect injection rate as a measure of quality. How to compute a defect injection rate is discussed in Appendix G of this book. While it is important to reduce the defect injection rate, achievement of the organizational productivity baseline is equally important.

Achievement of the lowest defect injection rate and the highest productivity should be the deciding factor for recognizing and rewarding employees for quality achievement. Sometimes an organization employs individuals who achieve a zero or near-zero defect injection rate for a considerably long duration but who may not rate high on productivity. Such persons should be rewarded if they meet the organizational productivity norm, even if they do not exceed it. Often, there is a champion in the organization who always scores high on both productivity and quality. I suggest the champion be promoted to a higher-level position so as to better utilize his or her talents. Not promoting a champion and only offering the person a reward every year has a two-pronged negative effect. The first is that the champion will likely become demotivated, believing that his or her talent is worth a reward but not promotion. The second is that it discourages others from even trying for the reward. While it is not my intention to define the entire scheme of recognizing quality achievements and giving rewards, I only offer some suggestions here to make the scheme effective.

All in all, it is necessary to define a scheme that truly recognizes achievements in the domain of quality and to reward achievement fairly and regularly. It does not augur well at all if the recognition and rewards for efforts in product quality improvement are given only sporadically or only when outstanding efforts are noticed.

COMMITMENT AND INVOLVEMENT OF SENIOR MANAGEMENT IN FOSTERING A CULTURE OF QUALITY IN THE ORGANIZATION

Although this aspect appears at the end of this chapter, it holds first place in importance. Without senior management support, quality efforts are a non-starter in any organization. Quality is a journey, never a destination. With so much competition and innovation in the market, it is natural that as soon as something great is achieved, somebody else will achieve something even greater. Therefore, an organization must constantly move forward, improving its performance in all four dimensions of quality (specifications, design, development, and conformance). To do this, senior management support is essential.

Quality initiatives consume monetary resources but do not generate any direct and tangible revenues. True, quality generates savings, but it is not easy to quantify and measure the savings. Whereas revenues are real, savings are, to a large extent, intangible.* There will always be pressure to cut costs incurred to maintain or improve quality in order to increase profits. This can tempt management to reduce staff in the QA department and embed QA activities within the delivery activities. It is senior management that bears the pressure of demands from top management (the board of directors) to cut costs. Without the support of senior management, the cost-cutting axe always falls on the quality initiatives.

There are many times in a software development organization when conflict arises between the delivery department and the QA department, especially when an organization is under delivery pressure. If the QA department is placed under the delivery function or if the delivery department does not support recommendations made by the QA department, it is the QA department that will be short-circuited. The most common argument for this is: "There are already some residual defects. What difference would one more make?" Not much, true, but

---

* An anecdote illustrates this point. A husband comes home from the office gasping and tells his wife, "I ran behind the bus today and saved 50 cents!" He hands the money to his wife, who sneers and replies, "You should have run behind a taxi. Then you would have saved a full dollar."

the objective of the QA department is to uncover and eliminate as many defects as possible and to prevent them from reaching the customer. In such situations, the counsel of senior management is essential. If the QA department is being unreasonable, it must be counseled, and if the issue is as serious as the QA department makes it out to be, then the delivery department should be counseled. Most importantly, however, senior management has to be impartial.

Since a QA department is a cost center, obtaining required resources is always an uphill struggle. This is especially so in the software industry, as it places less emphasis on QA, and no industry norms are available which require that a QA person is needed for every 50 developers, for example. Many organizations resort to having a QA department in name only. The head of the QA department is more often than not placed in a junior position in both rank and salary compared to the delivery head. This is a very counterproductive situation, as the QA head can never stand up to the delivery head in such an arrangement, even on important matters.

Another obstacle a QA department often experiences is not having adequate and qualified individuals to staff QA positions. Without proper staff, QA work cannot be accomplished competently. I know of an organization with a QA department certified at level 4 in CMM® (the predecessor of CMMI®) that is staffed with a journalism graduate, a biology graduate, and a mechanical engineering graduate out of a total staff of five. The person leading the QA department was designated "quality coordinator." How QA activities can be carried out effectively in such an organization, and how a qualified CMM® lead appraiser can rate it as having a maturity level of 4 is beyond my comprehension. Support from senior management is vital for QA efforts to be serious and to produce results.

Senior management support is essential for providing funding and resources for QA initiatives, for impartially judging conflict scenarios, and for instituting an effective, competent, and fully staffed QA CMM® in an organization.

FINAL WORDS

To achieve excellence in the quality of deliverables, organizations need to develop a culture that fosters quality. An organization's quality of deliverables is always commensurate with the culture prevalent in the organization. An organization that has developed a culture that fosters quality in its deliverables has senior management commitment to foster quality and provide the necessary resources to carry out QA activities, including a full-fledged QA department fully staffed with qualified and competent individuals; a well-defined and institutionalized software development process with standards and guidelines; a well-defined process for process improvement; and an effective system of recognition and rewards for quality achievement.

However, once such a culture is developed, entropy tends to set in—even in high-competence organizations—unless explicit efforts and mechanisms are in place to continually drive the improvement effort. Therefore, it is essential to carry out periodic appraisals and to initiate corrective actions in order to maintain an organizational environment that is conducive to achieving high levels of quality. Another way to maintain an organizational culture that fosters quality is to benchmark the organization's achievements in quality against those of similar organizations, in order to know where the organization stands in comparison. This facilitates improvement and allows the organizational environment to gear up for even better achievements and, ultimately, to become a leader in the industry.

SOFTWARE VERIFICATION

VERIFICATION

Verification is an activity that is carried out to confirm that something conforms to its documented specifications, standards, regulations, etc. It is confirmation that "the right thing is done" and that all the required components are present in the right quantity. Verification does not involve confirming functionality by testing the artifact. Verification is carried out by visual means and, at the most, by touch and feel, not by running or powering up the artifact.

Standard 610 of the Institute of Electrical and Electronics Engineers standard glossary of software engineering terminology defines the term "verification" as "the process of evaluating a system or component to determine whether the products of a given development phase satisfy the conditions imposed at the start of that phase" and also as "formal proof of program correctness."

The Capability Maturity Model Integration (CMMI®) model document for development (version 1.2, August 2006) defines the term "verification" in its glossary section as "confirmation that work products properly reflect the requirements specified for them. In other words, verification ensures that 'you built it right.'"

Walkthroughs (reviews), inspections, and audits are the tools commonly used for verification. Verification plays an important role in most forms of human endeavor for quality control. Most of the quality assurance (QA) activity in the manufacturing and construction industries involves verification. Testing has limited applicability in these industries, especially in heavy manufacturing such as large turbine, shipbuilding, aircraft, etc. In the service industries, verification plays a larger role and testing a lesser one. For instance, in a catering service, it is a costly waste of time to prepare a food item and then test it to find out how it tastes. If it tastes bad, the dish would have to be thrown out and a new dish cooked. In this example, testing is cursory to see if the taste of the dish is acceptable. Inspection before cooking to ensure that all the ingredients in the recipe are in the right quantity and in the right proportion is vital to the quality of the dish. In construction, it is not practical to test the strength of a structure, as it might lead to the destruction of the structure itself. Inspection to ensure that the right materials are being used in the right proportion and that the structure is being built in the right manner is the only way to ensure the quality of the structure. Verification is a vital tool for QA in all industries, including the software development industry.

However, testing in the software industry is nondestructive, and fixing defects does not necessitate physically breaking and remaking the product. Therefore, testing is the preferred QA activity in the software development industry today. Because of this, though, many companies neglect verification activity, and such neglect is risky because it is well recognized that 100% testing is not practical. Software verification has an important place in software development, and neglecting it is detrimental to the quality of deliverables.

For certain software artifacts, verification is the only possible QA activity. For example, the requirements documents, design documents, and various plans can only be subject to verification or review. With the exception of source code (which can be tested), there is no way these documents can be "tested." Some software developers (especially those who detest documentation) argue that verification of code is a waste of time, as it is the testing that can reveal any defects, and testing is always carried out even if rigorous verification is carried out as well. What is the point of performing both activities? Consider the following cases where testing would not be able to detect any defects:

★ Unnecessary declaration of variables and constants, which are not used in the code, may be harmless, but it ties up RAM and has the potential to slow down the system, especially in Web applications.

★ Inclusion of unwanted libraries not used by the application also may be harmless, but it increases the size of the setup file. It also occupies unnecessary disk space at the target location.

★ There are always multiple algorithms for achieving a given functionality. Whether the algorithm used is efficient cannot be detected by normal testing.

★ There are multiple control structures (go to, if, while, do while, case, etc.) available in programming languages, and each has its own efficiency. With the possibility of any one control structure being used in place of any other, programmers tend to use the control structure they are most comfortable with rather than the right one. Normal testing cannot determine if the right control structure was used.

★ Testing can ensure that the product performs stated actions, but if some unstated and undesirable actions are built into the product, even negative testing might not be able to detect them. This is called *malicious code*, which includes "time bombs" (their activation is based on a date or a clock hour), "event bombs" (their activation is based on a specific and rare event trigger), "random bombs" (their activation is based on a random number generation technique), etc. Needless to say, malicious code performs undesirable actions that are detrimental to the safe usage of a product and can even cause damage. Verification of source code is the only way to detect malicious code, which justifies the activity if for no other reason than this one.

★ It is normal for programmers to insert statements to debug logical errors, self-directed comment statements, unnecessary documentation statements, superseded code that is commented in the source code, etc. This is called *trash code*, and it does not have any function; its insertion is purely temporary. Programmers often neglect or forget to delete trash code before bringing the artifact into configuration control. Testing cannot detect trash code. Trash code might be harmless, but it could cause issues during software maintenance.

Therefore, software source code verification should not be skipped.

The objectives of verification are primarily to ensure that the right thing is built, and the following specific confirmations are sought from verification:

1. **Achievement of the core functionality set for the artifact**—This ensures that the artifact contains all product-related functionality that it is supposed to and that no specified functionality has been left out.

2. **Comprehensiveness and completeness of the artifact**—This ensures that any aspect that is required in the artifact is not left out. All sections are filled in. All explanations are given. All aspects of the artifact are self-contained and all references are correctly given to external artifacts. There is traceability for all aspects to the upstream artifacts and downstream artifacts.

3. **Conformance to standards and guidelines defined for the type of artifact in the project plans**—There are standards and guidelines for documentation, coding, naming conventions, etc. for all software artifacts. These standards and guidelines ensure uniformity in interpretation, completeness of artifacts, and maintainability. This aspect ensures that the artifact conforms to these standards and guidelines.

4. **Efficiency and effectiveness of the solution presented by the artifact**—The efficiency aspect ensures that the solution alternative selected is best suited to the situation in terms of ability to implement, maintainability, accuracy, and response times. The effectiveness aspect ensures that the solution alternative selected delivers the results expected of it.

5. **Clarity and correctness of the artifact**—This aspect ensures that the artifact is easily understandable by other people, as it might need maintenance later on. That is, the artifact is not open to multiple interpretations. It also ensures that what is contained in the artifact is correct and that no mistakes have crept in.

6. **Achievement of all ancillary functionality that is expected of the artifact**—The artifact is likely to contain ancillary functionality that is required for defect prevention, protection against misuse or unintended use, security functions for restricting access rights, etc. Reviewers confirm that all ancillary functionality is properly built into the artifact.

7. **No unnecessary functionality is present in the artifact**—Reviewers also need to confirm that the artifact contains only the necessary functionality and no other functionality, whether harmless or not.

8. **No malicious functionality is contained in the artifact**—This is, again, unnecessary functionality, but functionality that could be malicious with the potential to cause damage. Reviewers need to exercise extra care to ensure that no malicious functionality has crept into the artifact.

9. **The format of the artifact adheres to organizational standards or customer specifications**—Sometimes customers specify the format, especially for information artifacts such as design documents. When no such customer specification is mandated, organizational standards become operative. Proper formatting assists in maintenance. Therefore, reviewers need to ensure that the artifact is formatted properly. Often, the code formatting is neglected in code artifacts, which causes issues during software maintenance. Reviewers need to ensure that the formatting is properly done and that it conforms to specified standards.

10. **Fulfillment of the requirements of downstream functions of the artifact when it is to be used downstream**—This is especially important for information artifacts such as requirements documents, design documents, test case documents, etc. that are to be used by other people downstream to carry out subsequent work. Such artifacts need to be verified to ensure others can understand them in the proper context without misinterpretation and can carry out their work effectively and efficiently.

The tools and techniques for verification adopted in software development organizations include the following:

1. Walkthroughs (also referred to as peer reviews)
2. Inspections
3. Audits

Each of these verification methods is discussed in greater detail in the following sections.

WALKTHROUGHS (PEER REVIEWS)

A walkthroughs is an activity in which people other than the author walk through every sentence of the software information artifacts (mainly documents) and every line of code for the software code artifacts (source code, table scripts, stored procedures, interface routines, etc.). The CMMI® model document for development (version 1.2, August 2006) defines *peer review* in its glossary section as "the review of work products performed by peers during development of the work products to identify defects for removal. The term 'peer review' is used in the CMMI® Product Suite instead of the term 'work product inspection.'"

The people (peers) conducting a walkthrough normally have experience and expertise similar to that of the author. They deliver a report at the end of the walkthrough, known as a review report. A review report contains the following information:

1. The defects uncovered during the walkthrough, which include logical errors, any trash code and malicious code, unused but declared variables and constants, the presence of hard coding, nonconformance to standards and guidelines, etc.
2. Opportunities for improvement, if any, uncovered during the walkthrough, such as better constructs, syntax improvements, etc.
3. Suggestions for improvements that might result in greater clarity or robustness or better efficiency of execution, using reusable components, eliminating redundancy of code in the artifact or the end product of the artifact, etc.
4. Other information, such as the name of the artifact reviewed, date of the review, names of the author and the reviewer, information pertaining to closure of defects, and a place to provide answers to opportunities for improvement as well as suggestions for improvements

Figure 5.1 offers a suggested format for a review report.

There are five types of walkthroughs:

1. Independent walkthroughs
2. Guided walkthroughs
3. Group walkthroughs
4. Expert reviews
5. Managerial reviews

Each of these is discussed in greater detail in the following sections.

Independent Walkthroughs

This type of verification is also sometimes referred to as a *postal review*. It is carried out in the following manner:

Review Report

Project name:

Name of the artifact being reviewed, with version number:

Name(s) of the reviewer(s):

Name of the author of the artifact:

Date(s) on which the review is conducted:

Type of review: ☐ Independent/guided

☐ Individual/group

☐ Postal/meeting

Defects uncovered during the audit (use an additional sheet if necessary)

Defect ID	Defect description	Reference to process for the defect	Defect origin	Closed on	Status (open or closed)

Signature of lead reviewer:

Date of signature:

Figure 5.1. Review report format (page 1 of 2)

Closure Action by the Author

Corrective actions implemented

Corrective action implemented	Defect IDs covered by this corrective action	Comments

Preventive action implemented

Preventive action implemented	Defect IDs covered by this corrective action	Comments

Signature of author:

Date of signature:

Defect closure actions (to be filled in by the lead reviewer)
I have verified and found that all the defects described above are closed satisfactorily, except the following defects, which are retracted or pending:

1.

2.

3.

Signature of lead reviewer:

Date of signature:

Figure 5.1. Review report format (page 2 of 2)

1. The author of the artifact completes the work and informs the project leader (PL) or software project manager (SPM), who arranges for the review.
2. The PL or SPM brings the artifact into configuration control.
3. The PL or SPM allocates the work of reviewing the artifact to a peer of the author of the artifact.
4. The artifact to be reviewed is made available to the reviewer. This can be done by pointing out the location of the artifact to the reviewer or by physically transferring the artifact to the reviewer. When the location is pointed out, the access rights are limited to "read only."
5. The reviewer reviews the artifact, prepares the review report, and hands the review report over to the PL or SPM.
6. The PL or SPM scrutinizes the review report and arranges for the defects pointed out in the report to be fixed.
7. The PL or SPM requests that the reviewer verify the efficacy of the defects fixed.
8. The reviewer verifies the rectifications.
9. If all the defects are closed, the reviewer records the details in the review report and closes the report.
10. If defects remain in the artifact, steps 6, 7, and 8 are iterated until all defects are fixed.
11. When all defects are closed, the review activity for the artifact is completed.

The process of an independent walkthrough is depicted in Figure 5.2.

The notable aspect of this review is that the author of the artifact need not be present while the review is being conducted. If the reviewer needs any clarification, he or she contacts the author to obtain the required clarifications. This way, the author is free to devote time to another activity while the artifact is being reviewed. However, if the artifact is poorly developed or if it uses complex algorithms, the reviewer might not understand and might not be able to unearth all defects effectively.

Guided Walkthroughs

A guided walkthrough is conducted in the presence of the author of the artifact being reviewed. In this method, the author of the artifact guides the reviewer through the artifact.

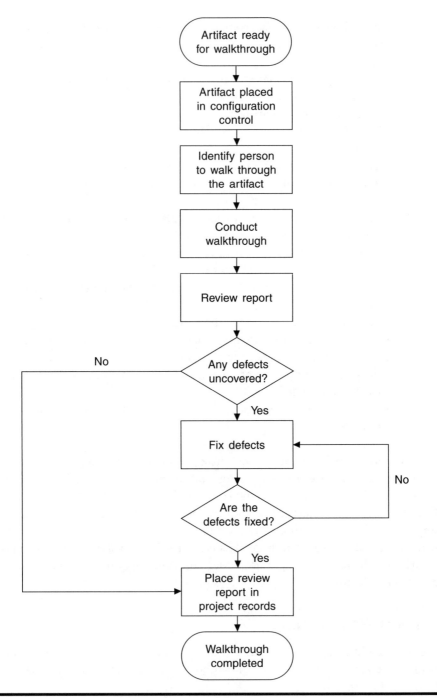

Figure 5.2. Independent walkthrough process

A guided walkthrough is conducted in the following manner:

1. The author of the artifact completes the work and informs the PL or SPM, who arranges for the review.
2. The PL or SPM allocates the work of reviewing the artifact to a peer of the author of the artifact.
3. The author interacts with the reviewer and they agree on a time slot for the review.
4. The author then walks the reviewer through the artifact, explaining the contents of it.
5. The reviewer seeks additional explanation wherever necessary.
6. Wherever the reviewer finds an opportunity for improvement, the author and the reviewer discuss the opportunity, and if consensus is reached, the author makes a note of the correction to be carried out.
7. By the end of the walkthrough, the author will have noted all opportunities for improvement and accepted the manner in which improvements are to be carried out.
8. Optionally, the author can implement the corrections at the time of the review, closing each defect as it is uncovered.
9. The author implements the accepted corrections and closes the defects in concurrence with the reviewer.
10. The reviewer informs the PL or SPM that the artifact has passed the review.
11. The PL or SPM brings the artifact under configuration control.
12. Optionally, the reviewer might prepare a formal review report.

The advantage of this method is that the duration of the review is much shorter compared to an independent walkthrough. The total turnaround time for completion of the review is also shorter. One disadvantage, however, is that there is a possibility that the author and the reviewer may disagree about an opportunity for improvement, which can end up in an argument that requires resolution from a higher level of authority. Another disadvantage is that the author might convince the reviewer that a defect is in fact not a defect!

Group Walkthroughs (Group Reviews)

A group walkthrough (also referred to as a group review) is used when it is determined that the knowledge of more than one person is necessary to review the artifact. This type of walkthrough is used in particular for strategic artifacts, such as product specification documents, software architecture design documents, and test strategy plans.

A group walkthrough is conducted in one of the following three modes:

★ **Postal review**—In this method, the PL or SPM takes responsibility for coordinating the review. The advantage of this type of review is that the reviewers can conduct it at their convenience and location rather than try to find a time when the reviewers can meet, which could delay the review. In addition, with each member of the review group focusing on the artifact, knowledge from different areas can shed more light on possible improvements, which might not be possible when just one person reviews the artifact. The disadvantage, however, is that the review might take longer, because the process cannot be completed until the slowest member finishes. The following steps are carried out in this type of review:

1. When an artifact is constructed and ready for review, the PL or SPM selects a review team consisting of members slightly more experienced than the author(s).
2. A review coordinator is nominated either by the review team itself or by the PL or SPM. Sometimes the PL or SPM acts as the review coordinator.
3. The artifact is handed over to each member of the review team.
4. The review team walks though the artifact, and each member hands over his or her individual review report to the review coordinator.
5. The review coordinator consolidates the review reports by eliminating duplicates and prepares a final review report.
6. Alternatively, the review coordinator might organize a meeting to collate the review findings and prepare the final review report.
7. The final review report is handed over to the author(s) of the artifact.
8. The author interfaces with the review coordinator, obtains clarifications where required, and implements corrections based on all the review report findings.
9. The author interfaces with the review coordinator and closes all the review report findings.
10. The review is completed and the artifact is promoted to the next stage in configuration management.

The postal review process is depicted in Figure 5.3.

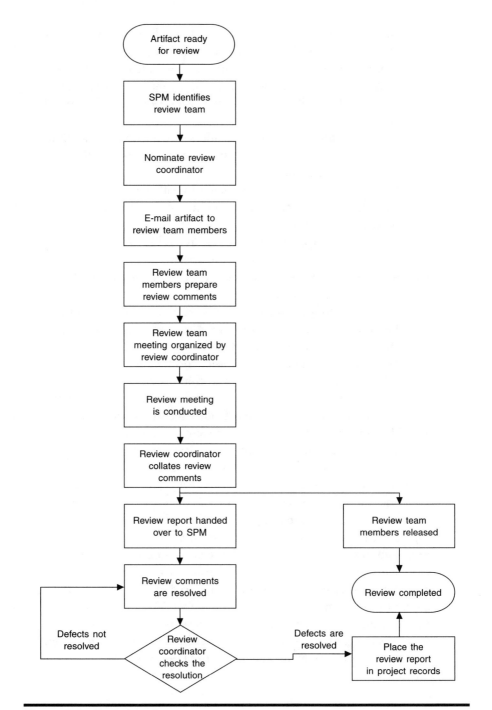

Figure 5.3. Postal review process

★ **Meeting review**—A meeting review is used to reduce the review turn-around time. One disadvantage, however, is that, except for the review coordinator, some review group members might not focus adequate attention on the artifact, thereby not contributing fully to its improvement. The following steps are carried out in this type of review:

1. When an artifact is constructed and ready for review, the PL or SPM selects a review team consisting of members slightly more experienced than the author(s).
2. A review coordinator is nominated by either the PL or SPM.
3. The artifact is handed over to each member of the review team in advance of the meeting.
4. The review coordinator arranges for the review meeting in consultation with all review team members.
5. All review team members come to the meeting prepared with their review comments.
6. The review coordinator collates the review comments from all the group members, and they are discussed in the meeting.
7. The review report is finalized in the meeting.
8. Review team members are released, and the review coordinator continues the subsequent steps in the process.
9. The review coordinator submits the report to the PL or SPM, who has the author(s) of the artifact rectify the defects.
10. The author interfaces with the review coordinator until all defects are fixed and closed by the review coordinator.
11. The artifact is moved to configuration control.

★ **Guided meeting review**—This type of review is conducted in the same manner as the meeting review, except team members do not have to come to the meeting prepared with comments. The artifact is presented by its author, and the review team members discuss each topic and offer their comments. The review coordinator collates the comments and prepares the review report. The advantages of this method are that the turnaround time is reduced to the shortest possible amount of time and the review team members do not have to spend time reading the artifact and forming their comments before coming to the meeting. One disadvantage, however, is that the review team members might not focus adequate attention to add value to the artifact.

Expert Reviews

Sometimes there is no one on the project team or in the organization who is knowledgeable in and has experience in the domain or technology in which the artifact was constructed. This is especially true when the artifact involves a new technology. The artifact could be a program developed in a new language (or one that is new to the organization) which only the author has learned and mastered, or the organization might be working with a domain for the first time. There is always a first time for working with every technology or domain for an organization.

In some projects, it might become necessary to include complex mathematical algorithms in some of the artifacts. In this case, only the complex algorithms might need an expert mathematician. The rest can be reviewed within the project team.

In large projects, the software architecture plays a vital role in the robustness of the product. Once built with a specific architecture, it is impossible to correct a product without major overhaul. This fact becomes all the more crucial when developing a commercial off-the-shelf product, as inefficient software architecture can spell doom for the success of the product. In such cases, it is advantageous to have the software architecture (or the high-level design) reviewed by experts external to the project.

When such a situation occurs, the review becomes critical to ensure completeness and effectiveness of the artifact. In order to ensure that the artifact is reviewed effectively, an expert from either within the organization or outside the organization is identified to conduct the review. Some organizations (especially large ones) have centers of excellence or pools of experts from which resources are drawn to assist project teams in times of project difficulty. If no internal expert is available, an external expert, possibly from an academic institution, can be engaged to conduct the review.

Organizations use experts to develop applications as well as to verify them. Experts can be any of the following types:

1. **Domain experts**—People who have many years of experience in a field and who have seen all possible situations.
2. **Subject matter experts**—People who are experts in a specific subject, such as mathematics, and who normally come from academia. These experts might not be experienced in the field, but they are well versed in the theory and can aid in the development or review of algorithms.
3. **Technology experts**—People who are highly skilled in the development platform. They may have many years of experience in the programming language, database, or target platform on which the product functions.
4. **Social experts**—People who have expertise in the areas of social behaviors, market forces, and anthropology. They help organizations in product acceptance by the target market as well as in product usability aspects and its possible social impact. These experts can assist with such products as games and multimedia applications.

Expert reviews are costly, as the expert is external to the project and is paid for his or her expertise. Expert reviews should be scheduled carefully so as to utilize the expert's time effectively and fully. If a postal review (independent review) is used, the expert might need more time to understand the artifact and will charge for that time. Still, the expert might need clarification from the author, and therefore interaction between author and expert reviewer is inevitable. For this reason, a guided walkthrough is the usual mode of review for conducting expert reviews.

Expert reviews can involve a single expert or a team of experts, depending on the artifact being reviewed. Especially in the case of product specifications or software architecture documents in new domains or new technologies, it is normal to use multiple experts. In other cases, a single expert will suffice.

Normally, expert reviews are conducted to supplement peer reviews. A detailed peer review can be conducted in addition to an expert review to ensure that all defects lurking are unearthed and fixed. The methodology of an expert review is similar to that of an independent walkthrough and a guided walkthrough, except that the reviewer is the selected expert. All other aspects are the same.

Managerial Reviews

A managerial review is performed by the person who directly supervises the author of the artifact. This review is the final step before promoting the artifact to the next level in configuration management. A managerial review is a cursory review, and it does not delve into the details of the artifact.

The objectives of a managerial review include the following:

1. It gleans over the artifact to ensure that the right product is built.
2. Using the well-developed hunches of the supervisor, it specifically looks at possible problem areas and ensures that everything is alright.
3. It ensures that no required information is missing from the artifact.
4. It ensures that all the essential preceding activities have been performed before according approval to the artifact or promoting the artifact to the next level in configuration management.
5. It ensures consistency with other artifacts in the project as well as in the organization.
6. It also ensures traceability with both upstream and downstream artifacts, where applicable.

There is no hard-and-fast rule that prohibits supervisors from delving into the details of an artifact, and sometimes they do just that, especially when the individual conducting the peer review is slightly inexperienced in the review process.

A managerial review starts once the peer review has been conducted and all defects are fixed and closed. A managerial review can take the form of either an independent walkthrough or a guided walkthrough, depending on the size and type of the artifact.

Normally, a managerial review does not generate a review report. If defects are unearthed during a managerial review, the work is reassigned either to the same person (or team) who conducted the peer review or to another person to redo the peer review. The managerial review is not expected to uncover any defects, but if defects are found, then another round of peer reviews is conducted.

Best Practices in Walkthroughs

The first and most common pitfall I have seen many organizations fall prey to is treating walkthroughs as a mere formality to create a review record rather than using them to improve product quality. Such organizations mostly use independent or guided walkthroughs conducted by a peer. Group walkthroughs and expert reviews are rarely, if ever, performed. A best practice is to treat walkthroughs as an effective tool for uncovering as many defects as possible and to give the activity the importance and seriousness it deserves in the organization. In addition, where necessary, group walkthroughs and expert walkthroughs should be used in an organization.

The second pitfall I have seen is the omission of group walkthroughs for even the most important artifacts, such as requirements documents and software design documents. A best practice is to subject important artifacts to both group walkthroughs and expert reviews.

Another pitfall I have observed is not conducting both a peer review *and* a managerial review. Organizations either subject an artifact to a peer review followed by a cursory managerial review, if there is one at all, or completely skip the peer review and conduct a thorough managerial review. Each of these reviews has its own objectives. While a peer review focuses only on the artifact, a managerial review treats the artifact as a part of a whole series of artifacts and links the information contained in the artifact being reviewed with the information contained in other artifacts. Whereas a peer review focuses on details, a managerial review focuses on the big picture. Therefore, a best practice is to skip neither the peer review nor the managerial review.

In most organizations today, defect reporting is automated through a defect resolution software tool. Some organizations use this mechanism only to report defects uncovered during walkthroughs, and they omit the review report altogether. This is another pitfall. Even if defects are reported using a defect manager software tool, a review report still needs to be prepared and delivered. A review report contains information in addition to identifying defects, such as opportunities and suggestions for improvement. If only a defect manager tool is used, reviewers are discouraged from making observations about possible improvements. Therefore, a best practice is to prepare a review report for each walkthrough conducted in the organization, whether or not a defect manager software tool is used to track and close all defects.

INSPECTIONS

Inspections play an important part in software QA. They ensure that all required components are ready for the next stage. The output of an inspection activity is an inspection report which specifies whether the system passed or failed. Figure 5.4 offers a suggested format for an inspection report. If the report

---

Inspection Report

Project ID:

Type of inspection carried out: ☐ Readiness for system testing
☐ Acceptance testing
☐ Delivery

Name of inspector:

Date of inspection:

List of components inspected

Name of component	Nature of component	Type of inspection carried out
Database server	Hardware	Visual and power-on inspection
	RDBMS	Checked for existence of database and tables
	Master data	Checked for existence of data
Software components	Software	Tallied with configuration register
		Verified all QA records and ensured that all planned QA activities are performed and all defects uncovered are closed
Web server	Hardware	Visual and power-on inspection
	Web server software	Checked for existence of Web server software as well as the Web site
User documentation	Documentation	Verified review records and approvals

Figure 5.4. Inspection report format (page 1 of 2)

Defects uncovered

Defect description	Location of defect	Corrective action	Defect closed on

Inspection result: ☐ Pass
                    ☐ Fail
                    ☐ Needs rectification and reinspection

Signature of inspector:

Date of signature:

Defect closure action (to be filled in by the inspector)
I have verified all closed defects and approve the closure action.

Signature of inspector:

Date of signature:

Figure 5.4. Inspection report format (page 2 of 2)

indicates the system passed the inspection, it means that the system can proceed to the next step. If the inspection report indicates that the system failed, it means that some rectification needs to be carried out on the system under inspection. After rectification, the system is resubmitted for inspection. To be able to proceed to the next step, it is essential that the inspection report indicate that the system passed inspection. Figure 5.5 depicts the inspection process.

The scenarios in which inspections are to be carried out are discussed in the following sections.

System Testing Readiness Inspection

System testing readiness ensures that all required components are in place for conducting the system testing. Especially in Web-based applications, many configurations are needed for a thorough system testing. If any of the required components are missing, the testing process will be stalled and the defect must be fixed immediately. A delay in fixing a defect leaves testers idle and waiting.

System testing readiness inspection ensures that the server is equipped with the following:

1. Hardware (the Web server, database server, app server), which has adequate RAM, hard disk capacity, and networking hardware
2. System software, including the operating system and other software, which is loaded and in working order
3. Security software, such as antivirus, antispyware, firewalls, etc., which is loaded and in working order
4. Connectivity and bandwidth, meaning the servers are connected together and are connected to client machines through the Internet or an intranet
5. Master data, meaning the tables that store master data are filled in with appropriate data and have been subjected to the necessary QA activities to ensure data integrity and accuracy
6. Software product, meaning the software product being tested has undergone all the planned software QA activities, with all defects uncovered fixed and all items reported as nonconformances closed
7. All the client machines, which are in place with the specified configuration and are connected to the servers through the Internet or an intranet

In addition, system testing readiness inspection ensures that the following conditions are met:

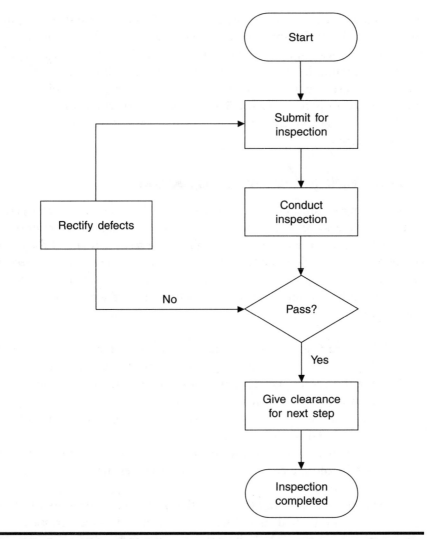

Figure 5.5. Inspection process

1. The test plans and test cases are in place, and they have been subjected to QA activities as planned. All defects are fixed and all nonconformances are closed.
2. All testers have been briefed on the testing to be carried out.
3. The criteria for closing the testing activity are approved and are known by the individuals concerned.

This inspection should be carried out by QA department personnel. Alternatively, an SPM or a PL from another project in the organization can carry out this inspection. A system testing readiness inspection report is prepared and handed over to the project SPM or PL; the report lists defects uncovered, if any. The SPM or PL rectifies the defects and closes the inspection report, in order to move forward with carrying out the system testing.

Acceptance Testing Readiness Inspection

Acceptance testing is conducted as a prerequisite for obtaining the customer's acceptance of product delivery and, thus, for receiving payment. This is a very crucial stage, as any defect uncovered here reflects poorly on organizational quality and delays dispatch, consequently delaying receipt of payment. Therefore, inspection carried out at this stage ensures that everything is right and ready for acceptance testing.

The following aspects are ensured during an acceptance testing readiness inspection:

1. The software is complete in all respects.
2. All the planned QA activities, including other inspections, reviews, and tests, are exhaustively conducted, and all nonconformances reported have been rectified and closed satisfactorily.
3. The test data has been created and inspected for its suitability and is found to be accurate.
4. The approved acceptance plan is in place.
5. Approved acceptance test cases are ready for use.
6. All the requisite hardware, with the right configuration as specified in the acceptance test plan, is in place.
7. All system software and middleware as well as the database are properly loaded on the hardware and are functioning as they should be.
8. Test data is loaded and ready.
9. The customer's confirmation to conduct acceptance testing on the scheduled dates is received.
10. All concerned organizational entities are informed of the acceptance testing schedule, and all necessary support is in place.
11. Fallback plans are in place for fixing any bugs that are uncovered during acceptance testing as well as for addressing failure of any hardware.

Acceptance testing readiness inspection normally is carried out by the QA department. In the absence of a QA department, a peer SPM or PL from another project can carry out this inspection. An acceptance testing readiness inspection report is prepared by the inspector and is handed over to the project SPM or PL; the report lists defects uncovered, if any. The SPM or PL arranges for rectification of any defects uncovered and closes the inspection report. Then the acceptance testing is carried out as planned.

Delivery Readiness Inspection

The purpose of delivery readiness inspection is to ensure that the delivery package has all the components and that the right versions are included in it. Delivery for a project can be carried out in one of three modes: (1) single-shot delivery, meaning all components are delivered at one time; (2) interim delivery, meaning one of multiple deliveries; or (3) final delivery, meaning the last of a series of deliveries.

The following aspects are covered in delivery readiness inspection:

1. The project configuration register is used as the reference.
2. The executable code, if part of the delivery, is inspected for the date and time of build and to ensure that it agrees with the configuration register. If there happens to be a "build routine" that is used to prepare the executable build, it is inspected to ensure that the right versions of source code and libraries are used in preparing the build.
3. In an interim delivery, inspection ensures that all components mentioned in the software delivery note are in fact included in the delivery set.
4. All planned QA activities are performed on all components of the delivery set, and all defects uncovered are closed.
5. The version numbers of each of the components of the delivery set are checked against the software delivery note and the configuration register.
6. In a final delivery, inspection ensures that all components mentioned in the customer purchase order have been included in earlier deliveries or are included in the current delivery and that there are no components left pending delivery to customer after the current delivery. This is in addition to ensuring the aspects previously mentioned.

7. In a single-shot delivery, both the customer purchase order and the configuration register are used as references. Inspection ensures that all components mentioned in the customer order are included in the current delivery set and that no further deliveries are needed. This is in addition to ensuring the correct version numbers and the veracity of the build routine, if any.

8. The medium of delivery is as specified in the customer's purchase order, and the right number of copies is included in the delivery set.

9. All necessary approvals to effect delivery are in place.

10. The delivery is being effected to the right persons, as specified in the customer's purchase order.

Delivery readiness inspection normally is carried out by the QA department. Sometimes marketing department personnel also take part in this type of inspection. In the absence of a QA department, a peer SPM or PL can carry out this inspection. Upon completion of a delivery readiness inspection, a delivery readiness inspection report is prepared and handed over to the project SPM or PL; the report lists defects, if any. The SPM or PL arranges for rectification of any defects and closes the report. Delivery is then effected to the customer.

Inspections at other points in the software development phases can be carried out as necessary depending on the nature of the project and the need for inspection. These inspections are determined by the SPM during the project planning stage, and the details are recorded in the project software QA plan.

Best Practices in Inspections

Most software organizations use inspections, as they are an effective tool for ensuring that a major activity is conducted smoothly. Some organizations argue that inspections are superfluous, as the same objective is achieved through phase-end audits. This is somewhat true, but audits are mainly document verification systems. Inspections not only look at documents, but also examine physical entities to ensure their correctness and readiness. For example, a system testing readiness inspection looks at the configuration register, work register, review reports, and test logs, to ensure that all components are built and all QA activities have been performed completely. It also looks at the systems to ensure that all necessary system software is loaded and that all master data is ready, along with the state of the current software product on the system. These functions combined make inspections indispensable. A common pitfall in many organizations is exclusion of inspections altogether, using the argument that phase-end audits achieve similar objectives.

Best practices for inspections of any type include:

1. Conducting inspections at least before system testing and acceptance testing and before delivering the software product to the customer.
2. Staffing the QA department with specialist inspectors to carry out inspections. This is more effective than having a software developer from within the project or from another project conduct inspections. Having a software developer carry out an inspection often ends up being an exercise in filling out forms rather than a serious inspection aimed at uncovering deficiencies.

AUDITS

Audits are used mainly in organizations that have a defined software development process that has been implemented in their projects. Audits are document verification systems in which project documents and records are compared with the organization's standards or defined processes. They generally are short in duration, with about one to two hours spent on auditing a project or a function. Audits are used as a QA tool mainly to ensure conformance of project execution to the organization's defined software development processes. They ensure that a project is being executed in conformance with the organization's defined processes and that it is ready for the next phase of execution.

Audits are conducted for the purpose of uncovering nonconformances (NCs), if any, in a project. If project documents or records show deviations from the process described in the organization's defined processes, these deviations are treated as NCs and project execution is considered as not conforming to the organization's defined processes. The output of an audit is a nonconformance report (NCR). An NCR lists all NCs uncovered during an audit. Figure 5.6 shows a sample NCR.

Audits consist of auditors (the people who conduct the audit) and auditees (the people whose project is being audited). Auditors should have specialized training in conducting audits. Auditors who conduct audits within an organization must receive internal audit training, whereas auditors who conduct certification audits or surveillance audits for other organizations must be trained and certified to do so.

The usual duration of a project audit is one to two hours. During this time, the auditor verifies all the project documents and notes any NCs found in order

Nonconformance Report

Project name:

Name(s) of the auditor(s):

Name of the auditee:

Date on which the audit is conducted: _____

From (time) _____ to (time) _____

Type of audit: ☐ Periodic/phase end   ☐ Vertical/horizontal

Nonconformances uncovered during the audit (use an additional sheet if necessary)

NC no.	NC description	Reference to process for the NC	Closed on	Status (open or closed)

Opportunities for improvement observed, if any

Description of improvement opportunity	Artifact reference	Reference to section of the artifact for improvement opportunity

Figure 5.6. Nonconformance report (page 1 of 2)

Suggestions for improvement

Description of the suggestion	Reference to artifact or area for the suggested improvement

Signature of auditor: Date of signature:

Closure Action by the Auditee

Corrective actions implemented

Corrective action implemented	NC numbers covered by this corrective action	Comments

Preventive action implemented

Preventive action implemented	NC numbers covered by this corrective action	Comments

Signature of auditee: Date of signature:

Nonconformance closure actions (to be filled in by the auditor)
I have verified and found that all the nonconformances described above are closed satisfactorily, except the following, which are retracted/pending:

1.

2.

3.

Signature of auditor: Date of signature:

Figure 5.6. Nonconformance report (page 2 of 2)

to prepare an NCR later. The completed NCR is handed over to the auditee. The auditee then must take the necessary action specified in the NCR to address the NCs and have them closed by the auditor within the time allowed. Necessary action as specified in an NCR involves the following:

1. Taking corrective action so that the NC is resolved
2. Putting in place preventive action so that the NC is not repeated in the project later

Figure 5.7 depicts the audit process.

Audits can be classified in a variety of ways, as discussed in the sections that follow.

Conformance Audits versus Investigative Audits

Conformance audits focus on the efficacy of implementation of organizational processes during project execution. They are conducted to compare and contrast the project documents with the organizational processes, uncover NCs, prepare an NCR, and track the NCR to its resolution.

Investigative audits usually focus on finding the causes for a failure, but sometimes focus on finding the causes for an extraordinary success. The project execution documents are carefully verified and in-depth interviews are held with the project personnel to uncover the specific reasons that caused a failure or grand success. They are used in special scenarios only.

Vertical Audits versus Horizontal Audits

Vertical audits are conformance audits conducted across the organization on either a few selected projects or on all projects; they focus on all aspects of the project(s).

Horizontal audits are also conformance audits conducted across the organization on either a few selected projects or on all projects, but they focus on only one aspect of the project(s). Configuration management audits are a good example of this kind of audit, which are conducted in most organizations. Horizontal audits focus on the efficacy of implementation of one crucial aspect of project execution in the organization.

Periodic Audits versus Phase-End Audits

Periodic audits are conformance audits that are conducted at the organization level based on calendar duration. Normally, ISO-certified organizations conduct

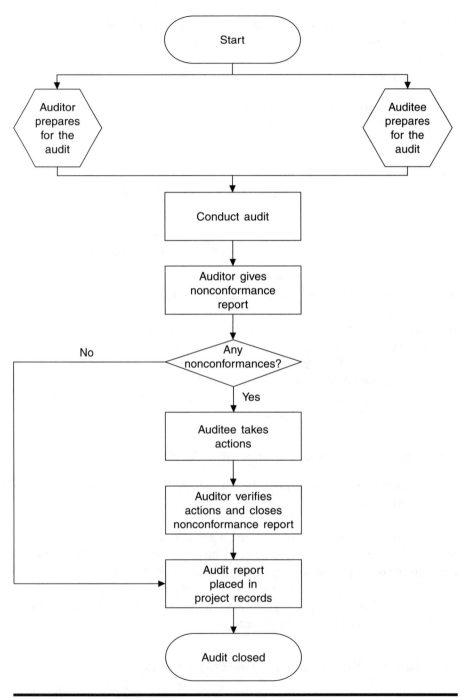

Figure 5.7. The audit process

these audits once every two or three calendar months. Each audit covers a few of the organization's current projects, and all projects under execution (not closed projects) in the organization are covered within a one-year period. At the end of every cycle of audits, the audit findings are consolidated and presented to management and to the auditees.

The process for periodic audits is as follows:

1. Periodic audits normally are coordinated at the organization level by the QA department.

2. At the beginning of every year, an audit plan is prepared and approved by the appropriate authorities. This plan includes details such as probable dates for the audits, probable projects to be included in each round of audits, probable auditors, etc.

3. At the beginning of each audit, an audit opening meeting that includes all the auditors, auditees, and management representatives is held. The QA department representative explains the auditing process in general, the objectives of the audit, the NCR resolution process and timelines for closing NCs, etc. QA clarifies any issues raised by the auditors or the auditees. Optionally, the management representative also explains management's viewpoint on these audits.

4. Auditors conduct the audits, in conformance with the organizational audit process and audit guidelines, and record NCs found, if any. The NCs are explained to the auditee and the NCR is handed over to the auditee. The QA department also receives a copy for follow-up.

5. The QA department consolidates all the NCRs and carries out analysis of the NCs uncovered in the audits. The QA department conducts an audit closure meeting with the same attendees who were in the audit opening meeting and presents the audit findings as well as the analysis of NCs. The efficacy of process implementation in the organization is discussed, and opportunities for improvement in process definition or implementation are agreed upon. The QA department notes the decisions made during the meeting, if any, and tracks them to resolution.

6. Auditees resolve any NCs by taking corrective action and also put in place preventive action so that they do not recur in the project.

7. Auditees approach the auditors to close the NCRs and show auditors the resolution of all NCs raised on the project.

8. The auditor verifies the resolutions, closes the NCR, and hands over the closed NCR to the QA department.

9. The QA department consolidates all NCRs and carries out an analysis of NC resolution. This analysis is then presented to management at a suitable opportunity.
10. The periodic audit is then complete.

Figure 5.8 shows a consolidated audit report that would be prepared at the end of a cycle of periodic audits. Figure 5.9 depicts the periodic audit process.

Phase-end audits are triggered by project events. The SPM arranges for these audits in coordination with the QA department when a project execution phase is completed. Typically, these audits are conducted after the following phases:

★ **Project initiation**—This audit is conducted soon after the project initiation activities are completed. It ensures that the project is initiated in adherence with the organizational process for project initiation, which ensures that the subsequent phases of software development move forward without any issues. A project initiation audit is conducted for all projects.

★ **Software requirements analysis**—This audit is conducted on projects that have a significant requirements analysis, but would be skipped for smaller or short-duration projects. It ensures that the process of gathering and analyzing project requirements was carried out in conformance with the organizational process for software requirements analysis, that required QA activities were performed, and that NCs, if any, are properly resolved. A software requirements analysis audit ensures that the next phases of software development are issue-free.

★ **Software design**—This audit is conducted on projects that have significant software design activity, but would be skipped for short-duration projects or those projects that do not have a significant software design component. The audit ensures that the software design was carried out in adherence with the organization's software design process, that required QA activities were performed, and that NCs, if any, are properly resolved. A software design audit ensures that the next phases face no issues.

★ **Software construction**—This audit is conducted once the software construction is completed, which means that software development, independent review, and unit testing of the developed code are completed. The audit ensures that the software construction was carried out in conformance with the organizational processes for software construction and that integration, peer review, and unit testing were

Audit Report

Audit cycle reference (month and year):

Type of audit: Vertical/horizontal

Dates on which the audit is conducted: From: _____ To: _____

Executive highlights of the audits:

1.

2.

3.

Projects covered during the audit (use an additional sheet if necessary)

Project ID	Names of auditors	Names of auditees	Conducted on	No. of NCs

Figure 5.8. Consolidated audit report (page 1 of 2)

Types of nonconformances uncovered

Process area	No. of NCs	Comments*

* Describe if the nonconformances are due to drawbacks in the process, training, negligence, etc.

Proposed improvement actions

Proposed improvement action	Timeline

Any other significant points:

1.

2.

3.

Signature of QA head:

Date of signature:

Figure 5.8. Consolidated audit report (page 2 of 2)

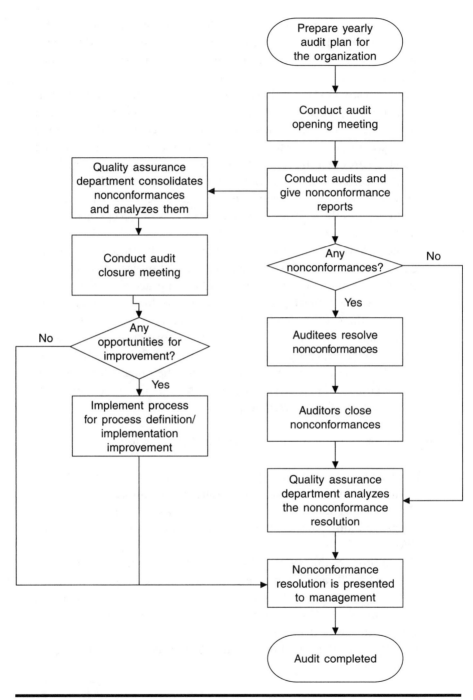

Figure 5.9. Periodic audit process

carried out in conformance with the organizational processes for peer review and unit testing. A software construction audit is conducted for all software development projects and ensures the software product's readiness for system testing.

★ **System testing**—This audit is conducted after system testing is completed. It may be skipped on projects that are small and that do not have a significant component of system testing, especially when the software product is expected to function on one platform only. The audit ensures that the system testing was successfully completed and that all defects uncovered were satisfactorily resolved in conformance with the organizational system testing process. A system testing audit ensures the software product's readiness for acceptance testing by the customer.

★ **Project closure**—This audit is conducted for all projects, just before a project is formally closed. It ensures that all project closure activities, such as documenting the best and worst practices of the project, archiving the artifacts, identifying the reusable components and handing them over to the appropriate organizational entity, and knowledge sharing, were carried out in conformance with the organizational process for project closure. A project closure audit ensures that the project experience is shared with the other SPMs and that it is documented properly to be part of the organizational knowledge repository for future reference.

The steps for carrying out a phase-end audit are as follows:

1. When a project phase is completed, the SPM coordinates with the QA department to conduct the appropriate phase-end audit.
2. The QA department identifies an auditor, assigns the audit to the selected auditor, and schedules the audit in consultation with the SPM.
3. The auditor conducts the audit on schedule, records any NCs, prepares the NCR, and hands the NCR over to the SPM.
4. The SPM resolves the NCs and, in coordination with the auditor, closes the NCR. The auditor gives clearance to move the project forward to the next phase.
5. The SPM adds the closed NCR to the project records, concluding the phase-end audit.

Figure 5.10 depicts the phase-end audit process.

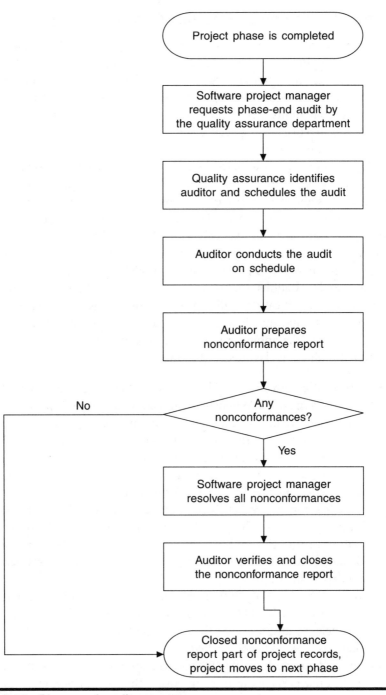

Figure 5.10. Phase-end audit process

Internal Audits versus External Audits

Internal audits can be conformance audits, investigative audits, periodic audits, or phase-end audits, but they are conducted by people internal to the organization. However, the internal auditors are independent of the project being audited, meaning they can be from either the QA department or from other projects. Internal audits are conducted to either ensure conformance or investigate the occurrence of a special event. The audit process is similar to the processes previously described.

External audits are conducted by an external agency that specializes in the audit process. Organizations that seek certification for compliance with the ISO 9000 series of standards or any other similar standards use external auditors. Individuals who are certified as *lead auditors* can conduct audits for certification or to ensure continued compliance with ISO standards. Optionally, an organization can engage external consultants to conduct audits in order to obtain an unbiased opinion about its process and its implementation in the organization. Sometimes external audits are conducted to ascertain the readiness of the organization for a certification audit. External audits consist of the same process as internal audits, and the NCR is the vehicle for recording and reporting NCs uncovered during the audits as well as for closing the NCs.

External audits are classified as follows:

★ **Precertification audits**—These audits are conducted as a prelude to certification audits. When an organization has multiple projects running concurrently, an external consultant is engaged to ascertain its readiness for a certification audit. The precertification audit serves as a rehearsal for the organization so that it can pass the certification audit. It also allows the organization to smooth out any uncovered rough edges in preparation for a certification audit.

★ **Certification and recertification audits**—These audits culminate in either awarding or denying the coveted certificate to the organization. A certification audit is conducted only once, unless it results in denial of the certificate to the organization. Most quality certification models mandate periodic recertification, such as once every three years. A certification audit is conducted for an organization that has never been certified. A recertification audit is exactly the same as a certification audit, except that it is conducted for an organization that has already been certified.

★ **Surveillance audits**—ISO 9000 certification mandates a surveillance audit once every six months to ensure that process implementation is at the same level it was at the time of the certification audit. The same external agency that originally awarded the certificate conducts these surveillance audits. They are scaled down slightly from the certification audits, and a smaller sample of projects is audited.

Audits are very useful tools for effective implementation of organizational processes, and they are used in most software development organizations.

Best Practices in Audits

In many organizations that conduct periodic audits, the exercise becomes more of a ritual than an earnest attempt to assess the level and seriousness of process implementation and conformance across projects in the organization. Since in most companies peers conduct the audits, the audits becomes *quid pro quo* (you scratch my back, and I'll scratch yours!) among peers in that not all the NCs uncovered during an audit are reflected in the NCR. Each auditor typically lists two or three NCs so that the audit appears authentic, but most NCs uncovered are informally pointed out to the auditee and not recorded. When all NCs are not recorded, the post-audit analysis does not reflect the true picture of process implementation and compliance. This is a most common pitfall I have observed in organizations that conduct periodic audits.

This problem can be addressed in a couple of ways. First, include in the audit team specialist auditors who are not software developers. These auditors can come from either the QA department or from outside the organization. They will make known all NCs, as they are not subject to the *quid pro quo* that exists among peers. When specialist auditors are rotated among projects, inevitably all project NCs are uncovered and recorded. Using the findings of these specialist auditors, the peer auditors can be counseled on the necessity to record all NCs. Another way to address the problem is to randomly subject the NCRs submitted by peer auditors to a verification audit by a specialist auditor. The fact that an NCR might be selected for random verification will compel peer auditors to diligently record all NCs. This second solution is a best practice.

Another pitfall is that the people in charge of overseeing process implementation consider these audits a necessary nuisance that must be endured rather than a tool for assessing process implementation and compliance. In one ISO 9000–certified company, the technical head (who is usually in charge of effecting software deliveries to the customer and who oversees all software developers in the organization) had not even read the organizational processes! If the most senior person does not believe in process implementation and compliance, the result can only be audits that are performed as a ritual for record-creation purposes.

A best practice is to have senior people in place who believe in quality and process implementation and compliance. If those in senior posts do not believe in process-driven software development, it might be better not to conduct audits at all.

A common pitfall in phase-end audits is assigning them to a peer from within the project itself. This also leads to audits deteriorating into record-creation exercises. A best practice is to engage a specialist auditor to conduct phase-end audits.

Two arguments in favor of using peer auditors are (1) the auditor has the opportunity to learn best practices and pitfalls from other projects and (2) a peer better understands process implementation than a specialist auditor does. Both arguments are valid if and only if the peer auditors exercise complete professionalism and do not resort to a *quid pro quo* approach. Peers learn from other projects during the audit closure meeting, where the audit findings are shared with all persons concerned. A best practice is to have at least some specialist auditors on the audit team.

Yet another common pitfall is the organization blaming the SPM if the project receives a large number of NCs or the SPM *having the impression* that management blames him or her for the NCs. Counseling SPMs whose projects are found to have a large number of NCs must be handled very carefully. Senior management needs to ascertain whether the number of NCs is unduly large in the first place, because absolute numbers do not tell the whole story. Expecting the number of NCs for a large project to be on a par with a small project is unrealistic. Senior management also needs to ascertain whether the NCs are chance errors and oversights or if negligence is involved. Counseling needs to be given only in the case of negligence, as chance errors uncovered by audits are automatically corrected—after all, the purpose of audits is to uncover such chance errors and oversights.

VERIFICATION PROCESS

Verification is a very important QA activity in software development organizations, and it therefore should not be carried out with an informal or ad hoc approach. A professional software development organization should have a well-defined process for driving verification activity in the organization. A separate process is needed for each of the following verification activities:

1. Walkthroughs
2. Software inspections
3. Audits

Walkthrough Process

The walkthrough process describes the types of walkthroughs an organization conducts, the roles and responsibilities in arranging for and conducting the walkthroughs, and the analyses to be carried out on the defects uncovered in the walkthroughs. The walkthrough process also includes a procedure for each type of walkthrough:

1. Independent walkthrough
2. Guided walkthrough
3. Group walkthrough
   ★ Postal review
   ★ Meeting review
   ★ Guided meeting review
4. Expert reviews

The walkthrough process also includes guidelines for selecting the type of review to be conducted for an artifact, the recommended reviewers for each walkthrough method, meeting guidelines, defect-reporting guidelines, etc. In addition, the walkthrough process offers various checklists for each walkthrough method, as well as formats for review reports, defect collation formats for group reviews, and any other formats specific to the organization.

Software Inspection Process

The software inspection process describes the types of software inspections to be carried out in the organization, the roles and responsibilities in arranging for and conducting the inspections, defect-reporting guidelines, analyses to be carried out on the defects uncovered during the inspections, etc. The software inspection process also offers a procedure for conducting each of the following types of software inspections:

1. System testing readiness inspection
2. Acceptance testing readiness inspection
3. Delivery readiness inspection
4. Any other organization-specific inspections

It also indicates the format for the inspection report and guidelines for reporting defects uncovered during inspections.

Audit Process

The audit process describes the types of audits to be conducted in the organization as well as the roles and responsibilities in requesting and conducting audits. It offers a procedure for conducting each of the following types of audits:

1. Periodic audits
2. Phase-end audits
3. Investigative audits
4. Any other organizational audits

The audit process also offers guidelines and checklists for conducting each of the following phase-end audits:

1. Project initiation
2. Software requirements analysis
3. Software design
4. Software construction
5. Project closure
6. Any other organization-specific phase-end audits

In addition, the audit process includes a training course outline and a training procedure for instructing internal auditors. It also includes guidelines for various audits to be conducted in the organization, as well as formats for NCRs and audit reports to be used for periodic audits. A sample audit process and audit guidelines are given in Appendix A.

IMPLEMENTATION OF VERIFICATION ACTIVITIES IN PROJECTS

While it is possible to implement verification activities in projects using an ad hoc approach—and some organizations do so, it is not advisable. When using an ad hoc approach, verification activities are not explicitly planned and the SPM will implement the verification activities that are convenient for the exigencies of the project execution.

A better approach is the planned approach. When using this approach, verification activities for a project are planned by the SPM during the project planning stage, and they are recorded in the software QA plan. The software QA plan, also referred to as a *software verification and validation plan*, is described in greater detail in Appendix K. It records the following details of verification activities to be implemented in the project being planned:

1. A list of all verification activities planned for implementation in the project
2. A list of project execution phases, after which phase-end audits are to be conducted
3. A list of stages at which software inspections are to be carried out
4. Artifacts that are to be subjected to peer reviews, along with probable individuals who will conduct the reviews and the type of peer review that will be utilized
5. Metrics and measurements that are to be carried out to ensure the efficacy of verification activities

The verification activities planned for a project need to conform to the organizational verification process. The peer review of the software QA plan ensures that the planned verification activities do in fact comply with the organizational verification process. All these activities must be implemented during project execution in conformance with the software QA plan. Verification activities also must comply with various procedures, guidelines, formats, and templates defined for each of the planned verification activities in the organizational verification process. The progress and status of implementation of verification activities in the project must be monitored along with other project activities, using the project status report as the mechanism. These activities are subject to the usual progress-monitoring meetings held by senior management.

In addition to the verification activities planned in the software QA plan for a project, other verification activities planned at the organizational level also must be carried out for the project. Such verification activities include periodic audits, external audits for certification or surveillance, horizontal audits such as the configuration management audit, etc. These verification activities might also uncover NCs, and the SPM should arrange for necessary corrective and preventive actions in order to close the NCs.

VALIDATION

CHAPTER OVERVIEW

★ The meaning of the term "validation"
★ Validation of designs and specifications
★ Validation of a software product
★ The definition of testing and various types of tests that can be conducted on software products
★ Testing basics, testing techniques, and approaches to testing
★ Test strategy and design of test cases
★ Testing different types of software applications
★ Best practices and pitfalls in software testing

Undetectable errors are infinite in variety in contrast to detectable errors, which by definition are limited.

—Gilb's third law of uncertainty

DEFINITION OF VALIDATION

Validation indicates confirmation or corroboration of a claim. In the context of software development, validation refers to the activities performed on a software product to confirm that all the designed (or required) functionalities are indeed built and are working in adherence with the original specifications (intended use), along with other implicit functions for ensuring safety, security, and usability.

Standard 610 from the Institute of Electrical and Electronics Engineers standard glossary of software engineering terminology defines the term *validation* as "the process of evaluating a system or component during or at the end of the development process to determine whether it satisfies specified requirements."

The Capability Maturity Model Integration (CMMI®) model document for development (version 1.2, August 2006) defines validation as "confirmation that the product, as provided (or as it will be provided), will fulfill its intended use. In other words, validation ensures that 'you built the right thing.'" It also states that "the purpose of validation is to demonstrate that a product or product component fulfills its intended use when placed in its intended environment."

Synonyms for the word *validate* include authenticate, certify, corroborate, confirm, endorse, bear out, substantiate, and support, among others. One definition of validation is *the act of ensuring that something is valid*.

To understand the term "validation" correctly, consider the following scenarios that involve validation:

★ You are entering into a contract with someone. Before you sign the contract, you show it to a lawyer for validation (not verification). Only after the lawyer certifies that it is valid (that is, legally valid and that it would be valid in a court of law) do you sign it.

★ You are affirming something in writing. You have a notary authenticate your affirmation. Once authenticated, your affirmation becomes an affidavit and is legally valid.

★ You are taking a trip to the North Pole. After studying the literature on the subject, you make a plan. You take your plan to an expert on the North Pole and ask the expert to "confirm" that your plan is sound. Once the expert confirms that your plan is workable, you set out on your adventure.

★ You have authored a spy-thriller novel. Before you publish it, you have a real-life spy read it. After the spy approves it, you go ahead with publishing the book.

★ An automobile manufacturer claims that its new model car is capable of achieving a fuel consumption rate of 230 miles per gallon. The marketing department demonstrates this claim in front of a select set of journalists, and the journalists substantiate it.

Therefore, under this definition, validation is a precaution normally taken before taking a risk—especially a strategic risk. The above scenarios share the following characteristics:

★ There is a claim that needs validation.
★ The originator of the claim arranges for validation.
★ The validation is not made against the specifications of the originator of the claim. It is made against the specifications that might have been formulated by an external agency:
    ☆ In the first scenario, the contract is validated against the law of the land.
    ☆ In the second scenario, the affirmation is validated by an independent, government-authorized individual.
    ☆ In the third scenario, the plan is validated against the expert's firsthand experience.
    ☆ In the fourth scenario, the novel is authenticated based on the spy's firsthand experience.
    ☆ In the fifth scenario, the claims are certified through the journalists' firsthand observation.
★ There is a risk involved that necessitates the act of validation.

Validation gives outsiders the confidence to be able to say "this is indeed true" or "it really works."

Validation performed in a software development scenario carries out the same functions listed above. The software development team or organization makes the claim that its software product works without defects. That claim is then substantiated by validation of the software product.

To achieve the full worth of validation, the following three factors must be applicable:

1. Validation is performed by independent persons who are not the same persons as those making the claim.
2. Validation is performed not just against the specifications of the claimant, but also against external specifications.
3. Validation is a planned and coordinated effort performed for the purpose of substantiating a claim and instilling confidence in stakeholders; it is not performed for self-assurance.

During software development, validation of important software artifacts is carried out. Normally, software designs and software products are validated in a contract development scenario. In a commercial off-the-shelf product scenario, product specifications are validated in addition to the software design and the software product itself.

VALIDATION OF SOFTWARE DESIGNS

Similar to the adage "the proof of the pudding is in the eating," the proof that the design is robust is in the building of the product and then the testing of the product. How do other industries validate their designs? In cases where the design is used to produce a large quantity of products, a prototype (one sample unit of the product) is built and subjected to all necessary tests, and the design is improved based on the results of those tests. This method is often used in the automobile and electronics industries, among others. But what about such industries as shipbuilding and aircraft manufacture? They cannot afford to build a wrong product, even for testing. In such industries, they make a scale-model prototype and subject the model to tests. Before building a large ship, for example, a shipbuilding company makes a much smaller model of the ship it plans to build and tests the prototype in a scaled-down environment. The results of the test are to validate the design of the proposed ship. Before making a new model of a large aircraft, an aircraft manufacturer builds a smaller, scaled-down prototype and subjects it to tests in a wind tunnel. Based on the results, the design is improved and the product built.

Today, computer models allow testing of designs through computer simulation, and improvements in designs are made based on those simulations. Yet software vendors that provide simulation software to test rockets, ships, and aircraft, for example, do not provide simulation software that validates software designs!

A development methodology that uses prototyping exists in software development too. This methodology uses two types of prototypes: build-and-improve prototypes and use-and-discard prototypes. In *build-and-improve prototypes*, skeletons of the software product, such as screen layouts, report layouts, and simple navigation, are built on the actual development platform. Software developers continue to improve the design based on the results of validation of the prototype. In *use-and-discard prototypes*, a prototype is built on a mockup using drafting tools. The requirements are validated, and then the actual software product is built on the real development platform.

Although the software industry is presently using a prototyping methodology for eliciting user requirements, it is not using one for validating designs. Software designs are validated through group reviews by peers or experts. Only if the members of the review team are carefully selected does this method become effective for validating software designs. It makes sense to have the review team made up of more external (outside of the project team) experts, as they would validate the product not just against internal standards but also against field requirements and field usage. It also makes sense for domain experts who are users of the software product to be included as members of the review team instead of the team being made up solely of software designers.

The results of validation would be much more insightful if both prototyping methods mentioned here and group reviews using domain experts were used for validating software designs. This is, in fact, a best practice.

VALIDATING THE PRODUCT SPECIFICATIONS

Product specifications, especially for a software product built to meet the demands of more than one customer, are very important, as all other software development activities are downstream to product specifications. Improper definition of specifications has serious repercussions. Product specifications are the precursor to the software design on which product construction depends. When the specifications are not right, obviously the right product cannot be built. Since defining product specifications is the first step in software development, product specifications need to be validated.

As with software design, validation of product specifications also often is achieved through group reviews that include domain experts. Postal reviews and meeting reviews can be used as well. The advantage of using a postal review is that geographically dispersed experts can be included, although it might take longer to obtain feedback from them and to finalize the product specifications. The advantage of meeting reviews is that finalization of product specifications can be cut to a shorter time, but the drawback is that all the geographically dispersed experts have to be transported to the organization at the organization's expense. The alternative is to use only local experts.

Brainstorming is yet another technique used to validate product specifications. In brainstorming, concerned experts gather in an informal meeting and deliberate to validate the artifact at hand. Brainstorming is used when the activity is performed for the first time and in research and development type of activities.

VALIDATING THE SOFTWARE PRODUCT

Software testing is the main tool for validating the final software product. In the British Standards Institution's Standard BS7925-1, testing is defined as "the process of exercising software to verify that it satisfies specified requirements and to detect faults." Software testing is defined as "the process of executing a software item to detect the differences, if any, between its behavior and the desired behavior."

Testing is carried out using a set of chosen inputs for which the expected result or output is known. It is performed primarily to unearth any and all defects present in the system and to prevent a defective product from reaching the customer. Testing also is carried out to assure the customer that the product conforms to the specifications and functionality initially agreed upon. Testing is used to *confirm* quality rather than achieve it. It can detect errors, but it cannot confirm that there are no other defects lurking in the software product.

Exhaustive testing means trying out all possible combinations of inputs and outputs, and ensuring that the results are correct. Figure 6.1 depicts software testing pictorially.

Software development is one domain where the flexibility for testing is unparalleled. To test a car's behavior in a crash, a perfectly running car is destroyed when it is crashed into something during the test, resulting in the loss

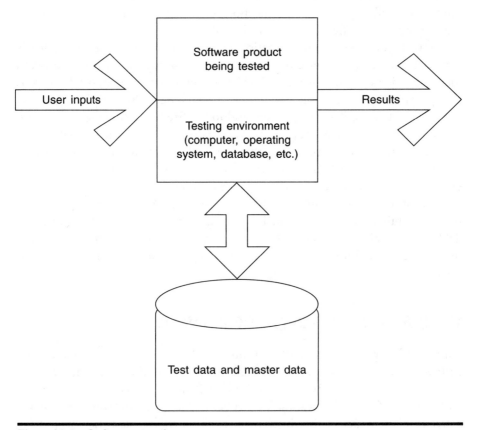

Figure 6.1. Software testing

of the car; retesting requires that another car be built and tested. Testing the behavior of a building in a tornado is impossible because a limited tornado cannot be created. Testing the ability of a building to withstand such circumstances must be done either through computer simulation or with models in labs. In the software domain, however, software can be subjected to any type of testing without the fear of damaging the product or database or injuring the testers. This flexibility allows extensive use of software testing as the main tool for quality assurance in the software development domain.

Software also happens to have a large array of functionality, as it sometimes covers an entire business process, such as finance, materials management, or marketing management. The number of functions that need to be tested is perhaps the highest compared to other domains, such as manufacturing or construction. This flexibility for exhaustive testing coupled with a wide range of functionality makes testing a costly activity, and sometimes the cost of testing equals or even surpasses the cost of development itself.

Software testing is recognized as an essential activity in software development. Lately, the importance of *independent testing* (testing by persons not involved in the development of software) has been gaining wider acceptance, so much so that software companies specializing in software testing have been established and are quite successful. The increasing complexity and size of software have resulted in more complex testing as well as more types of testing.

TESTING DIFFERENT TYPES OF SOFTWARE PRODUCTS

Software testing appears deceptively easy, but it is actually a complex activity because it covers a wide array of software products, and the software that needs to be tested is multifaceted. The following sections describe the different types of software, all of which require testing.

Batch Processing Systems

Batch processing software systems receive inputs from stored data and process them with minimal intervention from the user to produce results. Examples include weekend processing systems, monthly processing systems, yearly processing systems, etc. These systems are found in such mundane applications as Microsoft Office's print functionality (converting text into a format the printer understands, sending line feeds and page feeds, checking printer status and paper outages, etc.) and in such advanced applications as payment processing on the Internet (authorization, debiting the account, crediting the account, funds transfer, etc.), electronic billing (authorization, communicating billing details, receiving acknowledgment, receiving payment, etc.), sending and receiving e-mails, etc.

The main attribute of batch processing systems is that the data is entered offline. When the data is submitted to the software, it is expected to have been validated, is certified to be accurate, and is in the right format. Therefore, batch processing systems do not provide for extensive data validation and error handling routines. If an error is encountered, a batch processing system fails. Therefore, the main precaution that needs to be taken in testing batch processing systems is preparation of accurate data in the right format expected by the software.

Black box testing (explained later in this chapter) is the main testing technique for this type of software. To carry out structural testing using the black box testing technique, test data that forces the software to traverse each path in the code must be created. As stated earlier, the key aspect in testing these systems is preparing the "right" test data for carrying out exhaustive testing and for uncovering all possible errors. The testing steps are identical in all test cases; the one differentiator between test cases is the test data. Test data preparation is the main task in testing batch processing systems.

In this type of software, unit testing is the type of test normally carried out. Batch processing systems can be integrated into other software products, and in such cases, integration testing is carried out on the software product. However, a set of batch processing programs can be run in a stream, one after the other. Each program is tested in unit testing, and the set is tested in "stream testing," which means all programs are run in a stream. The final results are verified for any differences from the desired or expected results.

Online Systems

Online systems also are referred to as event-triggered systems. All online applications, wherein the user interacts directly with the computer through a graphical user interface (GUI) screen to enter or retrieve data, are online systems. The user can follow any sequence to enter data. When a user clicks the mouse interface to set focus to a control on the screen, an event is triggered and a response is generated by the software. Examples of this type of system include online reservation systems, online purchase systems, and all online business applications.

Online systems are expected to be replete with data validation and error handling routines, especially in the inputs. To test online systems, test cases are prepared that send positive inputs which prove that the software does what it is supposed to do and that send negative inputs which show that the software has all the data validation and error handling routines to prevent wrong data from entering or failing the system. This type of system necessitates extensive testing, including all the types of tests mentioned subsequently in this chapter.

In testing online systems, the key aspect is the design of the test cases. The test cases are numerous and consume a significant amount of time to design and document. Some of the testing is carried out intuitively using such testing guidelines as GUI testing guidelines, negative testing guidelines, and report testing guidelines. These tests are described later in this chapter.

Real-Time Systems

Real-time systems interact with machines and control them to perform the desired functions. They are used for process control applications in process flow manufacturing industries, aircraft, weapon systems, and in computer numerical controlled machines (CNC machines).

Since real-time systems interface with hardware, it is sometimes not possible to use the hardware in testing because a wrong signal from the software might damage the machine or its surroundings if the machine malfunctions. Therefore, machine responses have to be simulated during testing, and a test bed that simulates responses from the machine must be created. The significant aspect here is the creation of the test bed, which sometimes is a software product that receives the hardware interrupts placed by the main software and responds to those interrupts exactly as the machine does. Thus, to test the software, another software product needs to be developed.

Scientific Applications

Scientific application systems are built around complex mathematical equations that process large algorithms with a few inputs. They are processing intensive rather than data or transaction intensive. They are found in such applications as weather forecasting and image processing.

The major work in testing these systems is preparing the expected results by hand. For a software product that is capable of carrying out linear programming and matrix algebra that involves a thousand rows and a thousand columns, working out a solution by hand is extremely tedious, and without an expected result against which to compare, it can never be known if the actual result is accurate. Data with a solution that is known and that has been worked out on a reliable existing system can be used in testing this type of software system. For a computer-based system being developed for the first time, it is imperative that the solution is manually worked out to ensure that the actual results of the test are accurate. Precision becomes an issue when using numbers that consist of 16 significant digits or more.

Mobile Applications

Mobile applications are message-processing systems used predominantly in mobile communications. Mobile software needs to be cryptic and brief, due to the small amount of memory available in mobile phones. Again, to test this type of software, either an interface to the hardware is needed or test software that simulates the hardware responses has to be developed. When system testing is carried out, the developed software product must be interfaced with the actual hardware that facilitates mobile communications.

Software Simulators

These systems are yet another type of mathematical processing system that, using special hardware, simulates a real-life scenario. A flight simulator is a popular type of simulation software, but there are many practical applications for simulation in various industries. Simulator software offers both graphics and animation.

Simulators also interface with the input hardware of the actual hardware systems. To test this software, either the actual hardware has to be brought in or a test bed that generates signals identical to those generated by the actual hardware must be prepared. Once this test bed is prepared, the test cases can be executed, and the expected results are those of the actual system. The significant aspect in testing this type of software is the preparation of the test bed.

Testing with Special Hardware

Testing the types of applications discussed above differs based on which of the following classes an application falls into: (1) software that can be tested without special hardware and (2) software that requires special hardware for testing. Business applications, whether batch systems or online systems, can be tested without special hardware. Real-time software, scientific applications (which sometimes might not need special hardware), mobile applications, and simulators all require special hardware. Special hardware in this context means hardware other than the normal computer system and networking hardware.

TESTING BASICS

There are six principles pertaining to software testing that guide organizations:

1. Customer requirements should be the basis for all testing.
2. Software testing should be planned prior to the start of testing.
3. Software testing is subject to the Pareto principle or the "significant few and insignificant many." That is, a few (about 20%) units or modules contain most (about 80%) of the errors.
4. Software testing should start with the smallest unit of software and progress gradually toward the entire system.
5. Exhaustive (100%) testing—that is, testing all possible cases—is not practical.
6. To be effective, software testing should be conducted by independent testers who are not involved in the development.

There are two types of testing techniques: black box testing and white box testing, as discussed in the following sections.

Black Box Testing

In black box testing, the software is treated as a "black box," and its internal logic for processing the data is not considered. A set of inputs is fed to the software, and the outputs delivered by the software are compared with the expected outputs. To use this technique, the tester considers the functionality of the software and administers the test. Black box testing is depicted in Figure 6.2.

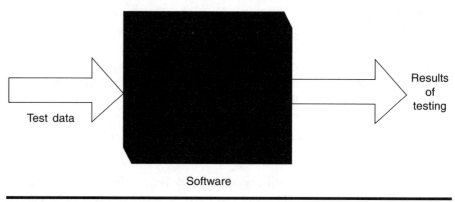

Test data

Results of testing

Software

Figure 6.2. Black box testing

Black box testing normally is conducted from the user interface or command line. The program is invoked, and necessary inputs are given to the software so that it processes the test data and user inputs to generate outputs that can be compared with the expected outputs. This determines whether the software functioned correctly. The efficacy of black box testing depends on the care with which the test cases and test data are designed. If test cases were exhaustive, the testing is exhaustive and has a better chance of detecting anomalies in the software. Test case design is dealt with in greater detail in subsequent sections of this chapter.

The following are the steps for conducting black box testing:

1. Prepare the software unit for testing by creating the executable file or by receiving the executable file from the development team, and install it on the test system.
2. Prepare the master data that is required to run the test. This data can be copied from the development environment or the necessary master data can be entered into the master data files and tables.
3. Study the test plan and note the test objectives.
4. Study the test cases designed for the test.
5. Run the program from either the command line or the user interface.
6. Execute test cases in the sequence specified. At the end of every test case, log the actual results and determine whether test execution failed or passed the test. Record the result.
7. When in doubt about the results of a test case execution, restore the test data to the pretest image and re-execute the test.
8. After all test cases are executed and actual results logged, along with the pass or fail decision, arrange for a managerial review of the test results and submit the report to the originator of the test request.
9. Provide clarification to the originator of the test request, and help the individuals involved in defect resolution to properly understand the defects uncovered during the testing.
10. As required, carry out regression testing to ensure that the defects are resolved satisfactorily. When they have been resolved, clear the software unit for the next stage.
11. If regression testing uncovers fresh defects or old defects that are not resolved satisfactorily, iterate steps 7 to 9 until all defects are satisfactorily resolved.

One precaution that should be taken in black box testing is to preserve the pretest image of the master data and test data, as both are likely to be altered during the course of testing. Whenever a retest is required, the master data and test data need to be set to the pretest image.

White Box Testing

White box testing considers the internal logic and program statements of the software. It involves stepping through every line of code and every branch in the code. To use this technique, the tester should be knowledgeable in the software programming language and should understand the structure of the program. White box testing ensures that all program statements and all control structures are tested at least once. White box testing, depicted in Figure 6.3, also is referred to as *glass box testing.*

White box testing can be conducted from the command line, the user interface, or from within the program. If testing is conducted from the command line or user interface, the exhaustiveness of testing depends on the test cases to traverse through every path in the software. The other way is to conduct white box testing using the interactive development environment (IDE) or a language-specific debugger. These tools have facilities to perform the following:

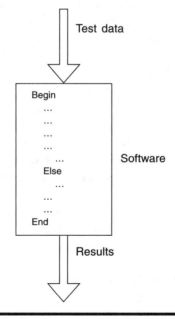

Figure 6.3. White box testing

★   Step through every line of code

★   Set break points in the code where the execution waits for the tester to resume execution

★   Set the initial value or change the value of variables or constants, without the need to change the program

★   Traverse through every path for control structures by dynamically setting control variable values

★   Stop execution at any point in the program and resume testing from the beginning or anywhere in the program

★   Move the execution from any point to any other point in the program

Using these facilities, white box testing is easy to conduct. In fact, the IDEs or debuggers make it possible to thoroughly test software at the unit testing level.

When white box testing is conducted from the IDE or the debugger, the following steps are involved:

1. Prepare the master data and load it into master data files or tables.
2. Study the test plan and note the objectives.
3. Study applicable testing guidelines, if any.
4. Obtain applicable checklists and keep them handy.
5. Study the test cases and be ready to execute them.
6. Receive the software unit to be tested from the development team, and load it onto test system.
7. Launch the IDE or debugger, and open the software unit to be tested in the IDE or debugger.
8. Set break points where a pause in program execution is desired.
9. Run the test cases in the specified sequence and log the actual results.
10. Determine the pass or fail result for each test case by comparing actual results with the desired results, and log the pass or fail result.
11. Run all tests as suggested in the applicable testing guidelines and checklists, if any, and log the results.
12. Arrange for a managerial review of the test results, and submit the test report to the originator of the request.
13. Assist the defect resolution team in properly understanding the defect report.
14. When requested, conduct regression testing to ensure satisfactory resolution of all defects.

15. If the regression testing uncovers fresh defects or original defects that are not resolved satisfactorily, iterate steps 12 to 14.

Sometimes an IDE or a debugger might not be available to carry out white box testing. In such cases, test software that will test the software unit under consideration needs to be developed. Such test software performs the following functions:

★ It calls the software unit under consideration and passes the required parameters to it.
★ It receives the final values produced by the software unit under consideration and presents them to the tester for evaluation of their efficacy.
★ It allows interaction, if required, with the software unit under consideration during execution.

When the IDE or debugger cannot be used to display intermediate values or to suspend and resume execution, temporary statements might have to be inserted into the software unit under consideration. In such cases, the tester also needs to be a programmer, and the test is to be conducted on a copy of the program, not the original program.

APPROACHES TO TESTING

There are two basic approaches to software testing:

1. Intuitive testing
2. Process-driven testing

Intuitive Testing

Intuitive testing is carried out by an experienced tester who uses his or her common sense. A general description of the functionality and suggestions or guidelines for intuitive testing that explain how to go about unearthing defects might be available. Testing is carried out using the experience and intuition of the tester. A certain amount of creativity or common sense is expected from the tester. For example, while testing an input screen, the tester enters values based on the labels provided for the input boxes. It is easy to decipher what to enter:

- ★ If the label indicates dates, enter a date appropriate to the screen. For example, labels such as date of birth, date of application, date of marriage, etc. are easy to recognize, which makes it easy to determine the right and wrong data inputs.
- ★ If the label indicates numeric data such as salary, price, cost, length, height, weight, zip code, etc., it is easy determine the right and wrong data inputs.
- ★ If the label indicates reference to alphanumeric data, such as the name of a person, the person's address, title, e-mail ID, city, etc., again, it is easy to determine the right and wrong data inputs.
- ★ If the label indicates making a choice using radio buttons or check boxes, it is easy to determine the right and wrong inputs.
- ★ The tester can ensure that when wrong data input is given, the software rejects it.
- ★ The tester verifies if the data entered is properly stored and retrieved.

If testing a report, the tester generates a report that contains the desired data and ensures the following:

- ★ The columns are properly aligned.
- ★ No data is clipped or truncated.
- ★ All totals are accurate.
- ★ The report headings, page headings, page numbers, and report dates are properly and fully displayed, without any spelling errors.

If testing an inquiry screen, the tester generates a few inquiries and ensures that the required information is retrieved and displayed properly.

The tester, using common sense, determines the error conditions, generates the test log, gives the test log to the author of the code artifact, and arranges for resolution of defects.

The advantage of this approach to testing is that much of the time usually spent on test planning and test case design is saved. The disadvantages of this approach to testing include the following:

- ★ It requires an experienced tester to conduct the tests and uncover all defects lurking.
- ★ It is almost impossible to test all functionalities without a test plan.
- ★ It is almost impossible to conduct thorough testing, even for critical functions.

Some organizations still use this approach to testing. I have seen it used in an organization that conducts independent validation for products produced by other companies, and the organization certifies them quite successfully.

Process-Driven Testing

In this approach, software testing is conducted in adherence with a defined validation process using a test plan and a set of test cases. For each project, a software test strategy is decided upon during the project planning stage, and it is recorded in the test plan or software quality assurance plan. Test strategy is explained below.

Test Strategy

Test strategy is concerned with uncovering as many defects as possible within the allocated time and cost budgets and with maximizing the impact of such testing. The test strategy for a project generally is included in the test plan for the project.

The first step in finalizing the test strategy is to set testing objectives, such as the following:

1. **Quality objectives**—These relate to the level of unearthing defects:
   ★ Uncover all defects, irrespective of time or cost
   ★ Uncover almost all possible defects within the time available, with cost and time being the main criteria
   ★ Uncover all possible defects within the time available, with time being the main criterion
2. **Customer acceptance objectives**—The main objective of testing is to convince the customer that the product is built in accordance with the customer's requirements and that all functionalities are working without any defects and to obtain customer sign-off and be paid by the customer for the product.
3. **Product certification objectives**—The tests are carried out as specified by the customer, and the product is certified as requested by the customer. A product can be certified in any of the following areas:
   ★ Virus- and spyware-free
   ★ Functionality
   ★ Usability
   ★ Comparison and relative position
   ★ Product rating

In addition to objectives, the following also are part of test strategy:

★ **Types of tests to be included in testing**—Determine which tests need to be conducted on the software product to achieve the project quality objectives.

★ **How to test**—Determine the testing methodology, such as:
  ☆ Test-plan- and test-case-based testing or intuitive testing
  ☆ White box or black box testing
  ☆ Manual testing or tool-based testing

★ **Regression testing**—Determine the number of iterations for regression testing (only once or iterated until all defects are fixed).

★ **Criteria for successful completion of testing**—Define the criteria in order for testing to be declared successful. Sometimes the elapsed time is the criterion for completion of testing. That is, as much testing as possible is conducted until the deadline is reached. Another criterion is testing be conducted until a preset budget is spent. Another is testing is conducted until no more defects are uncovered. Still another is all the defined test cases are executed. Such criteria would be defined and recorded in the test plan or software quality assurance plan.

★ **Mechanisms for defect closure and escalation, when necessary**—Mechanisms include who will close defects, how to close defects, who will escalate, when and to whom to escalate, how to escalate, etc.

★ **Progress reporting**—To be performed during project execution.

★ **Defect analysis**—Determine whether such analyses as ABC analysis, category analysis, defect criticality analysis, etc. are required.

Test strategy for a project is documented in the test plan for the project. Figure 6.4 shows a sample test plan format.

TEST CASE DESIGN

After the test strategy and plan for the project are defined and recorded in the software quality assurance plan, for every intended test there should be a set of test cases against which testing is carried out.

The Institute of Electrical and Electronics Engineers Standard 610 defines a test case as "a set of test inputs, execution conditions, and expected results developed for a particular objective, such as to exercise a particular program path or to verify compliance with a specific requirement, and as documentation

Test Plan for a Project

Project ID:

Revision history of the test plan

Version no.	Description of release and modifications	Prepared by	Approved by	Date of approval

Reference documents: *Enumerate all the documents that were used as reference for preparing this plan. The documents may include project plans, requirements documents, design documents, customer specifications for software testing, etc.*

Software test environment: *Describe the configuration of hardware, servers, client machines, network connectivity and system software, and other software such as database management system, Web server, app server, etc.*

Objectives for software testing: *Enumerate all the objectives, including quality objectives, customer acceptance objectives, certification objectives, and time and expenditure budgets, that are applicable to the present testing.*

Test case preparation

Test	Person responsible for preparing the test cases	Probable reviewer	Schedule of preparation (specify dates)
Unit tests for software units	Program author	Project leader or software project manager	After the unit is coded
Integration tests for each module	Project leader	Software project manager	At the beginning of module integration
System tests	Software designer	Quality assurance department	After software design is approved but before the product is built
Acceptance testing	Software project manager	Quality assurance department and customer	After user requirements are finalized but before system testing is completed

Figure 6.4. Test plan format for a project (page 1 of 4)

Tests to be conducted for the project

Test	Probable testers	Test objectives	How to test	Criteria for completion
Unit testing	Independent peers from the project team	Ensure that the code is defect-free	Based on test cases and white box testing using IDE	All defects uncovered are closed
Integration testing	Project leader	Ensure that the interfaces are working without defects	Every time a unit is integrated with the module using black box testing and test cases	All defects uncovered are closed
System testing	Project leader and software project manager for the project	Ensure that the product works on Windows 2000, XP, and Vista, using Explorer, Firefox, and Chrome	Using system testing test cases	All defects uncovered are closed

Regression testing strategy: *Specify whether regression testing, whenever required, is to be conducted until all defects uncovered, whether in the main test or in the regression test, are closed or if regression testing is to be conducted only once after all defects are closed. If regression testing is conducted only once, specify the strategy to handle residual defects uncovered in regression testing.*

Escalation mechanisms: *Describe the criteria for escalation of unresolved issues in testing or defect closure. Include situations where the author disputes the defect, defect closure is not satisfactory, the defect classification is disputed, etc. Specify the executives, both in the delivery department and the quality assurance department, to whom issues can be escalated and the mechanism for communicating the escalation, such as e-mail, phone call, progress-monitoring meeting, etc. Also specify the timeline allowed for resolution of an escalation.*

Progress reporting: *Specify the timeline for reporting progress and status of testing (such as weekly or daily), to whom the progress report is to be communicated, responsibility for preparing the report, and so on.*

Figure 6.4. Test plan format for a project (page 2 of 4)

Risks identified: *Enumerate all the risks identified, along with their mitigation plan activities*

Risk ID	Risk description	Probability of occurrence	Mitigation plan

Tools to aid in testing

Name of tool	Purpose	Administrator	Reference to tool documentation
PMPal	Defect reporting, resolution, and defect metrics	Software project manager	Project information folder
IDE for programming languages	Unit testing	Program author(s)	Available with the IDE itself
Microsoft Office Suite	Prepare test cases, test logs, and reports and carry out analyses	Concerned persons	Available inside the suite itself
Doors	Load testing	Software project manager	Available in the tool itself

Proposed analyses for the project

Analysis	Person responsible for carrying out the analysis	Schedule for carrying out the analysis
Defect injection rate for programmers	Quality assurance department	Once every calendar month on the last working day
Rework effort for defect resolution	Quality assurance department	Once every calendar month on the last working day
Defect category analysis	Quality assurance department	Once every calendar month on the last working day
Defect by origin analysis	Project leader or software project manager	Once every calendar month on the last working day

Figure 6.4. Test plan format for a project (page 3 of 4)

List of waivers: *Enumerate all the waivers from implementation of organizational process, if any, obtained.*

1.

2.

3.

Any other information relevant to conducting software testing of the project: *Record any other information not covered in any of the above sections but that is relevant to the project testing.*

Figure 6.4. Test plan format for a project (page 4 of 4)

specifying inputs, predicted results, and a set of execution conditions for a test item." From this definition, the following can be deduced about test cases:

★ Test cases are used for executing a test on a software product.
★ Test cases are comprised of user inputs that are provided to the application and the procedure for executing the test case during the test.
★ Test cases detail the expected outputs from the software when the test is executed with the specified user inputs.
★ Test cases are specific to a software code artifact or a class of software code artifacts.
★ Test cases facilitate and ensure compliance of the software code artifact with a specific requirement.
★ Test cases are documented.

The usual practice is to document the test cases in a spreadsheet such as Microsoft Excel or in a tool such as TestPal. (This tool is available as a free download from the Web Added Value Download Resource Center at www.jrosspub.com.) The general practice is to document the test cases for one software component (software code artifact) in one document. Figure 6.5 shows a sample test case definition format.

List of Test Cases

Project ID:

Module name:

Component to be tested:

Type of component: ☐ Screen   ☐ Report   ☐ Stored procedure
                    Describe if other:

Test case ID	Description of test case	Expected results	Actual results	Pass or fail

Figure 6.5. Test case definition format

A condition table is another way to describe test cases. A *condition table* describes the behavior of the system for different combinations of inputs. For example, in a log-in screen, the user enters a user ID and a password and clicks on either the OK button or the Cancel button. When the Cancel button is clicked, the log-in action needs to be canceled, but when the user clicks the OK button, the system behaves as described in Table 6.1.

Test case design is extremely important in software testing. Properly designed test cases can uncover all defects, and poorly designed test cases leave residual defects in the software product. The objective of test case design is to uncover all defects lurking in the software and to test the entire software completely, with the constraint being minimization of effort and time.

Test cases should be derived from the software information artifacts. Table 6.2 lists the artifacts that assist in deriving a test case.

Table 6.1. Condition table for a log-in screen

Condition	User enters user ID and password and clicks OK button
Valid user ID and valid password	Accept
Valid user ID and invalid password	Reject and prompt for valid password
Invalid user ID and valid password	Reject and prompt for valid user ID
Invalid user ID and invalid password	Reject and prompt for valid user ID and password
Empty user ID and valid password	Reject and prompt for user ID
Valid user ID and empty password	Reject and prompt for password
Empty user ID and empty password	Reject and prompt for user ID and password

The number of test cases to be designed and documented is quite large. Consider the following implications in designing test cases:

★ For every numeric data input (including date-type data), five test cases, using the partitioning and boundary value analysis techniques explained later in this section, are needed.

Table 6.2. Software information artifacts that assist in deriving test cases

Type of test	Information artifacts	Remarks
User acceptance testing	User requirements documents	User acceptance testing needs to prove that all user requirements are met by the software
System testing	Software design description— high-level design (software requirements specification)	Target system specification portion of design documents gives this specification
Integration testing	Software design description— high-level design (software requirements specification)	Interface description portion of design documents gives this specification
Unit testing	Software design description— low-level design or detailed design	Specification for the unit in the design gives this specification

★ Size checks must be performed for all nonnumeric data, one per data item.

★ All nonnumeric data must be checked to ensure it has been entered and that the entry area is not left blank.

★ Logical testing is needed to check for the presence of invalid data, such as two decimal points in numeric data, numeric and special characters in name data fields, etc.

Therefore, the test case set for even a moderately complex unit is huge.

Modern projects are large in size, and the effort required to prepare exhaustive test case sets is extensive. For this reason, it is common to prepare test cases where it is expected that the tester cannot intuitively figure out the test cases on his or her own. Guideline-based testing is commonly used for the following types of software testing:

★ GUI testing
★ Navigation testing
★ Negative testing
★ Load testing
★ Stress testing
★ Parallel and concurrent testing

Organizations use these guidelines to avoid having to prepare exhaustive test cases. Integration testing, system testing, and acceptance testing normally are carried out against test cases.

Some of the techniques for test case design which help to ensure that test cases are comprehensive are discussed in the following sections.

Equivalence Partitioning

In equivalence partitioning, the input space is partitioned into *valid inputs* and *invalid inputs*. The following example illustrates this technique. In a human resources application, employee age can be a minimum of 16 (minimum employable age) and a maximum of 65 (retirement age). The partition of valid values is between 16 and 65. There are two partitions of invalid values: one below 16 and the other above 65. Therefore, there are three partitions for this case—one valid and two invalid. One test case can be designed for each partition, resulting in three test cases. The possible outcomes are as follows:

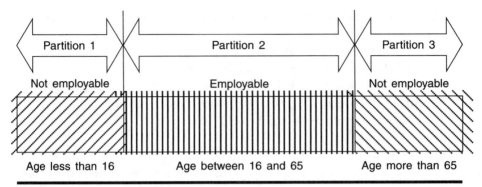

Figure 6.6. Equivalence partitioning

★   If the input conditions specify a range of values (such as 16 to 65), there are three partitions, as stated above.

★   If the input conditions specify a single value (such as 16), there will be three partitions: one valid partition, one invalid partition above the valid value, and one invalid partition below the valid value.

★   If the input conditions specify a Boolean value (true or false), there will be two partitions: one valid partition and one invalid partition.

★   If the input conditions specify a set of valid values, there will be one partition for each of the valid values and one invalid partition for an invalid value.

Figure 6.6 depicts equivalence partitioning.

Boundary Value Analysis

"Bugs lurk in corners and congregate at boundaries," a wise statement attributed to Boris Beizer, is the basis for this technique. Again using the equivalence partitioning example, there are two boundaries: the minimum employable age and the maximum employable age (retirement age). These two boundaries—16 and 65—must be accepted, and all values below 16 and above 65 must be rejected. Therefore, test cases are designed that combine the techniques of equivalence partitioning and boundary value analysis. In this example, there are five test cases:

1. One value between 16 and 65—valid value
2. One value at the lower boundary of 16—valid value

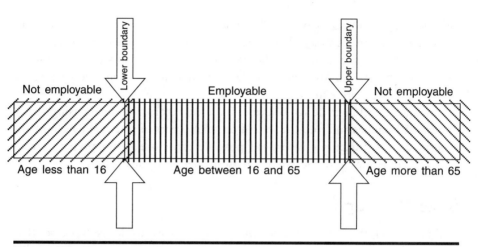

Figure 6.7. Boundary values

3. One value just below the lower boundary (that is, less than 16)—invalid value (normally this value would be given as 1 day less than 16)
4. One value at the upper boundary of 65—valid value
5. One value just above the upper boundary (that is, greater than 65)—invalid value (normally this value would be given as 65 years and 1 day)

Figure 6.7 depicts boundary values.

Error Guessing

As it is generally accepted that exhaustive testing of all possible scenarios is not practical, organizations try to ensure defect-free product by designing test cases for such instances where defects are possible. Generally, a guideline for error guessing is developed. In this technique, the test case designer uses experience, intuition, and common sense to design test cases that are likely to detect errors. As the name itself suggests, there is some amount of guessing involved, which means software engineers are likely to commit errors. Using this technique certainly requires many years of experience in developing and testing software.

Examples of areas in a date field where errors are likely to occur include an invalid date such as February 30 entered, a month set to 13, or a wrong year such as 9999 entered. An example in a human resources application is entering an invalid age for employment. Chronology is another area where errors are likely crop up. For example, when material receipt should precede material issue and the date of issue is prior to the date of receipt, the transaction should be rejected by the system. Another example is negative numbers entered where only positive numbers are expected.

Software developers design test cases to detect errors in software using highly developed hunches and intuition based on many years of software development experience. Organizations record all possible error areas and prepare error-guessing guidelines and checklists for use in designing test cases.

Logic Coverage

In this method, the logic of the software design is used to derive test cases that evaluate the software to ensure that the logic is producing the desired results. The test cases designed either prove or disprove the logic built into the software design.

Consistency Checking

Consistency checking involves designing test cases that check for consistency of processing from different points in the software. For example, in a warehouse information management software application, the stock balance for an item can be obtained from any of the following:

1. Stock inquiry for an item
2. Monthly stock report
3. Priced stores ledger
4. Material issues
5. Material shortages report

Although each of these processes could be governed by a different unit of software, each provides the stock balance information, and the stock balance for an item must be the same, irrespective of the process from which it is obtained. Consistency of information from these different units is checked. If there is a difference in the values produced, it is a clear indication of an error in those software units.

Therefore, test cases are designed to ensure consistency of values. They are applicable wherever there is a requirement to display the same information through different functionalities of the software.

Requirements Tracing

Requirements tracing is the most common method for designing test cases. The requirements, from the user requirements specification to the software detailed design, are traced, and the test cases to test the software product are designed to confirm that the software does in fact meet and fulfill the user requirements.

The following example of a log-in screen component illustrates how test cases are derived from software requirements by tracing them through high-level design, low-level design, and finally design test cases. Table 6.3 shows how these requirements transform in various artifacts.

Test cases are needed to test the log-in screen to ensure it is working to fulfill the requirement of the user and as designed. Here the user requirement is divided into three screens in the high-level design:

★ One screen ensures that the selected password is strong and captures questions and answers to be used to retrieve a forgotten password.

★ The second screen ensures that only authorized users access the application.

Table 6.3. Transformation of requirement for log-in screen

Artifact	Description
User requirement	Access to the product functionality is to be restricted by a user ID and password system. It should be secure enough to prevent unauthorized users from accessing the system. It also should restrict intruders from hacking the security through trial-and-error entry of user ID and password combinations. At the same time, authorized users must be assisted in a convenient manner to retrieve a forgotten user ID or password.
High-level design (software requirements specification)	Definition of the user details screen achieves password security by ensuring that the password is a combination of letters and digits and is not a dictionary word. The screen captures questions and answers for retrieving the user ID and password. The "Retrieve user ID/password" screen assists the user in retrieving a forgotten user ID or password. The log-in screen achieves the functionality of allowing or restricting access to the user. This screen has the facility to enter a user ID and a password. It should have two buttons: one to submit entries to the system and one to cancel entries. There should be a link to retrieve the user ID or password. Only three attempts from the screen should be allowed for invalid entries of user ID and password.

Table 6.3. Transformation of requirement for log-in screen (continued)

Artifact	Description
Software design description (low-level design or detailed design) for log-in screen component	Screen layout (not presented here) Program specs: 1. Display screen and set focus to the user ID box. 2. Set number of attempts to zero. 3. If the OK button is clicked, then perform steps 4 to 10 below. 4. Increase number of attempts incrementally by one. 5. If number of attempts is greater than three, then display the message "Reached maximum number of attempts. Please contact your administrator." Disable entry fields. 6. Verify if the user ID is blank. If so, set focus to the user ID box and display the message "User ID is blank." 7. Verify if the password is blank. If so, set focus to the password box and display the message "Password is blank." 8. Open the users table and verify if the user ID exists in the table. If the user ID is not found, set focus to the user ID box and display the message "Wrong user ID. Please try again." 9. If the user ID is found in the users table, verify if the password supplied by the user is the same as the one in the table. If the passwords do not match, set focus to the password box and display the message "Wrong password. Try again." 10. If the password supplied by the user matches the one in the table, close the log-in screen and display the next screen. 11. If the "Forgot user ID or password" link is clicked, close the log-in screen and display the "Retrieve user ID or password" screen.

★ The third screen facilitates retrieving a forgotten password and user ID for legitimate users.

The user requirements for this log-in screen component are as follows:

★ When the user ID and password combination is entered correctly, access to the system is allowed.
★ Intruders are prevented from gaining access through trial-and-error entry of user ID and password combinations.
★ The user is able to retrieve a forgotten user ID or password.

For each of these requirements, at least one test case needs to be written, but more are required to ensure that the requirements are fully met by the software.

Testing is easy for the first requirement. The correct combination of user ID and password is entered, and the expected result is access to the system. This is one test case. For the second requirement, all possible wrong combinations need to be entered, and the expected result is denial of access to the system. This means a number of test cases must be designed, one per each wrong combination. For the third requirement, the expected result is navigation to another screen. This is another test case.

Test cases can be designed using the format in Figure 6.5. The test cases for the log-in screen example are given in Table 6.4. Successful execution of the test cases represents confirmation that the user requirements are fully met by the log-in screen component of the software product. If the actual result is not the same as the expected result, the actual result is recorded in the "actual results" column. If the actual result is the same as the expected result, "pass" or a similar notation is recorded in the "actual results" column to indicate that the expected and actual results are identical.

This is how test cases are designed by analyzing the user requirements and the software design documents. As you can see, the purpose of testing is to ensure that user requirements are met. Design documents assist us in designing

Table 6.4. Test cases for a log-in screen

List of test cases:

Project ID: Sample project

Module name: Security module

Component to be tested: Log-in screen

Type of component: ☒ Screen   ☐ Report   ☐ Stored procedure
Describe if other:

Test case ID	Description of test case	Expected results	Actual results	Pass or fail
SL01	Enter the correct combination of user ID and password, and click OK button	Log-in screen is closed and the next screen is displayed		
SL02	Restart the application and click "Forgot user ID/password" link	Log-in screen is closed and the "Retrieve user ID/password" screen is displayed		

Table 6.4. Test cases for a log-in screen (continued)

Test case ID	Description of test case	Expected results	Actual results	Pass or fail
SL03	Restart the application, leave the user ID box blank, enter some characters in the password box, and click OK button	Focus is set to the user ID box and the message "User ID is blank" is displayed		
SL04	Enter some characters in the user ID box, leave the password box blank, and click OK button	Focus is set to the password box and the message "Password is blank" is displayed		
SL05	Enter some characters in the user ID and password boxes, and click OK button	Focus is set to the user ID box and the message "Wrong user ID" is displayed		
SL06	Enter the correct user ID and some characters in the password box, and click OK button	Since this is the fourth attempt, the entry boxes must be disabled and the message "Too many attempts. Contact your administrator." should be displayed		
SL07	Try to restart the application	The application should not restart		
SL08	Contact the administrator and reset the computer to facilitate restart	The application should restart		
SL09	Enter the correct user ID and some characters in the password box, and click OK button	Focus should be set to the password box and the message "Wrong password" should be displayed		

test cases with which we can ensure that user requirements are indeed met. The above example illustrates this aspect.

Response Time Checking

Response times are extremely important in real-time software systems that control such machines as aircraft, ships, and rockets, as well as robots and automated machines. Response times also have become very important for Internet-based businesses that offer such online features as booking reservations, purchasing, payment processing, etc. Take, for example, entering a credit card number to make a payment; a long response time may causes the user to wonder:

★ Has the payment been made and my credit card charged?
★ If I click twice, will my credit card be charged again for the same purchase?
★ Did the system hang?
★ Is it possible my credit card has been charged but payment has not been received?
★ Will I get what I paid for?

In an online shopping operation, if the system takes a long time to display, the customer might close the Web site and move to another merchant site or might altogether abandon the idea of online shopping. Therefore, in addition to real-time systems, response time has become crucial for online business systems. Test cases are designed to test the response time of a software product to ensure it is within acceptable limits.

Response time is understood as the elapsed time between when the customer gives a command (clicks the OK or Submit button or hits the Enter button) and the software begins to display a response. The rule of thumb in online business systems is that the maximum allowable response time should be between 15 and 30 seconds. The response time is checked either by using a stopwatch that shows seconds in one-hundredths of a second or by inserting statements in the program to display the time from as soon as the request is sent to as soon as the response is completed. The software's response time is arrived at by subtracting the final time from the initial time. Starting and stopping a stopwatch must be done quickly when using this method to check response time. In the system display method, the software needs to be altered to display the time of the system clock as soon as a command is given and just after the software responds, so that the time it takes the system to generate the response can be worked out.

TEST ENVIRONMENT

The software development environment is set up during the project initiation stage and typically includes the following items:

1. Servers for the database, Web server, and middle tiers
2. Client machines, one for each developer

3. Networking for all the machines
4. A software development tool kit for developing the software

The following steps are then performed:

1. Load all software information artifacts, such as requirements documents, design documents, standards and guidelines, etc., into a common area accessible to all team members.
2. Set up configuration management procedures to deal with change control and code promotion to the next stages. Typically, the code will move from the development state to the unit testing state, then to the product integration state, the integration testing state, the system testing state, the acceptance testing state, and finally to the delivery state. (The subject of configuration management is beyond the scope of this book.)
3. Set up the test environments necessary to conduct a minimum set of tests, specifically unit testing, integration testing, system testing, and acceptance testing. If other types of tests are planned, the test environments need to be set up for those additional tests as well.
4. Set up mechanisms for allocating work to team members and tracking the work allocated to completion.
5. Set up communication mechanisms for work allocation and completion, issue reporting and resolution, issue escalation, etc.

Development work is set to begin once the development environment is created, but what is of concern here is the test environment. The test environment should be a replica of the development environment, albeit at a scaled-down level. It needs a server that has all the necessary software for the database, Web server, and middle tiers, as well as a few client machines to conduct the testing. These client machines should have the same software development tool kit as the development client machines have. The server should have test data with an online backup facility so that it can be reset to the pretest image before conducting a test that would alter the test data.

Whenever a component of software needs to be tested, a copy of it is moved into this test environment. The component is then tested. After it passes in all test cases, it is removed from this environment, and the test data is reset to the pretest image. For testing client-server applications, the server should have the databases, and the software should be loaded onto the client machines. The testers then conduct the testing from the client software and data from the server. For testing Web applications, both the software and the database should reside on the server machines, and the tester should access the software using the designated Web browser to test the application. For mainframe applications, the front-end machines should use terminal emulation software, access the software and data from the server, and test the software.

The actual test environment is described in the test plan for the project. It is not uncommon to use the development environment itself as the test environment. However, this is not a best practice. The development environment would have other software to assist in debugging as well as other software that is not present on the customer's machines. The test environment should resemble as closely as possible the target environment at the customer's site. Therefore, a best practice is to have a separate set of machines for the test environment.

TESTING SCENARIOS

Independent software testing is carried out in two scenarios:

1. **Project testing or embedded testing**—Carried out as part of a software development project to ensure that the development work is defect-free. It is concurrent with software development.
2. **Product testing**—Carried out on a commercial off-the-shelf software product to ensure that the product works without any defects in a variety of customer scenarios. At the special request of the customer, this also can be implemented in contract development. This testing is conducted after software development is completed.

PROJECT TESTING OR EMBEDDED TESTING

When software is developed as a product either to be delivered to a single client or intended for use at a single location, testing of that product starts shortly after the start of its development. That is, a software unit is developed, and then that unit is subjected to the specified testing. As more and more units complete development work, those units undergo testing. As development work progresses, the testing work also progresses, albeit with a time lag between software development and testing. As development work is completed, the testing work is completed soon after. That is, the testing activity is embedded in the development activity itself. In the sections that follow, testing types normally conducted in embedded testing, in addition to software verification, are discussed.

Unit Testing

Unit testing is always carried out by the person who wrote the code and additionally by an independent peer, using the white box testing technique. The following steps are performed in unit testing:

1. The programmer constructs a component in adherence with the design document for the component, allocated to him or her by the project leader or the software project manager. The programmer reviews and tests the component to ensure that it performs the designed functions. The programmer informs the project leader or software project manager that the component is ready for unit testing.
2. The project leader or software project manager identifies a peer to carry out the unit testing, allocates the work of conducting the unit testing to the person identified, and provides that person with the test cases, guidelines, and checklists, if any, for conducting the unit testing.
3. A copy of the code is made available to the tester.
4. The tester loads the code for the component in the testing environment.
5. The tester executes all the test cases and logs the actual results for each test case, indicating a pass or fail result.
6. The tester hands over the test log to the project leader or software project manager, who arranges for rectification of any defects uncovered during the testing and requests that the tester conduct regression testing and close the defects.
7. The tester conducts the regression testing and closes the rectified defects and then hands over the test log to the project leader or software project manager for inclusion in the project records.
8. If regression testing reveals new defects or nonresolution of earlier defects, steps 6 and 7 are iterated until all defects are closed satisfactorily.

Certain development platforms, especially in Web application development, do not allow stepping through every line of code using an IDE or a debugger. White box testing in such cases has to be achieved by accessing the application from a browser and designing test cases in such as manner that all paths in the code are tested comprehensively.

Another distinct characteristic of Web applications is that their unit testing stage also should be used for system testing. Whenever a component in a Web application is constructed, the component has to be tested not only for functionality and structure but also from all target Web browsers and target client machines. If a Web application is tested on only one browser at the unit testing stage, the amount of functionality that needs to be tested at the system testing stage would be huge; it would be practically impossible to execute all test cases to ensure that the application works without defects on all target client machines and Web browsers.

Integration Testing

Integration testing is carried out either as a one-off (when all integration is completed) or incrementally (whenever one unit of software is integrated, its integration is tested until all units are integrated and tested). Black box testing is used for one-off integration testing, and white box testing is used for incremental integration testing. Integration testing should adopt the same approach used to achieve product integration testing by the development team. This should be documented in the project plan documents for the project.

There are two approaches to product integration: the top-down approach and the bottom-up approach. The top-down approach to product integration proceeds as follows:

1. The top-level component from where the product functionality would begin is developed first.
2. The top-level components for the modules of the product are developed next, and these are integrated with the top-level component of the product.
3. If there are any submodules, the top-level components for each submodule are developed and integrated with the top-level components of their respective modules.
4. Each component is developed and integrated with the top-level components of its respective submodule or module.
5. This process continues until all components are developed and integrated with the product.

In the top-down approach to integration testing, two aspects of integration would be tested:

1. The interface code for integrating a module with the product, a submodule with a module, or a component with a submodule or module is tested using the white box testing technique.
2. Functional testing and navigation checking are always carried out from the top-level component of the product toward the bottom of the product using the black box testing technique.

The bottom-up approach to product integration proceeds as follows:

1. Each component at the lowest level is constructed and tested first.
2. When all the components of a submodule are completely constructed and tested, the top-level component of the submodule is constructed, and all its components are integrated with it. Then the submodule is tested for integration efficacy.
3. When all submodules (or components) of a module are completely constructed, the top-level component of the module is constructed, and those submodules (or components) are integrated with the top-level component of the module. Then integration testing for the module is conducted.
4. When all modules are completely constructed, the top-level component of the product is constructed, and all modules are integrated with the product. Then integration testing for the product is conducted.

In the bottom-up approach to integration testing, testing is carried out as follows:

1. Integration testing is conducted whenever all components of a submodule or module are completely constructed and integrated.
2. The interface code for integrating components with a submodule or module is tested using the white box testing technique.
3. Functional testing and navigation checking are always carried out for each submodule or module using the black box testing technique, as and when all components are completely constructed and integrated with a module.
4. Functional testing and navigation checking are always carried out for each module using the black box testing technique, as and when all submodules (components) are completely constructed and integrated with a module.
5. Functional testing and navigation checking are always carried out for the product using the black box testing technique, when all its modules are completely constructed and integrated with it.

Integration testing is conducted as follows:

1. When an integration (either in the top-down or bottom-up approach) is completed, the project leader or software project manager arranges

for a peer review and then arranges for resolution and closure of the defects uncovered.

2. A copy of the code for the integrated submodule, module, or product is moved to the test environment by the project leader or software project manager.

3. The project leader or software project manager identifies a tester to conduct the necessary integration testing and provides the tester with test cases and any guidelines and checklists.

4. The tester conducts the testing in adherence with the test cases and any guidelines and checklists.

5. The tester logs the actual results and determines a pass or fail result for each test case, which also is logged.

6. The tester hands over the test log to the project leader or software project manager, who arranges for resolution of the defects uncovered.

7. The project leader or software project manager ensures that all defects are satisfactorily resolved and arranges for the tester to conduct regression testing and close the defects.

8. The tester conducts the regression testing and closes the defects. The test log is handed over to the project leader or software project manager for inclusion in the project records.

9. If the regression testing uncovers fresh defects or if previous defects were not resolved satisfactorily, steps 6 to 8 are iterated until all defects are resolved satisfactorily.

System Testing

System testing is carried out to ensure that the software works on all intended target systems. In mainframe applications, development usually takes place in a simulated environment on low-cost personal computers. Once development is completed, the software is loaded onto the mainframe computer and tested in the actual environment.

In client-server applications, system testing is carried out on all intended operating system versions, such as Windows 98, Windows 2000, Windows XP, and Windows Vista. It also is carried out on all applicable versions of the database, such as SQL Server 7, SQL Server 2000, SQL Server 2005, etc.

In Web applications, system testing includes testing on various client systems, such as Windows-based machines, UNIX- or Linux-based machines, and Macs. The applications also are tested on all popular Web browsers, such as Internet Explorer, Firefox, Google Chrome, etc. In addition, the different versions of these browsers also need to be used in the system testing. The combinations for system testing of Web applications are immense. In Web applications, most of the system testing is carried out during the unit testing stage. System testing of Web application software takes a significant amount of time to perform.

User Acceptance Testing

User acceptance testing (UAT) is carried out to obtain customer sign-off, so that the software can be delivered and payment received. This testing is unique to contract development. UAT normally is conducted using the black box testing technique. It is based on test cases designed to prove that the software performs all the functions specified in the user requirements document provided by or approved by the customer. It is positive testing.

The steps for conducting UAT are as follows:

1. Test plan and test cases are designed based on the user requirements document.
2. Sometimes the customer provides the test plan and test cases for UAT. In other cases, the customer approves the test plan and test cases provided by the vendor.
3. UAT is planned and scheduled during the project planning stage with the approval of the customer.
4. Normally, UAT is conducted at the vendor's premises and by the vendor's engineers. The customer representative is present during the UAT and ensures that the test environment and testing are as specified in the test plan and test cases designed for UAT.
5. Test results are logged, and any defects uncovered are resolved by the vendor's engineers.
6. Final clearance that the software product passed the UAT is obtained from the customer's representative. Usually, sign-off is in the form of an acceptance letter.

Optionally, many other tests can be conducted at the request of the customer. In Web applications, it is normal to conduct load testing, negative testing, and concurrent testing in addition to the four tests described in this section in contract software development. These additional tests are discussed in subsequent sections of this chapter.

PRODUCT TESTING

A software product in the context of this section is a product developed against specifications defined in-house rather than the specifications of a single customer. The product is to be marketed to multiple customers and delivered with or without customization. When a product is sold without customer-specific customization, it is referred to as a commercial off-the-shelf (COTS) product. There are many COTS products in the market alongside products that are subjected to customer-specific and site-specific customization. Since a COTS product is likely to function in disparate environments with differing system software (that is, different operating systems, browsers, networks, and servers), it requires more rigorous testing to ensure defect-free functioning on all target platforms.

A product is developed as a project first and undergoes all the tests that a project normally undergoes: unit, integration, and system testing. System testing is carried out more rigorously than unit testing and integration testing are and usually on multiple systems. In product testing, other more rigorous tests are carried out in addition to the usual testing. These tests normally are conducted using the black box testing technique. In the sections that follow, these additional tests are discussed in greater detail.

Load Testing

In Web and multiuser applications, large numbers of users are logged in and use the software in a random manner. The objective of load testing is to find out how the software manages multiple requests and whether it either serves up accurate results or mixes the results up. Load testing unearths issues connected with bandwidth, the database, RAM, hard disk space, etc.

Two methods are used for conducting load testing: manual testing and tool-based testing. In manual load testing, a large number of client machines are set up with the necessary software. A user is allocated to each machine and is asked to execute the test cases and then log the results at the workstation.

In tool-based load testing, the test tool is programmed with the necessary test cases and the tool simulates a large number of users by running the test cases on the software and logging the results. Load testing can reveal not only software defects but also hardware defects and limitations in supporting a large number of simultaneous users. Based on the test results, any defects uncovered are resolved.

Volume Testing

Volume testing subjects the software to a high volume of data to see if performance degrades as the amount of data increases. Normally during development and the usual testing, a small amount of test data is used mainly to prove the functionality is working as it should or to uncover defects in the software. In reality, however, the data continues to build up with actual usage of the software and can grow to huge levels. The performance of the software often degrades in such cases, especially when data-intensive reports are generated or when master data files and tables are maintained. Therefore, in addition to the usual tests conducted with a small volume of data, volume testing is conducted using a large volume of data.

In volume testing, functions that are likely to use large volumes of data are tested. Test cases are drawn from the software design documents. A large volume of test data is generated through a test data generator software product. A test data generator software product generates a large volume of test data by manipulating key values, but leaves the remaining data virtually similar in every record. The objective of test data is not to ensure logical results but rather to assess performance when a large volume of data is used. Using this test data, volume testing is conducted and the results are logged and tracked to satisfactory resolution. Volume test tools also are available in the market. These tools have to be programmed to generate a large volume of test data as well as to test the software and log the results.

Functional Testing

Functional testing tests the software to ensure that all its functions are working correctly. There are two types of functions: main functions and ancillary functions. Main functions fulfill product and customer needs as well as perform business processes. Ancillary functions ensure security, protection against intended or unintended misuse, maintenance of data integrity, etc. Functional testing ensures that all these functions are working when used as intended. Functional testing is positive testing.

End-to-End Testing

In end-to-end testing, one entity in the application is tracked from birth to death. In many applications, it takes many years for all functions to be performed on an entity. In a life insurance application, for example, when a policy is issued, it remains in force for a number of years. Some people diligently pay their premium and collect the benefit at the end of the policy period. Other people might borrow money against the policy, repay the money or not, stop paying the premium altogether, and so on. To ensure that all functions are working properly, this type of testing is conducted for one entity. For example, in a payroll application, an employee joins the system and may be promoted, demoted, or transferred; salary increases and decreases are effected or kept in abeyance; and the employee then either retires, dies, quits, or is terminated. End-to-end testing can have multiple paths from the birth to death of an entity, and all such paths are tested in this type of testing. End-to-end testing ensures that the state transitions designed for the entities in an applications happen as desired.

Parallel Testing

In parallel testing, a number of users access the same function and are either inputting or requesting the same data. Parallel testing assesses the ability of the system to handle requests made at the same time and to preserve the data integrity.

Two methods are used for conducting parallel testing: manual testing and tool-based testing. In manual parallel testing, a number of client machines are set up with the necessary software and the same set of test cases. Users are allocated to the machines and are asked to execute the test cases and log the results. In tool-based load testing, the test tool is programmed with the necessary test cases and the tool simulates a number of users by running the test cases on the software and logging the results.

Parallel testing can reveal the ability or inability of a software product to handle a number of requests for the same service or functionality. Based on the test results, any defects uncovered are resolved.

Concurrent Testing

Because of the emergence of Internet-based systems and the many functions being made available to different users, which they can access from the comfort of their home computer screens, the need for concurrency control has significantly increased. Concurrent testing ensures that the software product has adequate concurrency controls built in. This type of testing confirms that the software provides for concurrency control and that it does not malfunction with concurrent usage by multiple users. Concurrent testing is carried out to unearth any issues that occur when two or more users access the same functionality and update or modify the same data with different values at the same time.

Take, for example, a ticket reservation system. Suppose there is only one seat left on a flight and it is shown to two people as available. When both potential buyers of the seat confirm its purchase at the same time, the system should accept only one request and reject the other one. The system should not collect payment from both parties and reserve only one seat, because the credit card transaction of the rejected party will have to be reversed. Scenarios like this are tested with concurrent testing.

Another common scenario occurs when generating complex reports. When producing a report requires a number of tables (more than three) based on complex conditions, a report table is normally populated to be used by report generators to produce the required report. Consider the following example of generating a priced stores ledger in an online (not a batch system) warehouse management system. Normally, a priced stores ledger is generated for a period of time, such as a calendar month. It consists of the opening balance for each item (quantity and value), receipts during the period for each item (quantity and value), issues effected during the period for each item (quantity and value), and finally the closing balance for each item (quantity and value). The report is produced as follows:

1. Gather the information needed from the following sources:
   a. Material master, to ensure that every item in the warehouse is included in the report.
   b. Receipts information, for all receipts during the period for which the ledger is to be produced. This information normally is contained in two tables: the receipts master table (each receipt contains multiple items) and the receipt items table.
   c. Issues information, for all issues effected during the period for which the ledger is produced. This information normally is contained in two tables: the material issue requisitions table (each requisition contains multiple items) and the issue items table (each record contains issue information for one item).
   d. Material returns information, for items returned to the warehouse during the period. This information normally is contained in two tables: the material returns note table (each note contains multiple items) and the return items table (each record contains return information for one item).
   e. Purchase orders table, for pricing information to compute values of receipts, returns, and issues. This information normally is contained in two tables: the purchase order master table (each purchase order contains multiple items) and the purchase order items table.

2. Compute the opening balances and then include receipts, issues, and returns. Compute closing balances and then, finally, compute the totals for each page, the overall report, and the control statistics.
3. Consolidate information from each process using a report table. Common practice is to empty the report table when beginning to process the report request and fill the report table as the process executes. Then the report generator produces the report.

Suppose one person initiates a request for the system to produce the report, and while the process is in progress another person requests the same report from another computer. What happens then is that the second request deletes all the records included by the first process, and then both processes continue to fill the table with information. If this is not controlled properly, the result would be a mess. There are many methods to control this type of scenario, and these methods are called concurrency control methods. One concurrency control method prevents anyone else from generating a report when a request for the same report is already being processed; it keeps the second request on hold until the first one is completed.

Such reports once were produced in batch processing but now are made available to users online, to be produced at will. Many scenarios like the one described here occur in software development. Whenever required, it must be ensured through concurrent testing that adequate concurrency controls are in place in the software. Test cases for concurrent testing should be derived by analyzing the requirements and software design both at the high level as well as at the low level. Then those test cases have to be executed to ensure that the software has adequate concurrency control routines.

Stress Testing

Stress testing stresses the software by making expected resources unavailable, causing deadlock scenarios, not releasing resources, disconnecting the network, etc., to ensure that routines are built into the software to handle such stress. Stress testing assesses the response of the software to events such as machine reset, Internet disconnection, server time-outs, etc.

In Web applications, this type of testing becomes very important, as the user sitting in front of his or her system at a location remote from the Web site does not have any idea what is happening when an expected response is not forthcoming. This test helps to locate any deficiencies in the software that do not allow a smooth transition from an error condition caused by unavailability of expected resources.

Stress testing usually is conducted manually and involves disconnecting the resources in the middle of executing the test cases. It normally is conducted using a set of organizational guidelines and product-specific test cases. Appendix E offers such a set of guidelines for conducting stress testing.

Positive Testing

Positive testing tests the software as specified and does not try any actions that are not expected from a sincere user, to ensure that all defined functions are performing as expected. It is not designed to uncover defects in the software. Positive testing is performed mostly during customer and end-user acceptance testing, functional testing, and end-to-end testing. It is conducted based on test cases designed to prove that the software product is working as designed. This type of testing is used just before delivery of a product to customers, to ensure that the product is working.

Negative Testing

Negative testing involves using the software in a manner in which it is not expected to be used, thereby revealing all other hidden defects not related directly to the defined functionality in the software. This is to ensure that even malicious usage will not affect the software or data integrity.

With the advent of event-triggered software systems, negative testing has become very important. Each control on the screen, such as a text box, combo box, list box, etc., has a large number of events associated with it. For example, click, double-click, change, mouse up, mouse down, got focus, lost focus, key press, key down, key up, etc. are associated with a combo box. It takes great care to code the control so that the user action of triggering an event is validated by some code segment and failures are prevented.

Normally, negative testing is conducted using a set of guidelines, and Appendix F offers such a set of guidelines. Negative testing unearths deficiencies in the software focused on error handling and facilitates improvement of software so that unexpected failures do not occur at customer sites. I recommend carrying out this testing on all software products, be they in the project scenario or product scenario.

User Manual Testing

User manual testing involves using the software in conformance with the user manual to ensure that the manual and the software are in sync with each other.

It evaluates and validates the user documentation. The user manual is used as the test plan, and test cases and the software are used strictly as specified in the user manual. Any deviations found are logged. Using this test log, the user documentation is updated to reflect the functioning of the software. When the user manual is correct and the software is not functioning as designed, the software must be rectified.

Deployment Testing

Deployment testing simulates the target environment and deploys the software to ensure that the deployment specified is appropriate. It is conducted especially on large COTS products which have multiple software components that might have to be installed on separate machines to ensure that the product works without issue on all target platforms. This type of testing uses the final build file (or setup file) or the deployment CD of the product. The purpose of deployment testing is to find out if there are any defects in the build file or the deployment CD of the product. Web applications in particular require this type of testing, as there are many combinations of target platforms in terms of different versions of operating systems, databases, and Web servers. Each possible configuration of the target platforms is set up in a simulated manner, and the product is deployed. In deployment testing, only failures in deployment are considered. After deploying the software components on different machines, deployment testing ensures that the entire system is working satisfactorily.

Sanity Testing

This cursory testing ensures that the components of the software package are complete and the versions appropriate. Sanity testing is carried out before acceptance testing by the customer, before delivery to the customer, or before making a software build. However, this type of testing can be used in many other situations, such as before giving demos of the product to prospective customers. In sanity testing, the application is run and a few critical functions are randomly checked to ensure that the product is functioning as it should.

Regression Testing

Regression testing is carried out after defects uncovered by earlier testing have been fixed. In this test, only the defects recorded in the defect report are tested. The previous test is not repeated in its entirety.

Retesting

Retesting is conducting an entire test again. When testing is carried out and defects uncovered during the test have been resolved, retesting is conducted to ensure the process of fixing defects has not introduced any fresh errors in the software. Repeating the entire test consumes significant resources. Therefore, retesting is easy and practical only if a testing tool is used.

Security Testing

Security testing gauges vulnerability against the threat of viruses and spyware. This type of testing is performed on such software products as firewalls, antivirus software, antispyware software, e-mail software, etc. Security testing should be conducted using separate hardware because viruses and spyware are introduced into the system to see if the software is affected.

Performance Testing

Performance testing evaluates the overall performance of the system. Performance includes response times, report generation, turnaround times, etc. Performance testing is carried out on large-volume data processing, transaction processing, and Web applications. In this type of testing, test data is crucial for successful testing. Test cases are designed to test the system throughput based only on the software design.

Usability Testing

Usability testing involves testing the software for different types of usage to ensure that it satisfactorily fulfills the requirements of specified functional areas. Usability testing is performed especially if the software is expected to be used by persons with certain disabilities. This type of testing is carried out by testers who have the disabilities for which the software is targeted.

Install-Uninstall Testing

Install-uninstall testing tests the software on all target platforms to ensure that install and uninstall operations are satisfactorily performed. It is carried out for a single software component that is expected to be installed on a single machine. Install-uninstall testing differs from deployment testing in that deployment testing tests an entire software product that has multiple software components to be deployed on multiple machines. Install-uninstall testing ensures that the software components are properly loaded onto the intended directories during the install and all components are deleted from the system after uninstall. The install operation should not overwrite and render nonfunctional any files or dynamically linked libraries used by other applications resident on the computer, and the uninstall operation should not remove any shared files or dynamically linked libraries that might be required by other applications resident on the computer or render any applications nonfunctional.

Comparison Testing

Comparison testing involves testing the product with competing products to identify differences and to determine the relative position of the product vis-à-vis competing products. This type of testing normally is entrusted to independent verification and validation agencies, which determine the relative position of the product and certify the product's relative ranking. Comparison testing also is referred to as *benchmark testing* or simply *benchmarking*.

Regulation Conformance Testing

Regulation conformance testing ensures that the product conforms to all government regulations pertaining to minimum standards, such as Sarbanes-Oxley regulations for accounting and other regulations for safety, use by persons with disabilities, compatibility with earlier versions, etc.

Alpha Testing

Alpha testing is carried out after the product is ready for release. Actual prospective users of the software product conduct the testing at the facility where the software was developed.

Beta Testing

Beta testing also is carried out after the product is ready for release. Like alpha testing, actual prospective users of the software product conduct the testing, but at their respective locations, outside the organization that developed the software product.

Product Testing Summary

It is rare for all the tests described here to be carried out on every project executed/project produced in an organization, but it is common for product testing to include many of them. Every organization conducts some combination of the test types described here, but all organizations carry out at least the following four types of testing:

1. **Functional testing**—To ensure that all functionalities allocated to the software are working and that, when used properly, there are no inaccuracies
2. **Integration testing**—To ensure that the coupling between various software modules is in order
3. **Positive testing and acceptance testing**—For client acceptance of the software
4. **Load testing**—To ensure that the system does not crash when heavy loads are placed on it

Sometimes organizations carry out the other types of testing discussed in this section, but only if time and budget are available or if mandated.

BEST PRACTICES IN TESTING

It is not easy to define what the best practices are in testing, as they are relative to the situation and the objectives of the testing. The first overall best practice is to conduct independent testing, and the tests should be conducted in accordance with the following best practices:

1. White box testing should be performed at the unit testing stage, using either IDEs or debuggers or well-designed test cases, without exception.
2. Independent testers should conduct the unit testing.
3. White box testing should be used for testing of code that couples software units to modules and modules to the product.
4. A separate testing team in the organization, rather than developers, should conduct integration testing, system testing, and other selected types of testing. Developers should be limited to conducting independent unit testing only.

5. A well-defined testing process for conducting software testing in the organization should be established. The process should include process, procedures, guidelines, checklists, formats, and templates that will ensure testing is carried out thoroughly.
6. Negative testing should be made mandatory. This would ensure that the product will not fail unexpectedly in the field.
7. Testing should be conducted based on well-designed test cases. However, to reduce the effort spent on designing exhaustive sets of test cases, standards and guidelines should be defined to reduce the need for designing test cases.
8. Test cases should undergo thorough verification.
9. Test logs should be subjected to verification to ensure that the inferences of the results produced by testing have been accurately drawn and that the testing covered the entire spectrum of the product as designed by the test cases and organizational guidelines.
10. The organization should standardize a minimum set of tests to be carried out on software it develops. These tests should at least include independent unit testing, integration testing, system testing, and negative testing.

Additional best practices as well as pitfalls are discussed in the sections that follow.

Best Practices in Unit Testing

Unit testing conducted by an independent tester is itself a best practice. Use of an IDE or a debugger to step through every line of code is another best practice. If it is not possible to use an IDE or a debugger to conduct unit testing, a best practice is to ensure that the test cases used are designed in such a way that all paths in the software unit are tested at least once during the testing. Ensuring that every line of code and every path in the software unit is tested is referred to as the "100% coverage standard." This is a best practice. As the testing adage goes, "If you do not test it, you cannot find its defects."

If thorough unit testing is not carried out, defects not uncovered will surely surface during the next round of testing or, worse, at the customer location.

Not having an independent tester conduct the unit testing and relying on the testing conducted by the developer is a major pitfall. Quite a few organizations fall into this trap, and defects surface later on, resulting in extra effort to fix them as well as avoid embarrassment.

Not stepping through every line of code and not traversing every path in the software unit is another pitfall during unit testing. If a path is not tested, it very likely is left with defects that will continue to lurk in the software until that path is traversed in the field.

Best Practices in Integration Testing

Integration testing conducted by a specialist testing team is a best practice. Normally, in quite a few organizations, integration testing is conducted by project senior programmers or the project leader. These people are involved in the project and are emotionally attached to the product; therefore, they are likely to skip over minor aspects, and more often than not it is the minor aspects that cause major problems.

Another best practice to use both white box testing and black box testing in integration testing. The code that is developed to couple units with modules or modules with the product should be tested using white box testing, stepping through every line of code. Black box testing can be used for coupling and cohesion in integration.

Another best practice is to use incremental integration and incremental integration testing rather than doing all the integration in one shot (that is, as a "big bang") and conducting all the integration testing in one iteration. Conducting integration testing for all the integration in one iteration would require significantly more time. Such testing normally is conducted near the end of development work, and consequently, there is pressure to complete it quickly. This could mean not having enough time to finish the testing, resulting in not being able to uncover all the defects. A best practice is to carry out integration incrementally and align the corresponding integration testing with incremental integration.

Common pitfalls in integration testing include the project team conducting it, only black box testing used for it, and conducting it in one iteration as a "big bang."

Best Practices in System Testing

In Web applications in particular, putting off system testing until the entire product is ready results in inadequate testing. The combinations of target platforms are enormous, and testing all functionality for all target platforms at the system testing stage becomes impractical. In Web applications, system testing needs to be combined with unit testing. A best practice in system testing of Web applications is to combine system testing with unit testing and carry out a cursory system testing at the system testing stage. In other applications, system testing can be carried out after the entire product is constructed and integrated.

A best practice is to conduct system testing on all target platforms. Another best practice is to use a specialist testing team rather than the development team to conduct system testing.

A common pitfall in system testing is to conduct the testing on one representative target platform and assume that the product will work as well on other versions of the platform. For example, conducting system testing on Internet Explorer version 6 and assuming that it will work on versions 7 and 8 as well can cause defects to surface when the later versions are used. Another common pitfall is to entrust the system testing work to the development team rather than using a specialist testing team.

Best Practices in Regression Testing

Two aspects are involved in regression testing. The first is how many times a regression test should be run. One practice is to conduct a regression test only once and expect that no further defects will be unearthed; if any are uncovered, they can be left to the developers to fix. Another practice is to conduct regression testing as many times as required, until all defects uncovered are resolved satisfactorily. A best practice is to carry out regression testing until all defects are satisfactorily resolved.

The second aspect pertains to the limits of regression testing and whether to test only for the defects reported or to retest the entire software. Retesting is preferable, but repeating the entire test would take as much time as the first test took. If regression testing is conducted multiple times, then retesting every time would skyrocket the costs of testing. If testing tools are used for the first testing, the answer is clear: retest every time regression testing is needed. If no testing tools are being used and the regression testing has to be carried out manually, retesting is not practicable. However, a better practice is to extend the regression testing beyond testing only the defects and to include some sort of cursory testing in the final round of integration testing to ensure no fresh defects are introduced while resolving the defects reported.

Another best practice is to conduct regression testing after every round of defect resolution and change implementation. Many organizations totally do away with regression testing, and this is a major pitfall. They claim that their programmers are mature and can resolve defects completely without introducing fresh ones. Any exceptions are explained away as random aberrations rather than the result of human error. These organizations also argue that it is cheaper and quicker to fix a defect found at a later date than to conduct regression testing. They are focused more on making money than on providing products of excellent quality. I have seen many organizations fall into this major pitfall.

Minimum Set of Tests for a Software Product

It is essential to define a minimum set of tests to be conducted on a software product developed in the organization. These tests normally include independent unit testing, integration testing, and system testing. Negative testing and consequent defect resolution would add robustness and fault tolerance capabilities to the software. Similarly, end-to-end testing would ensure that state transition of data processing on entities is happening as designed. Load testing and volume testing also prevent unforeseen failures at the customer location. Therefore, it is a best practice to include negative testing, end-to-end testing, load testing, and volume testing in the minimum set of tests. Not having a defined set of minimum tests is a major pitfall.

Independent Testing Team

Should this be mentioned as a best practice at all? In manufacturing and other sectors, testers are always independent from the production team Testing is recognized as a specialty in itself. In the software development industry, however, many organizations do not have separate testing teams. They use developers to conduct all the testing. In fact, the testers are drawn from the development team that developed the software. These organizations argue that it is cheaper to use the development team, because its members are already knowledgeable about the product functionalities and can very quickly complete the testing. What they have missed with this argument is that the objective of testing is not to complete it quickly but rather to uncover all or as many lurking defects as possible. These organizations are the ones that receive midnight calls for customer support. They spend much more money on attending to defects uncovered in the field than on uncovering them in-house and preventing them from reaching the customer.

When separate testing teams are used, they grow into testing specialists and focus on uncovering defects, increasing their testing productivity. In fact, specialist testers have higher testing productivity than developers have. Another argument in favor of using specialist testers is that they conduct more thorough testing than developers would.

Having a specialist testing team would save an organization a significant amount of money—money that otherwise likely would be spent on attending to urgent calls for support from customers. It is a best practice to institute a specialist testing team in software development organizations.

However, before putting the testing group to work, developers have to ensure that their software works. I know of instances where developers have requested testing of the software as soon as it is compiled without errors, not after they have tested it themselves to ensure that it is fully functional and defect-free. This is misuse of independent testing. Software should be entrusted to the independent testing team only after the developers are reasonably confident that it is in working condition and without defects. The purpose of testing by the author is to ensure the functionality, and the purpose of independent testing is to uncover defects. Having an independent testing team test the software does not mean the developer is not responsible for testing his or her own code. Independent testing is meant to be supplementary to the developer's testing to confirm that the software does not have any defects. It is not intended to supplant the testing carried out by the developer. This is a common pitfall I have seen in organizations that have an independent testing team.

Best Practices in Beta Testing

Beta testing is very important in COTS products that are expected to sell a large volume. A best practice is to use a significantly large number of testers so that testing is as thorough as possible. About 1 to 3% of the sales volume can be used for testers to conduct beta testing.

One thing to keep in mind is that beta testing is not an alternative to thorough in-house testing. Beta testing is performed to uncover defects for which an in-house testing team might not be able to design test cases or when such a data combination cannot be generated in-house. A bonus of beta testing is suggestions for better usability of the software.

Therefore, best practices in beta testing are to entrust it to an adequate number of testers and to use it in addition to in-house testing. A major pitfall is the use of beta testing as an alternative to thorough in-house testing.

AUTOMATION OF TESTING AND USE OF TESTING TOOLS

Testing tools have entered the market in a big way. Even so, there is a misconception in the software development industry—especially among senior management—that a tool automatically does what is expected of it. There are a few facts to note here. The same misconception was prevalent when computers hit the market years ago; it was believed that by pressing a few buttons, the computer would accomplish every task the user wanted it to. It slowly dawned on users that quite a few buttons have to be pressed before the computer can accomplish in minutes what would take days to accomplish using manual methods. The same is true in the case of testing tools.

A tool helps a technician accomplish a quality job with much better productivity. A tool does not supplant the technician; it only assists the technician. For example, a plumber cannot do plumbing work without a pipe wrench. But having a pipe wrench alone doesn't make someone a plumber! Similarly, testing tools do not supplant the tester; they help the tester do a better job of testing. With this in mind, the following are prerequisites of testing tools:

1. Test cases have to be designed and test data, procedures to execute these test cases, and expected results have to be defined, and all this information has to be fed into the testing tool before it can execute test cases automatically. This is accomplished through a process referred to as test scripting.

2. Testing tools have to be programmed. Test scripts are essential if a tool is to be used for conducting testing in the organization. True, it is believed that writing test scripts is not as rigorous as programming is. There are many terms in use today, such as programming, defining macros, writing scripts, etc., which are all basically synonyms for programming. These terms denote defining a procedure that can be understood and executed by a computer. As in any programming, it takes time to script the tools. The simpler the testing, the simpler the scripting; the more elaborate the testing, the more elaborate the scripting that is required for the testing tool to do an effective job.

3. Just as good programming can be achieved with requirements analysis and software design, testing requirements have to be analyzed and test cases designed so that efficient and effective test scripts can be written.

4. If a test is conducted only once, then manual testing takes less effort and time than using a testing tool would, due to the effort required to prepare the tool to conduct the test. However, if it is necessary to conduct the same test a number of times, testing tools start to show benefits from the second iteration onward.

5. Most testing tools provide a "record and playback" (capture and replay) facility. That is, the test is conducted manually with the testing tool in capture mode, and the tool captures and stores every key-

stroke. When the testing tool is set to playback mode, it will execute the test automatically. In other words, the testing tool automatically generates the test script when a test case is executed when the tool is in capture mode. However, as with any automatic code generation tool, the script generated is difficult to maintain. When the testing requirements change, modifications have to be made in the test script.

6. Software engineers have to develop the test scripts for testing tools, and these engineers need training in writing efficient test scripts. Test scripts also tend to have bugs and require quality assurance to ensure they are defect-free.

Once it is understood that test scripting is required prior to using testing tools and organizations are ready to spend the effort and time necessary to accomplish that activity, the benefits of testing tools can be derived.

The benefits of using testing tools are as follows:

★ From the second iteration of testing onward, test execution shows a drastic improvement in terms of time and effort. That is, it takes much less time and effort to test.

★ Testing tools make retesting possible in every iteration of regression testing—something not possible in manual testing due to the amount of effort and time required for each iteration of retesting. This is a great benefit, as it ensures that the resolution of defects does not inject fresh defects, which unfortunately happens often enough.

★ Tools make it possible to conduct load testing, stress testing, parallel testing, concurrent testing, and others types of tests not possible or very difficult to achieve manually.

★ Testing tools are of great value during the software maintenance phase, because for every defect fixed or modification made, the effort and time needed for each regression testing are drastically reduced, and retesting can replace regression testing.

Testing tools provide benefits even with the concomitant effort spent on preparing the test scripts. In a contracted development project, wherein software for a single client is developed, it would be very costly to use testing tools. However, the customer might pay extra to have test scripts developed and delivered along with the software, so that they can be used with great benefit during the software maintenance phase. For in-house software development, use of testing tools is highly recommended, as the scripts can very profitably be used during the software maintenance phase.

I have one recommendation regarding testing tools: use less and less of the "record and playback" feature to generate test scripts; prepare test scripts only when a software product is developed, and subject them to all the quality assurance activities used in normal software development.

FINAL WORDS ABOUT SOFTWARE TESTING

Because no "break and make" is involved in testing software and test data can easily be set to the pretest image, there is practically no limit for software testing. With Web applications, an organization has no control over the environment in which end users utilize software. This makes it imperative to conduct exhaustive software testing; the alternative is unforeseen software failures and a resultant loss of reputation and possibly loss of business too. There is no other field in which such exhaustive testing is conducted or is feasible. The number of tests that can be executed in software testing is unheard of in other fields. This makes it a vast subject, and perhaps large volumes will be written about software testing alone in the near future. The purpose of this chapter is to provide as much information as possible on essentials of software testing as part of the overall subject of software quality assurance.

SOFTWARE PRODUCT QUALITY: RELIABILITY

SOFTWARE DISASTERS

Increasingly, more and more systems are being controlled by software. The pervasion of software in our lives is so extensive it might not be an exaggeration to say that there is no hardware that does not have software today. Such common items as televisions, washing machines, watches, clocks, security systems, etc. in our homes are software controlled. Airports, aircraft, rockets, weapon systems, factory machines, shopping malls—you name it, they are all controlled by software. We have labeled, whether rightly or wrongly, software development as "high tech," and therefore, we assume that it is flawless, because anything that is high tech must be flawless. Many of us either do not understand or do not try to understand the intricacies of software development; we place it on a pedestal. But the reality is that software is as prone to errors, defects, and failure as any of the hardware on which it resides.

It has been well proven in the manufacturing sector that human beings are the reason behind most failures, and machines are much better suited to achieve quality. The human element is crucial in software development, and it is not an overstatement to say that the highest cost in software development is expended on human beings. Therefore, it is clear that, due to its dependency on human beings, high-tech software is much more prone to errors than any hardware ever could be.

The Internet is replete with incidents of disaster whose origins can be traced to software flaws. This fact was glaringly depicted in the movie *Jurassic Park*. Consider the following incidents cited on Wikipedia:

★ Lufthansa flight number 2904 (http://en.wikipedia.org/wiki/Lufthansa_Flight_2904) landed at a speed of 170 knots (195 miles per hour)—20 knots (23 miles per hour) faster than the standard speed. The pilot had to steer the plane off the runway as it was reaching the end. The left wing hit an embankment and a fire broke out, spreading to the passenger compartment. As a result, the copilot and one passenger died. One of the reasons was a software flaw.

★ Patriot missiles in the Gulf War's Operation Desert Storm (http://en.wikipedia.org/wiki/MIM-104_Patriot) caused an accident. The battery from which the missiles were fired was in operation for 100 hours, during which time the system's internal clock drifted by one-third of a second. This resulted in a missile missing its target by a distance of 600 meters. Because of this, a scud missile was not intercepted and hit the U.S. Army barracks, killing 28 soldiers. The cause was traced to a software flaw.

★ In 1999, the mission to launch the Polar Lander to Mars failed, as the software misidentified vibrations in the vehicle's legs during touchdown and shut off the engines 40 meters (about 135 feet) from the surface. As a result, the Polar Lander was lost.

★ Y2K, as the approach of the year 2000 was labeled, was a widespread concern in the 1990s. This was because in the earlier days of computing, to save disk space and memory during execution, years were entered into systems using two digits only, with the understanding that any four-digit year began with "19." With the coming of the year 2000, all these programs had to be corrected—at an estimated cost of $500 billion. Some resolved the Y2K problem by assuming any year entered as "50" and above to be in the 20th century (1950 to 1999) and any year entered as "49" and below to be in the 21st century (2000 to 2049). The problem is, these programs are still running, and if they are not upgraded to another technology and rewritten, a similar type of problem will occur in 2049. All indications are that these programs will still be running in 2049.

★ The year 2038 problem pertains to computer systems using UNIX operating systems. UNIX stores system time as number of seconds from January 1, 1970 as a signed 32-bit integer. The number will reach its maximum on January 19, 2038. On that day, if this issue has not been corrected, the clock will be reset and the year will be treated as part of 20th century. This problem must be fixed in the near future.

The Web site The Daily WTF (http://thedailywtf.com), which records software disasters, offers many more examples of this nature.

These incidents are only a sample of the many problems (and disasters) caused by flawed software. Software issues in business are not that widely reported, as they do not cause loss of life or massive economic losses. I have witnessed a few incidents in business caused by problems with software:

★ A stock exchange computerized its operations. It took a little time to find out that some of the "sell" orders were resulting in "buy" orders. The stock exchange shut down the computer system and rectified the error before switching on computer-based operations once again. The loss of revenue was not clearly stated.

★ In a 1,400-bed hospital, the billing module was not including all services rendered to patients at the time of receiving payment. The hospital lost substantial revenue in six months before this anomaly was discovered and corrected. It took an investigative audit to discover this defect.

Both of these situations were traced back to software errors. Most people have had similarly frustrating experiences with their own PCs. The sudden hanging or crashing of a computer for no apparent reason often is caused by software problems. Software, even though it does not deteriorate with age or wear out with usage, still has reliability problems.

SOFTWARE RELIABILITY

The attribute a product must have in order to claim a quality tag, in addition to defect-free functioning, is reliability. That is, the product performs the designed functions diligently over the duration of its life. If a car is supposed to have a useful life of up to 100,000 miles, the car is said to be reliable if it continues to transport five people for 100,000 miles without requiring a major overhaul. The life of software depends on the life of the hardware that runs it. These days, hardware becomes obsolete within three years (the exception being high-cost mainframes), and maintenance is possible for perhaps another five years. During the eight- to ten-year life of hardware, many patches to the system software, such as the operating system, database management system, antivirus software, etc., may be required. These patches could cause the software to fail. Thus, the reliability of a software product depends on the reliability or stability of the system configuration on which it functions.

Software reliability is defined as the probability that the software will function without failure and defects, for a specified period in a specified environment. Reliability means delivery of the same level of defect-free performance during the life of the product.

A software product does have a finite life—which means the duration the product is likely to be used before it needs to be replaced. During the life of a product, software maintenance might be necessary for the following reasons: (1) to fix any defects unearthed during its usage or that arise as the result of system configuration changes such as updates to the operating system and other utilities, (2) to enhance the functionality necessitated by a changing business environment, or (3) to modify functionality to cater to business or environmental changes. Product replacement might be necessary when a product requires a massive change in functionality or when there is a paradigm shift in the environment, such as the explosion of Internet. These kinds of conditions are rare events, and therefore it can be expected that a product will be under software maintenance for a long time.

Software maintenance due to functional modification or enhancement does not render a product unreliable. However, any software maintenance carried out to fix defects that are unearthed while the software is in production *does* warrant a product unreliable. But if all quality assurance (QA) activities have been carried out, how can defects still remain inside a software product? Defects lurk in a product for various reasons, such as the following:

★ There could have been shortfalls in the specifications defined for the product.
★ The software design itself could be defective, or some of the design assumptions could have defects.
★ The construction of the software product could have been defective.

★ All QA activities may not have been carried out, or they could have been carried out without the necessary diligence.

★ As stated earlier in this book, it is a commonly accepted fact that 100% testing and uncovering 100% of defects are not practical. Some defects do still remain.

★ All software products are developed using a development platform, and that platform might harbor some defects which surface only when a specific set of conditions arises.

★ Changes in system configuration often bring about unforeseen conditions that cause the product to malfunction.

★ Updates and patches to system software such as the operating system and other utilities can cause the product to malfunction.

Reliability is achieved by building a software product so that it is not dependent (or is dependent to the minimum extent) on an operating system's shared libraries, which are likely to be changed or updated over a period of time. Minimizing the use of third-party tools or code libraries is another practice that helps to instill reliability in a product. Performing all QA activities on a product during its development stage is a must for producing a reliable software product. The reliability of a software product is confirmed through extensive software testing, which is described in greater detail in Chapter 6. When a software product is in production, it should be monitored for reliability using the following data:

★ **Failure rate**—Specified as the number of failures during a given time period, such as failures per calendar month or failures per quarter-year.

★ **Downtime due to software failure**—Expressed as the number of clock-hours the product is unusable. More often than not, software failure does not cause the product to be shut down. Sometimes the failure might cause a specific functionality to become unavailable. The downtime needs to be counted even if only one function is unavailable.

★ **Expenditure incurred for repair**—It is normal to dedicate a few personnel for maintenance work, irrespective of the occurrence of failures. This is a fixed cost, constant throughout the life of the product. Additional resources might be needed to fix defects and to attend to system breakdowns when the dedicated resources are unavailable or insufficient to carry out the needed maintenance.

Therefore, all costs expended toward software maintenance need to be taken into consideration. Cost per defect (the total software maintenance expenditure to fix defects divided by the number of defects fixed) is normally computed, and this value is monitored.

The values for all this data are monitored using moving averages and trend analysis to determine failure rate analysis.

CAUSES OF SOFTWARE FAILURES

Software failures can be caused by defects inherent in the software, such as errors, ambiguities, oversights, wrong assumptions, misinterpretation of requirements or specifications, malfunctioning of third-party tools, inadequate verification and validation, and incorrect or unexpected usage. Different types of software faults can cause reliability problems, as discussed in the following sections.

Software Design Faults

★ Architecture deficiencies
★ Exception handling issues
★ Traceability issues of specifications or requirements
★ Misinterpretation of specifications or requirements
★ Use of third-party tools without adequately testing them
★ Wrong assumptions regarding the end users or the target platform
★ Inadequate verification and validation of designs
★ Inadequate field size, such as the Y2K issue
★ Environmental changes, such as euro conversion

The best way to prevent software design faults is to implement verification and validation activities diligently for software design. These are discussed in detail in Chapters 5 and 6.

Coding or Construction Faults

★ Oversight
★ Missed steps
★ Errors of omission and commission
★ Inefficient code

★ Ambiguous code
★ Improper interpretation of comparisons due to wrong algorithms for data comparisons
★ Numeric precision issues

Prevention of software construction faults can be achieved through well-defined coding guidelines, followed by software verification and rigorous testing.

Quality Assurance Problems

★ Inadequate software verification
★ Inadequate software validation
★ Not using specialist software testers
★ Not verifying the test results
★ Not measuring the quality of the software product
★ Not having a QA department

It is true that QA activities cannot build quality into a product directly, but they certainly provide an environment that is conducive to producing high-quality software that is free of defects. The QA activities that are critical, in addition to verification and validation, are software process definition and improvement, software quality measurement, analysis and improvement, and definition of standards and guidelines for software engineering activities and their regular improvement.

Many organizations look at the QA department as a cost center and do not provide the funding, resources, and tools necessary for it to function effectively. Apart from this, senior management also does not allocate adequate time for QA activities. It is the norm for senior management to side with the development team in any conflict between the QA department and the development department. How to maintain an organization that is conducive to excellence in quality is discussed in detail in Chapter 4.

Data Failures

★ Master data errors
★ Ambiguous master data
★ Data precision problems
★ Data corruption
★ Data integrity and consistency problems

Bad or wrong data is one of the major causes of software failure, and the probability of software failure is very high, especially when data is entered offline, unless the data is thoroughly validated and cleansed of all bad data. Master data that contains reference data for making decisions is crucial for error-free operation of software. It was reported that a battleship was sunk because its radar software identified an incoming missile as a friendly object! Obviously, the software matched the attributes of the incoming object with the friendly objects contained in its master data files and determined the missile was a friendly object.

Another frequent problem in data quality is importing data from another application. When data is imported directly from one database to another, the programmatic controls are not operative to validate input data and ensure its quality. When importing data, it is important to diligently ensure that the data is clean and accurate. Otherwise, this is one way to inject bad data into the system.

PREDICTION OF SOFTWARE RELIABILITY

There are many reliability measurements and prediction metrics and models in the software literature. Standard 982 of the Institute of Electrical and Electronics Engineers *IEEE Standard Dictionary of Measures to Produce Reliable Software* provides a comprehensive set of such measures. In my opinion, however, most of them are too theoretical and complex to understand and implement, or they require an enormous amount of time to compute. Some measures which I believe are easy to derive and monitor include the following:

1. **Product metrics**—Such as the following:
   ★ Size of the software—The larger the size, the less reliable the software and the more likely it is to contain errors.
   ★ Program complexity using the cyclomatic complexity of McCabe's and Halstead's metrics.
   ★ Test coverage metric—Computing the amount of software code covered by testing. Ideally it ought to be 100%, but in practice, it is less than that.
2. **Project management**—The diligence with which project management activities are performed. As it is possible to cut corners during project execution, it is possible that the software will retain residual faults. The following are the critical aspects of project management that can influence the quality and reliability of a software product:

★ Quality management
★ Configuration management
★ Project management
★ Team morale

3. **Software development process metrics**—The quality of a software product depends on the software development process adopted in the organization. The stringency of the standards, guidelines, and QA activities has a direct bearing on the quality of the product. The following are the critical aspects of the software development process that can influence the quality and reliability of a software product:

★ Depth of the process
★ Stringency of standards and guidelines
★ Diligence of process implementation
★ Failure metrics
★ Number of failures in a time period, such as a quarter-year
★ Mean time between failures
★ Mean time to repair

The composite product quality rating (CPQR), detailed in Chapter 3, is a method to compute a software product quality metric. It is an excellent predictor of software reliability. As the CPQR moves downward from a value of 5, the reliability of the software product also slides downward. As the CPQR edges up toward 5, so does the reliability of the software product—it improves. I suggest using the CPQR to predict software product reliability.

SOFTWARE RELIABILITY IMPROVEMENT

Obviously, the reliability of a software product depends on all four dimensions of software quality detailed in Chapter 2. It is essential that software product specifications, software design, construction, and conformance of quality are all undertaken with equal diligence and are subjected to appropriate QA to ensure that quality is built into a product at every stage of its development. No one dimension can be given any greater or less importance than the others.

There are no silver bullets for achieving software reliability, but there are a few techniques that can help achieve a desired level of software reliability. In fact, all QA activities are designed to improve software reliability, and none of them can be ignored. Quality software product specifications ensure that a product is built with comprehensive and complete functionality, including both main functionality and ancillary functionality. Software design quality ensures that specifications are implemented in a robust manner, with built-in fault tolerance and protection from misuse. Software construction quality ensures that the software design is implemented and that the product is developed in full adherence with its design. Conformance of quality ensures that the other three dimensions of quality indeed conform to the best of the standards and practices available for the product. That is the reason why the chapter on the four dimensions of quality appears as Chapter 2, second only to the definition of quality and the explanation of the basics of quality.

PROCESS QUALITY

CHAPTER OVERVIEW

★ Evolution of the process quality concept
★ Process and process quality
★ Process definition approaches and steps in process definition
★ How to align the process with a selected certification model
★ Process improvement and stabilization
★ Components of a software development process
★ Process certification

PROCESS QUALITY EVOLUTION

The maturity of an organization in terms of quality is reflected in its products. Since customers focus on the end product or service for which they pay money, it is natural that providers focus on the quality of their product or service. They try to get it done "somehow," ensure that the end product is of acceptable quality, and deliver it. Although to a large extent customers are not aware of the processes by which products or services are prepared and delivered, these processes do in fact impact customers. For instance, if proper hygiene standards are not adhered to in a restaurant during the preparation of food, the food could become contaminated and the health of the people who dine in that restaurant could be affected. When food products are prepared and packaged in factories, food hygiene practices play a vital role in keeping consumers safe from illness.

This example clearly illustrates the importance of process quality. For certain products, however, it is not possible to test them to ensure that quality is built in. Take, for example, a lightbulb: it just is not possible to check the vacuum or determine the amount of inert gas inside the glass casing without breaking the glass and, therefore, the lightbulb itself. The shaft in an automobile, which is forged and annealed for strength, cannot be tested conclusively for proper annealing.

Recognition that the process by which a product is made is as important as the product itself gave rise to the adage "quality cannot be added; it has to be built in." It is this recognition that caused concepts of quality to evolve away from quality control to the more comprehensive quality assurance activities of today, with organizations developing processes and procedures that facilitate higher quality of product specifications and design. In time, the concept of total quality management emphasized the process aspect of quality assurance, shifting the focus from *quality control* of product quality to *making quality products*.

Software development introduced yet another dimension. Products in other industries either do or do not do what they are expected to; they never do what they are *not* expected to do. They either function or do not function. For example, a car either runs or it does not run—it does not fly! Software products, however, in addition to functioning or not functioning, can perform malicious operations they are neither expected nor intended to perform. An example of this is a download acceleration tool. You expect the tool to speed up the rate of downloading, but sometimes it collects your Internet usage information and sends it to the tool developer.

For this reason, quality assurance gained so much attention for its emphasis on process quality that the International Organization for Standardization (ISO) released its ISO 9000 series of standards in 1994, focusing on this process aspect. The software development industry embraced the standards enthusiastically. The release of the ISO standards was followed by the Software Engineering Institute of Carnegie Mellon University's Capability Maturity Model (CMM®) in 1998. CMM® focused purely on software development aspects, whereas ISO focused on process quality in general. The software development industry readily adopted CMM® and later Capability Maturity Model Integration (CMMI®). Both ISO 9000 and CMM® were centered on process quality, but they differed in their approach to assessing an organization's process compliance. While ISO certified an organization as compliant with its ISO 9000 series of standards, CMM® and CMMI® appraised an organization and rated its capability at one of five maturity levels. However, both encouraged a process-driven approach to organizational functioning.

PROCESS

Before discussing process quality, process itself has to be understood. When we attempt to make something, we follow a series of steps in order to produce the final product. Every activity in life follows a process, even if that process is not explicitly defined or documented. For some activities, the process must be strictly adhered to. For example, when using a recipe to cook a dish, the process is precise, and any liberty taken with the process is likely to result in either a poor-tasting dish or over- or undercooked food. For other activities, if a few steps are skipped or poorly performed, the result can still be acceptable, at least temporarily. For example, if a surface is not properly prepared before being painted, the paint might look alright once freshly applied, but it likely will peel off later on.

When it comes to organizational processes, the importance of process definition and process adherence was first recognized in such flow process industries as chemical manufacturing (the makers of fertilizers, drugs, petroleum products, plastics, etc.). Flow process manufacturing used machines to produce products, and workers would ensure that the process was being adhered to and effect necessary corrections when any deviation to process compliance was noticed. Any departure from the process, either above or below permissible limits, resulted in the disastrous consequence of unusable products being produced.

No significant importance was given to process compliance in the domain of discrete manufacturing, except in areas such as heat treatment, vacuum filling (in lightbulbs, for example), semiconductor components, etc. Process definition and its compliance became important only when correction of a product was not possible, as is the case in process industries. Where rectification of a defective product was possible, as is the case in discrete manufacturing, process compliance did not gain that much significance.

Nonetheless, it was found that process definition and documentation offered several benefits to an organization, such as the following:

★ They gave senior executives insight into how work was carried out on the shop floor.
★ They assisted analysis by experts in the field, and in doing so, this analysis helped to plug loopholes in the process as well as improve quality and productivity.
★ They facilitated tighter planning and scheduling of work.
★ They helped to uncover opportunities for automation and improvement of the manufacturing process itself.

★ They facilitated development of standards for methods of working as well as for components.

Recognizing the benefits that process definition and documentation offered, the discrete manufacturing industry began to use defined processes. This coincided with the development of the branch of industrial engineering that uses work study principles and techniques, and so it came to be accepted that definition and documentation of process improve quality and productivity. This process orientation was first referred to as *good manufacturing practices*, a term that is still used today.

Software development was considered to be creative work and was therefore viewed as not needing a framework of rigid standards and processes. Initially, no quality control activities were performed on developed software. The Institute of Electrical and Electronics Engineers software engineering standards were released only in the late 1980s, even though software development had existed for many years—which goes to show how prevalent the belief was that software was creative work.

The ISO 9000 series of process standards provided the software development industry with the much-needed push to embrace process-oriented working, which was already a norm in the manufacturing industry.

PROCESS QUALITY

Once process definition and documentation began to provide insight into how work was carried out on the shop floor, they were used as tools to improve quality and productivity. It was realized that most quality problems could be resolved by improving the process itself. Defect analysis was used to isolate frequently occurring defects and to trace their origins in the process. The area of the process where the same defects repeatedly occurred was changed (improved) to eliminate those defects. This was and still is achieved by improving methods, using better tools, or training personnel. Conformance to process was ensured through in-process inspections in flow process production, batch production, and mass manufacturing and through stage inspections in discrete manufacturing.

Today, instead of permitting defects to occur and using inspections and testing to uncover them after the fact, processes are developed to produce defect-free products so that defects are not injected into the product to begin with. The following are the three steps to achieve process quality:

1. Process definition
2. Process improvement
3. Process stabilization

PROCESS DEFINITION

The first step in process definition is to assign to an entity in the organization responsibility for championing process definition and improvement. Some organizations assign this responsibility to the quality assurance department; others assign it to a specialist process group. Whoever is entrusted with this responsibility to ensure process-driven working in the organization begins by carrying out process definition. Later on, the department responsible gathers suggestions for improvement, evaluates the benefits and costs of each one, and implements into the processes the suggestions deemed qualified. The actual definition of each process is carried out by the practitioners in the organization (specialists who have many years of experience in the area for which the process is being defined), with facilitation (tools, documentation guidance, coordination of quality assurance activities, etc.) provided by the process group.

There are two approaches to defining a process:

1. **Top-down approach**—This is suitable when the organization is new and the processes are being set up.
2. **Bottom-up approach**—This is suitable when the organization has been in existence and operations have been performed for some time.

Top-Down Approach to Process Definition

The top-down approach to process definition consists of the following steps:

1. Break down the organizational operations by function. The first level consists of the major activities of organizational operations. That is, software development is broken down into requirements analysis, software design, construction, testing, etc. at the first level. Then each major activity at the first level is further broken down to its next levels. For example, software design is broken down into architecture design, data modeling, database design, user interface design, report design, etc. Continue breaking down activities until it is decided that further breakdown does not add any additional value.
2. Define a process for each activity in the first level of breakdown.

3. Define a subprocess for the next level if it consists of sublevels.
4. Define a procedure for an activity that is not broken down into further levels.
5. Wherever possible, define standards and guidelines to aid practitioners in adhering to the procedures.
6. Define formats and templates to record and present information and to achieve uniformity among different practitioners in capturing, recording, and presenting information.
7. Define checklists to aid practitioners in adhering to the procedures and performing the activities comprehensively and exhaustively.
8. Define measurements and analyze the results of the defined process in order to evaluate the efficacy of it.
9. Arrange for review of the defined process by practitioners in the organization to ensure that it reflects reality and is accurately defined.

These steps are depicted in Figure 8.1.

Bottom-Up Approach to Process Definition

The bottom-up approach to process definition consists of the following steps:

1. Study how the practitioners are performing their tasks, and document this information. Obviously, there will be differences among practitioners in the way activities are performed. Therefore, include in the process document the most common practices and the practices of the people known to produce the best-quality deliverables.
2. Capture the formats and templates used by the practitioners. Study them and develop new formats and templates that include the best features of each format and template being used in the organization.
3. Capture the process details from project managers and senior managers, and document them, culling the best practices.
4. Organize the material into processes, procedures, formats, checklists, and standards and guidelines.
5. Release a draft version of the organizational process, and invite comments on it from all concerned persons in the organization.
6. Analyze the feedback received that serves to either enhance quality or productivity or simplify the work. After implementing the short-listed feedback, release the process for implementation in the organization.

These steps are depicted in Figure 8.2.

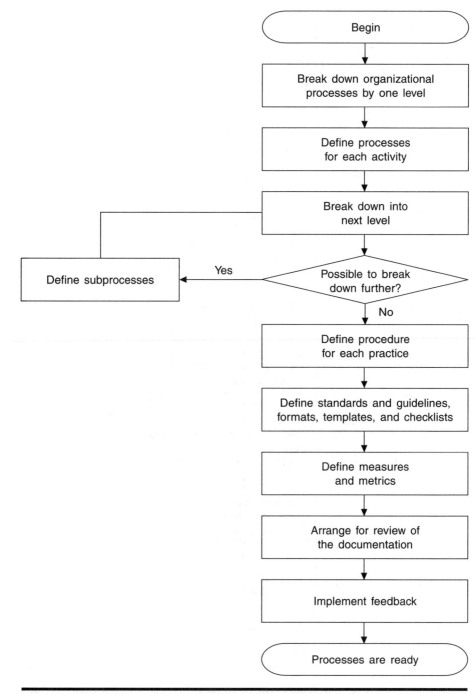

Figure 8.1. Top-down approach to process definition

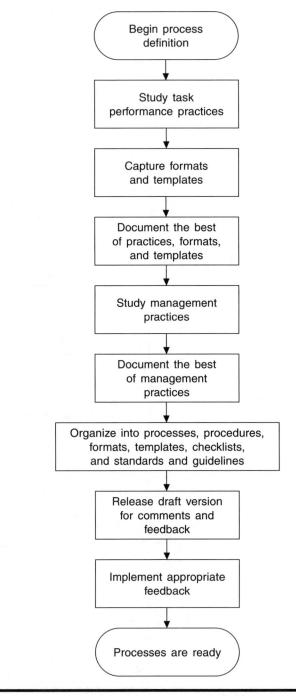

Figure 8.2. Bottom-up approach to process definition

Building Quality into the Defined Process

Once a process document is prepared, it should be subjected to scrutiny by experts in the field, either internal or external to the organization, before releasing it for implementation. These experts will evaluate each step and procedure of the process and compare it with the best practices in the industry. This evaluation and comparison produces a gap analysis document. The organization's in-house process group has to analyze each of the gaps uncovered for its feasibility to be bridged in the organizational process and practice. This in-house analysis might necessitate additional investment in tools, training for personnel, a change in methods of working, etc. Sometimes it might be possible to implement a best practice fully; other times it might need to be modified to suit the organizational environment. In some cases, the organization might need to completely reject a best practice if it does not suit its environment. In line with the decision on implementing the suggested best practices, the process documents should be updated and finalized. The inclusion of best practices in process documentation first and dovetailing them into practice second ensures that quality is built into the process.

The necessary quality assurance activities are then included in the process documents to ensure that the defined process is subjected to quality assurance during practice. These activities can include reviews, tests, inspections, and audits. Also included are the measures and metrics necessary to assess performance of the process. These activities build quality into the process.

ALIGNING THE PROCESS WITH A PROCESS MODEL

Aligning organizational processes with a process model such as ISO 9000 or CMMI® is becoming essential, as more and more customers are insisting on a certificate of compliance or a maturity rating as a prerequisite for participating in the bidding process for outsourced contracts. However, an organizational process that is defined comprehensively and includes industry best practices is adequate to meet the requirements of any model, as the main goal of all models is to ensure that an organization utilizes industry best practices in its functioning and in producing quality deliverables. Once it is ensured that the organizational process utilizes industry best practices, all that needs to be done is to confirm that the selected model and the organizational process are in sync with each other and that the organization's process meets or exceeds the requirements of the model's goals.

The following steps are required to align an organizational process with such a model:

1. Study the model requirements, especially the goals that need to be fulfilled by the organizational process and practice.
2. Carry out a gap analysis between the model requirements and the organizational process. Gaps can be positive, meaning the organization's practice exceeds the model's requirements, or shortfalls, meaning the organization's process does not meet the model's requirements.
3. Enumerate all shortfall gaps (the instances in the organization's process that do not fulfill the model's goals) in a gap analysis document.
4. Conduct a series of consultations with the organizational practitioners and management about the gaps and ways to bridge them.
5. Select the most suitable alternative solutions to bridge the gaps and implement them in the process.
6. Try out the improved processes on a pilot basis during the execution of a few projects.
7. Implement the feedback from pilot implementation into the processes.
8. Arrange for review by practitioners in the organization.
9. Release the new set of processes for implementation in the organization.

These steps, depicted in Figure 8.3, ensure alignment of organizational processes and practices with those of the selected process model.

PROCESS IMPROVEMENT

Once the organization has defined a set of processes, and if the organization has achieved alignment with a process model such as ISO 9000 or CMMI®, performance of the processes must be monitored continually in terms of actual performance vis-à-vis desired performance. Monitoring is important because an organization's climate can change frequently. Some of the reasons for this change include:

★ Changes in technology, which result in new paradigms for software development
★ Use of better tools and techniques by competitors to deliver higher quality software at a cheaper price
★ Government regulations for safety, usability, reliability, etc., which might make it imperative to deliver better quality
★ Availability of new development tools, which might save money or improve quality
★ Availability of new products for the back end, middle tiers, development platforms, etc.

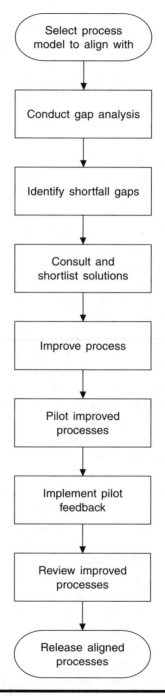

Figure 8.3. Aligning organizational processes with a selected model

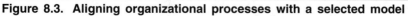

These are but a few reasons why organizations are driven to upgrade their processes to meet the changing environment and be competitive in the market. Therefore, improvement of organizational processes has to be approached in a disciplined manner—that is, by a process-driven approach.

A process for improving organizational processes must be defined, just like other organizational processes are. A process for process improvement should cover the following areas:

1. **Triggers for process improvement**—Triggers are either event based or duration based. An event-based trigger can be an audit report by an external auditor or external appraiser or a report from an organization-wide internal audit or appraisal. It also may be a new tool that has an impact on the process, or it might be the release of a new standard or a new version of the organization's adopted process model that impacts organizational operations.

   Duration-based triggers occur once every quarter, six months, or year or at the beginning of a new fiscal year, for example. These triggers are used to carry out an exercise to consolidate all process improvement opportunities, analyze them, and effect process improvement.

2. **Sources of opportunities for process improvement**—Various sources of information for process improvement are identified. These sources of information can include internal sources, such as suggestions from development team members, managers, and senior management, or external sources, such as suggestions from an external auditor or appraiser or a standards body or process model owner.

3. **Procedures for placing process improvement requests**—These procedures cover how to place a process improvement request, what the proper format or template is, what information needs to be included in the request, what approvals are required, etc.

4. **Authorized persons who can place process improvement requests**—This is a list that indicates the types of requests that can be placed by various persons in the organization. For example, the software programmer can place a process improvement request regarding coding guidelines or a testing practice. It is not appropriate for a programmer to raise a request to improve a defect analysis procedure, for example. That is, a person is best suited to raise an improvement request in the area in which he or she works. These criteria are enumerated in this section.

5. **Procedure for analyzing and accepting process improvement requests**—This section describes the type of analysis that can be con-

ducted on process improvement requests received by the process improvement group. The agency authorized to approve or reject process improvement requests analyzes a request and either accepts or rejects it. If the request is rejected, the originator of the request is informed of the rejection and the reasons why. If the request is accepted, the improvement is implemented in the normal manner.

6. **Procedure for implementing process improvements**—This section describes how to select people to implement suggested improvements in the process documents, the versioning norms for process documents, the reviews to be conducted for the improved process documents, and approval authorizations.

7. **Procedure for pilot implementation to obtain field feedback**—Once the process documents are improved and approved, they are implemented on a few projects to obtain feedback from the field. This section describes such a procedure, including how to select candidate projects, grant waivers necessary for deviating from the currently approved processes, obtain feedback from pilot implementations, collate and analyze the field feedback, etc.

8. **Implementing feedback from the field and releasing the process**—Once feedback from the field is obtained, it has to be implemented in the process. This section describes how to implement field feedback, organize the review, obtain necessary approvals, and release the improved process for implementation. It is normal practice to effect only a few releases per period, such as every quarter, six months, or year.

PROCESS STABILIZATION

Process stabilization is necessary for an organization to produce predictable results. That does not mean, however, that process improvement is not necessary. It only means that a process should be, by and large, stable. Improvements are effected based on a trigger, and they are implemented to either improve quality or productivity or to simplify work. Process stabilization becomes possible only after a process is defined.

An organization typically goes through the following stages before achieving a stabilized process:

1. **Initial stage**—This is when the organization is new and is just starting its operations. It is trying to establish commercial viability. Opera-

tions are performed based on the personal direction of the owners, chief executive, and senior management.

2. **Defining the process**—Once the organization has achieved commercial viability, it defines its processes for conducting operations using a process-driven approach.

3. **Implementing the process**—The defined process is implemented in the organization. All operations are run based on the defined process, and the process is institutionalized in the organization.

4. **Maintaining the process**—Once the process is implemented, it is monitored and improved as required, based on event or duration triggers, using the following steps:

   a. **Analyze results of the operations for any variances**—Variances can be beneficial if, for example, they result in higher quality or productivity. Undesirable variances result in more defects or diminished productivity, for example.

   b. **Conduct root cause analysis for variances**—When undesirable variances are discovered, root cause analysis is conducted. Some of these variances can be due purely to chance errors. Even in the most tightly controlled and machine-based processes, random variances do occur, with some due to assignable causes. Root cause analysis separates undesirable variances into chance errors and assignable causes and then uncovers the actual cause behind each variance.

      Undesirable variances due to assignable causes are analyzed to determine if they were due to process defects or other defects. If due to process defects, then improvement must be effected in the defined process. For undesirable variances due to assignable causes attributable to a defective process, improvement must be effected to plug the loopholes in the process so that those variances do not recur.

   c. **Pilot improved process**—The improved process is implemented in a few projects to observe the efficacy of the improvements. If the results do not produce the desired improvements, steps b and c are iterated until the desired improvements are achieved based on the pilot implementation.

   d. **Implement improved process**—Once the pilot implementation of the improved process shows the desired level of improvement, the process goes through the normal procedure for implementing a process in the organization.

5. **Stable process**—When most or all variances are due to random causes (chance errors), then the process is considered stable.

Figure 8.4 depicts process stabilization. Once a process is stable, statistical quality control techniques such as control charts can be used to monitor it.

SOFTWARE DEVELOPMENT PROCESS

As discussed in Chapter 4, a well-defined and institutionalized process is a prerequisite for fostering a quality culture in an organization. Such an organizational process is made up of four basic types of processes:

1. **Software engineering processes**—These processes define how the deliverable is built. They typically are comprised of processes for requirements management, software design, construction, and deployment.
2. **Quality assurance processes**—These processes define how quality is built into deliverables and also ensure that it is in fact built in. They typically are comprised of verification, validation, inspections, measurement and analysis, and audits.
3. **Management processes**—These processes define how all the other processes are managed. They typically contain the project management process, including project acquisition, project initiation, software estimation, planning, configuration management, quality management, work management, resource management, stakeholder expectation management, and project closure.
4. **Support processes**—These processes define how the other processes are supported by the organization. They are comprised of the network and systems administration process, human resources process, subcontractor management process, facilities management process, etc.

COMPONENTS OF A PROCESS

A process is an overall definition of a major organizational activity. It is an interrelated network of procedures for performing an activity and a top-level document under which other documents provide the details of the activity.

A process is an assemblage of the following components:

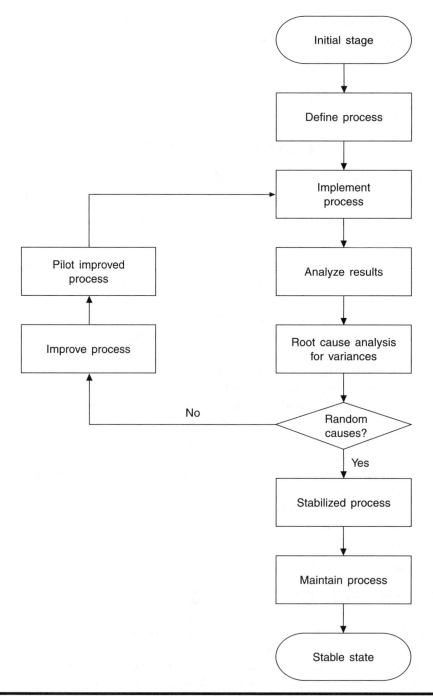

Figure 8.4. Process stabilization

1. **Procedures**—Procedures are step-by-step instructions for performing a subactivity of a process. Examples of procedures include the project planning procedure, software estimation procedure, phase-end audit procedure, progress-reporting procedure, etc.

2. **Standards and guidelines**—These define a common way of constructing the artifacts in the organization so that the output is uniform throughout the organization. Whereas procedures bring uniformity in performing an activity, standards and guidelines bring uniformity in the deliverables. Examples of standards and guidelines are screen design guidelines, database design guidelines, naming standards, coding guidelines, defect analysis standards, etc.

3. **Formats and templates**—These facilitate a uniform way of capturing, recording, and presenting information. Examples of formats and templates include estimation presentation templates, nonconformance report forms, review defect forms, estimation request notes, project management plan templates, etc.

4. **Checklists**—These assist the person performing an activity to carry out the task fully and help the reviewer to ensure comprehensiveness of the review. A checklist contains a number of items, with a space beside each to indicate "yes," "no," or "not applicable" as each point is completed or reviewed. When an activity is completed, this list should be referred to in order to ensure that all points have been addressed.

The hierarchy of the process documentation set is depicted in Figure 8.5.

PROCESS CERTIFICATION

Today, obtaining certification or a rating from a standards body or process model owner has assumed great importance, as many organizations that outsource high-value software development work use such certifications and ratings to short-list their prospective vendors. Therefore, a book on software quality assurance cannot be complete without touching upon this subject. Currently, there are two popular models: ISO 9000 and CMMI®.

A certificate of compliance with the ISO 9000 series of standards is awarded by an authorized lead auditor, who conducts an audit on a sample of projects, assessing project management and software engineering process compliance, and audits all other support groups. The auditor indicates a nonconformance wherever a practice does not conform to the applicable ISO 9000 standard. The authorized lead auditor

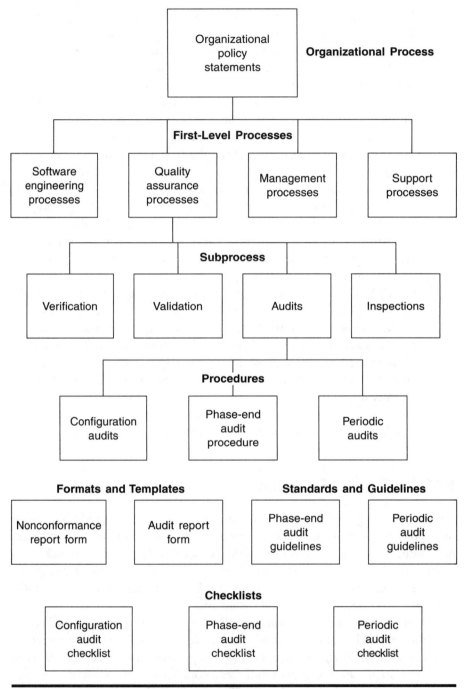

Figure 8.5. Process hierarchy

grants a certificate of compliance if there are no nonconformances or if nonconformances are not significant. If nonconformances are significant, the auditor either refuses to grant a certificate or withholds the certificate until the nonconformances are satisfactorily resolved by the organization.

The ISO 9000 series of standards have undergone one revision since their original release in 1994. A copy of the standards is available for purchase from ISO.

A CMMI® capability maturity rating is awarded by the Software Engineering Institute (SEI) of Carnegie Mellon University upon receiving a recommendation from an authorized lead appraiser. SEI revised the methodology for the maturity rating once, and the present methodology is called the Standard CMMI Appraisal Method for Process Improvement (SCAMPI®).

An authorized lead appraiser conducts the SCAMPI® appraisal with a team of people who are qualified based on SCAMPI® norms and trained by an authorized lead appraiser. The appraiser points out to the organization opportunities for improvement if any are uncovered during the appraisal. The appraisal team, working under the guidance and direction of the authorized lead appraiser, gathers evidence from a sample of selected project documents and then corroborates that evidence by interviewing organizational personnel involved in process implementation. If, in the opinion of the appraisal team and the authorized lead appraiser, process implementation is found to indicate that the CMMI® model is largely implemented, the appraiser and the appraisal team submit a recommendation to SEI to grant a maturity rating to the organization. SEI then reviews the assessment conducted and grants the maturity rating recommended by the appraisal team and the appraiser.

The CMMI® model document has been revised twice since its original release. The latest versions of the CMMI® model definition document and the appraisal methodology document are available free of charge to those interested in learning about the model and the appraisal process in detail.

Both methodologies are based on an organization's process-driven manner of working. Although the appraisal method and the final award differ, the steps followed to attain the award are similar:

1. Define the process.
2. Implement the process.
3. Improve the process based on feedback obtained from the field about the process implementation.
4. Stabilize the process, which includes internalization and institutionalization of process-driven working.

ISO grants a certificate of compliance and performs a surveillance audit once every six months to ensure continued compliance.

SEI grants a capability maturity rating; level 2 is the minimum rating awarded and level 5 the maximum. In CMMI® adaptation, an organization starts out at level 2 and graduates to level 5 over a period of time and successive appraisals. A maturity rating is valid for a period of three years.

For software development organizations, CMMI® is required more often in the United States and the ISO 9000 certificate is accepted in most other parts of the world.

Books have been written on these two models; covering the subject thoroughly is beyond the scope of this book. To learn more about them, obtain their documentation for study or contact an ISO 9000 or CMMI® process consultant for more information.

NEW PARADIGM FOR SOFTWARE QUALITY

CHAPTER OVERVIEW

★ The present state of certification paradigms
★ The fallacy of certifications
★ Criticisms of certification models
★ A proposed new paradigm for quality

CURRENT CERTIFICATION PARADIGMS

Whenever there is leeway for providers to take shortcuts, governments step in to formulate regulations and checks and balances to protect potential victims if professional associations or industry bodies fail to do so. For example, if you want to start a company, the company has to be registered with a government agency, and you must submit periodic reports. If your company borrows money, then you have to periodically submit reports on its financial position to the government as well as to lenders. If your company raises money through a public offering, there are a host of agencies that will be regulating it. A public company needs internal departments just to comply with those regulations. Why? Because a company that accepts money from the public is answerable to the public through the good offices of the government.

A public company must be audited by an accredited auditing firm to certify that its accounts are in order even though the company has a qualified internal officer who prepares the accounts and an equally competent internal auditor who audits those accounts. This process is much the same as periodically having your car certified as roadworthy by an accredited agency, even if you are an automotive engineer and know that your car is fit to drive. An external auditor first examines the existence and diligence of the internal controls in a company and then audits a random sample of financial artifacts. If the external auditor finds that the internal controls are unsatisfactory, the audit is stopped and the auditor reports the company to the appropriate government authorities. These activities are carried out without fail, because how a company uses its money (and the public's money) affects the public, and governments try to protect the public from potentially being swindled.

The quality of products also affects the public. Consumer associations, re-dress forums, criminal codes, etc. exist to protect the public from poor-quality products. When a building is constructed, it has to be certified as safe before people can occupy it. The construction industry is regulated by inspections and certifications. The certifying agencies inspect the construction records as well as the actual structure to ensure that the right quality of materials and the right methods are being used. Once the certifying agency is satisfied with its findings, the building is certified as fit to be occupied.

In the past, manufacturers developed internal controls for quality through a quality assurance (QA) department. The manufacturing industry formed as-sociations, such as the National Electrical Manufacturers Association, the Inter-national Telecommunications Union, the Solar Energy Industries Association, the Biotechnology Industry Organization, etc., to develop a host of standards for quality and good manufacturing practices to ensure quality in products. Orga-nizations in the services sector also formed associations to define their own quality standards (the Hotels Associations and the Association of Travel Agents, for example) and to ensure compliance with those standards. Even the media have their own council to oversee the conduct of their members.

In short, there was voluntary recognition in the manufacturing, services, and construction sectors that quality is an important aspect of any product, and efforts were readily made to continually improve product or service quality by setting up internal controls. It is not an exaggeration to say that a reputable manufacturing or service organization that does not have a quality department is rare.

In 1994, the International Organization for Standardization (ISO) released its ISO 9000 series of standards, which deal with process quality. There are many areas of manufacturing and construction where process is of paramount impor-tance, such as pouring concrete and forging and heat treatment of metals. Take, for example, manufacturing a lightbulb: the internal vacuum cannot be tested after a bulb is sealed. Many processes such as this cannot be inspected or tested without destroying the component. Still, no standards body developed process quality standards until software began to play an increasing role in our lives. Only then did it become obvious that software quality left much to be desired, and the need for process quality standards was recognized.

It is not common for software development companies to have a quality department, and for this reason, internal controls for ensuring quality of deliverables are, more often than not, absent. The importance of this fact is highlighted by the vital role software now plays in our lives. Software controls most, if not all, communication, travel, weapons, power distribution, and home equipment. It is disturbing to realize that quality takes a back seat in the organizations that develop software. Yet, to the best of my knowledge, no consumer has sued for losses caused by software and been awarded compensation for damages.

There are no government regulations or agencies to play the role of watchdog over the quality delivered by software development organizations. They submit no reports regarding quality to anyone. The dictum "let the buyer beware" is most apt for software products, as a buyer cannot test a software product comprehensively prior to purchasing it. In contrast, for example, when you buy a car, you can test drive it, and you can bring the car back to the dealer and demand repair if it malfunctions during the warranty period or take it to a service station after the warranty period has expired. But can you bring a software product back to the company that developed it and demand repair? Is there such a thing as a software service station? A driver can drive a car—which costs much more than most software—for 15 minutes and know whether or not it is a quality vehicle. Can a user test a computer operating system and really know in a couple of hours if there are any defects? Can a consumer truly understand the differences between a Windows-based computer, a Linux-based computer, and a Mac and decide which best suits his or her needs?

Software organizations aim to earn either a certificate from a lead auditor to show they are compliant with the ISO 9000 series of standards or to earn a level 2, 3, 4, or 5 capability maturity rating from a Capability Maturity Model Integration (CMMI®) lead appraiser. But such attainments are no guarantee of software quality, as detailed in the next section.

THE FALLACY OF CERTIFICATIONS

The state of standardization in the software development industry is not up to the level in manufacturing. True, the Institute of Electrical and Electronics Engineers (IEEE) released software *engineering* standards, but these standards are not software *quality* standards. Rather, they are more guidelines than standards in the strict sense of the word and are therefore open to interpretation and adaptation. The concept of total quality management suggests that adhering to a defined process will ensure software quality, and the ISO 9000 series of standards and the Software Engineering Institute's (SEI) Capability Maturity Model (CMM®) and CMMI® are frequently used by software development organizations to instill quality in their products. However, these standards, guidelines, and models all have their limitations and flaws. Definitive standards developed by industry associations, similar to the level of those that exist in the manufacturing, construction, and services industries, do not exist in the software development industry.

With the release of the above standards and guidelines, many organizations looking to outsource their development work began to insist that software development organizations be certified, especially for CMMI® (though certification is actually a capability maturity rating). Holding a certificate opened the doors for bidding, and lack of a certificate closed those doors. Software development organizations began to actively seek certification just to retain their market share. Not surprisingly, certification organizations began to sprout up like mushrooms. Plenty of software development organizations received the coveted ISO 9000 certification and in many cases both ISO and CMMI®.

Software development organizations also can obtain a maturity rating from other maturity models, such as the Testing Maturity Model, People Capability Maturity Model, Software Engineering Capability Maturity Model, IT Service Capability Maturity Model, etc. Lee Copeland lists 34 maturity models in his article "The Maturity Maturity Model™ (M3)" on the StickyMinds Web site (www.Stickyminds.com).

The original focus of the ISO 9000 series of standards was on quality, with the "Quality Management System" as its main document and "Quality Policy" the backbone for organizational processes. Industry, however, diluted these processes to mean only organizational operations processes, thus reducing the emphasis on quality and shifting the focus from organizational quality policy to organizational vision and from quality goals to organizational goals. CMMI® goes one step further by stating that the purpose of a process should be to achieve organizational goals. The quality of deliverables has clearly taken a back seat.

I have been associated with certified organizations in the past, either as a consultant, a member of an audit team, or an employee. A significant number of these organizations do not adhere to their own defined processes. I was horrified to find that the management representative (the person responsible for driving the quality initiative in the organization) in one ISO 9000–certified organization did not read the process documentation. The quality head of a CMM® level 5 organization did not know how to open the URL for the organizational process on the intranet. A CMM® level 4–certified organization did not collect or maintain any metrics. I heard the CEO of an organization certified for ISO 9000 and aiming for CMMI® level 3 state that he did not want any managers in his organization; I was left wondering who would manage the company's software projects if everyone was a coder. This organization also did not have a quality department. In the words of that CEO, the organization is truly "lean and mean." That organization was ultimately granted a level 3 maturity rating by the SEI.

Today, the disconcerting reality of certified software development organizations often follows this pattern: organizations unearth loopholes in the models, consultants advise how to "cook the books" to get certified, and appraisers who certify for a fee are available. I once posed the following question to the CMMI® discussion group (which has about 4,000 members) on Yahoo!: Had anyone ever heard of an appraiser refusing to grant a certificate or a maturity rating to a software development organization? Only one or two members replied affirmatively; the rest maintained a dignified silence.

CRITICISMS OF MATURITY MODELS

One of the main criticisms of the maturity models mentioned in this chapter is that they all emphasize the organizational business objectives, not the quality of the product (or deliverable)! The confidence that a process-driven organization delivers quality is misplaced. Consider these factual issues: (1) the process itself might be flawed, (2) each process has loopholes, (3) developers are focused more on conforming to the process than achieving excellence in quality, and (4) management focuses more on delivering and selling than on quality.

The job of the unfortunate quality head, if there is one, is only to coordinate with certifying agencies, as he or she has no control over product quality. In many organizations, the person who holds the title "quality head" (often under other designations, such as software engineering process group head, quality coordinator, quality manager, director of quality, etc.) is either not really qualified or experienced enough to hold this post or does not possess enough knowledge about quality concepts and tools.

Maturity models focus less on the development of software and ensuring that quality is built into it and more on support processes. CMMI® for development (version 1.2) has more process areas for project management (project planning, integrated project management, risk management, configuration management, project monitoring and control, quantitative project management, supplier agreement management, and requirements management—eight in total) than it has process areas for quality (process and product QA, validation, and verification—three in total). It has only three process areas (product integration, requirements development, and technical solution) for software development. It has only two process areas (organizational process focus and organizational process development) for organizational process definition and only four process areas (causal analysis and resolution, decision analysis and resolution, measurement and analysis, and organizational process performance) for measurement and analysis. The remaining two process areas are organizational innovation and deployment and organizational training. Thus, the focus on quality is diluted, as it is part of only 3 of the 22 process areas a software development organization needs to receive a rating.

Furthermore, maturity models do not insist that the model be completely implemented. They accept "largely implemented" as adequate for granting a certificate or rating. The models themselves are not tightly defined and are made so flexible that the required practices are open to interpretation. Some allow "alternative practices" in place of the practices defined in the model. This degree of flexibility allows organizations to do what they want and still be certified as conforming to the model.

A second criticism of current maturity models is that they do not define any quality thresholds for achieving certification. Conformance to self-defined process is adequate. For example, suppose the standard for an electrical appliance defines the insulation resistance in quantitative terms (say one megaohm) so that people do not get an electric shock when handling the appliance. Yet no software engineering standard defines what the defect density, for example, should be for a financial application.

Another criticism of process models or maturity models is that they do not specify the number of years an organization must be in operation before it can be *mature* enough for certification. Therefore, even a one-year-old organization can obtain certification. In fact, single-person organizations can be certified.

Still another criticism of maturity models, as noted earlier, is that they do not specify any quality objectives that must be achieved in order to obtain certification. Mere conformance or showing evidence of conformance in just six projects or less is enough for an organization to be certified, with no need to demonstrate it has achieved the required state of quality.

The owners of maturity models do not monitor the actual performance of organizations once they are certified. ISO performs cursory half-yearly surveillance audits, but CMMI® requires an organization to be reappraised every three years. Maturity model owners do not know whether the quality of an organization's processes has improved or whether the number of customer complaints has decreased because they do not keep track.

Some of the more key issues regarding these certifications are discussed in the following sections.

Financial Considerations

Certification agencies charge a high fee ($200 per hour is an average rate, with an appraisal period ranging from two days to three weeks). Suppose an auditor or an appraiser rejects certification of one of his or her clients. What do you think the chances are that this auditor or appraiser will receive many calls from other organizations in the future? Slim to none. Therefore, the best an appraiser can do to keep his or her appraisal business from closing is to cancel an assignment with an organization if he or she is dissatisfied with its preparation. In other words, an auditor or appraiser is not likely to risk being branded as too strict. The auditor or appraiser that offers certification with a minimum of fuss is the one that is most sought after.

The certificate accorded to auditors and appraisers that allows them to issue certificates to organizations is handed out too easily. The norms are not very rigorous, and they do not mandate software development experience at all. Without software development experience, how can an auditor or appraiser knowledgably assess the capability of a software development organization?

Certifying organizations, like most organizations, are for-profit businesses that have expenses to meet, targets to reach, and growth to be achieved. These organizations make their money by issuing certificates, and that is one reason why so many certificates are being issued and are issued rather easily.

Method of Appraisal

Criticisms can easily be made of the appraisal process itself. Appraisers evaluate the evidence presented to them, which makes the method of appraisal more of a conformance audit rather than an investigative audit. What guarantee is there that the data is not biased to suit the requirements of the appraiser? If the accounting books (which are subject to statutory independent audits) can be "cooked," why not the data that will be presented for certification? I once was asked to adjust data for a certification audit. The head of the organization told me—with a straight face—that the certification agency knew the information would be false and that it was a willing partner in the sham. Of course, I told the organization to find somebody else to alter the data. In many cases, the appraiser organization also becomes the process consultant for an organization.

Surprisingly, neither the model definitions nor the appraisers acknowledge any conflict of interest in such an engagement, as long as the individual performing the appraisal and the consultant are two different people.

Appraisal is invariably performed by sampling. However, a sample offers an accurate picture of the universe only when the following aspects are inherent in the whole:

★ The universe is homogeneous.
★ The sample is selected randomly.
★ The sampling method is appropriate for the purpose.

The appraiser does not ensure that any of these prerequisites are met before beginning an appraisal, and none of these prerequisites exist in software development organizations. The population is not homogeneous because:

★ All projects are perhaps similar, but not identical.
★ All project managers are not uniformly qualified or trained, nor do they have similar experience.
★ The candidate projects are hand-picked by the organization being appraised.

When the universe is not homogeneous, more rigorous sampling methods, such as stratified sampling or cluster sampling, offer better results. However, these methods are not usually used when selecting candidate projects for audits or appraisals.

There is no guideline that specifies when 100% project appraisal (that is, all projects) becomes mandatory. In none of the appraisals I have witnessed, whether I was personally involved or not, was a random sampling technique used to select candidate projects. The appraisers simply accepted the projects offered by the organizations. The norms followed by most organizations are two projects for ISO and six projects for CMMI® for one location. In fact, software development organizations internally refer to projects as "CMMI® projects" and "non-CMMI® projects" (or alternatively, "ISO projects" and "non-ISO projects"). The appraiser assumes that all the organization's other projects are identical to the projects presented and accords the organization a certificate or a rating, which the organization then flaunts to attract customers.

Another criticism of these appraisal methods is that the final result is too vague. In some cases, the outcome is the granting of a certificate of compliance which states that the organization presented adequate evidence that compliance to the selected model is satisfactory. In other cases, the outcome is the according of a capability rating. In either case, the quality capability is not expressed in numbers so that prospective customers can draw their own independent inferences as to the quality level of an organization. There are now virtually thousands of software development organizations that are certified for compliance with the ISO 9000 series of standards. Would it be accurate to say that the quality level of all these organizations is identical, within a small margin of variance? Similarly, there are many organizations that have been given a CMMI® level 3 maturity rating. Again, is the quality level of all such organizations identical, within a small margin of variance?

Even if the quality level cannot be inferred from these certifications or ratings, can it indicate the magnitude of software development projects these organizations are capable of executing? Suppose an organization is certified as compliant with the ISO 9000 series of standards. Can a prospective customer infer that the organization would be able to execute a software development project of any size? Similarly, can a prospective customer infer from a CMMI® rating the size of projects an organization can execute? For example, does a level 2 CMMI® rating mean an organization can execute a project size of 5,000 function points, a level 3 up to 10,000 function points, a level 4 up to 20,000 function points, and a level 5 any size? Obtaining a certificate or an appraisal rating does not allow any of these inferences to be drawn about an organization's capability to successfully execute software development projects, nor does it indicate the quality level of the organization.

Liability of Appraisers

Suppose a company outsources its software development to an organization based on that organization being certified or having a certain maturity level rating. If, after some time and expenditure, the company realizes that the organization does not deserve the certificate or rating, is there any way for the company to claim consequential liability from the auditor or appraiser because it had been led to believe in the capability of the subcontracted organization based on its certificate or rating?

I am afraid the answer is no. An auditor or appraiser does not have the liability an external financial auditor has.

A plumber is liable. An electrician is liable. A doctor is liable. A lawyer is liable. But a process auditor or appraiser who provides a certificate or rating to an organization is not liable for any consequential damages. It does not matter that the organization has flaunted its certificate or rating as proof of its capability or has used it for marketing and sales purposes. An auditor's or appraiser's license is not revoked; he or she can continue to provide certificates or ratings.

Redress Mechanisms

Customers have no place to go if they wish to lodge a complaint or if they have something to report about a certified organization. The e-mail IDs of the officials responsible for looking into complaints about certified organizations that use their certificates to obtain business are not publicly available. Nor do those officials take action on their own against errant organizations. For example, CMM® was retired more than two years ago, and its rating should no longer be used. Yet many organizations still tout their CMM® level on their Web sites, and no official has corrected them.

Postcertification Reporting Requirements

Certified organizations are not required to submit compliance reports to anyone. In contrast, a company is mandated to submit financial reports every quarter to the stock exchange and to the Securities and Exchange Commission just for the privilege of allowing its shares to be traded on a stock exchange. ISO mandates surveillance audits twice a year, and the nonconformance reports raised by the auditors can be cleared by the next surveillance audit. In the meantime, the certificate is not suspended. Very few certificates, if any, are ever revoked. More doctors are stripped of their licenses to practice medicine than software organizations are stripped of their certificates.

CMMI® requires reappraisal once every three years, which means an organization can exploit its maturity rating for three full years. Public companies (that is, companies certified by a registrar of companies or by an equivalent authority that issues certificates of incorporation) are mandated to publicize their financial achievements, which are audited by an independent auditor once every quarter in addition to yearly publication.

Shouldn't certifying models for software development mandate the same requirement as for public companies? None of the models require a certified organization to make its quality data (such as its sigma level, defect density, nonconformance reports raised by auditors, or "opportunities for improvement" pointed out by appraisers) or quality performance public on either its own Web site or that of the model owner.

Any Revocations So Far?

I have searched the Web sites of SEI and ISO to locate a list of organizations for which they have rejected, revoked, or canceled a certificate or rating. I could find none; nor could I locate a link to such information through Google's search engine. This can mean one of two things: they have not rejected, revoked, or canceled a single certificate, or they keep this list confidential. Public display of such a list would go a long way toward improving the credibility of certification.

Auditing the Auditors

The way in which certifying agencies themselves are audited leaves much to be desired. Model owners periodically audit certifying agencies, but this is merely a conformance audit, not an investigative audit. Thus, surveillance of the certifiers is lax.

Final Words about Criticisms of Maturity Models

Based on the criticisms of maturity models discussed so far, it becomes evident that the objectives of a model definition and certification are not to ensure quality and that possession of a certificate by an organization does not guarantee the quality of its deliverables. Consider the following incidents:

★ Satyam Computers of India has all the certificates from all types of certifying agencies. Still, those certificates did not prevent the chairman from committing massive fraud (he publicly confessed in early 2009). If the certification processes were working properly, how could this have happened?

★ The World Bank banned several organizations that possessed the highest levels of certification from carrying out any work for it. If these organizations delivered quality so inadequate to an institution like the World Bank, then what level of quality are these organizations delivering to customers that do not have the same clout as the World Bank?

Do these incidents tell us something about the credibility of certificates?

Clearly, certification has failed. I know I will be ridiculed for this, but someone has to shout "the Emperor is naked!" The time has come to develop a different paradigm for quality for software development organizations—a paradigm that is focused more on the quality of the deliverable than on the achievement of organizational goals. The following section proposes such a paradigm.

A NEW PARADIGM FOR SOFTWARE QUALITY ASSURANCE

Why is a new paradigm needed? As detailed earlier in this chapter, the present certification and maturity rating models do not provide objective data on an organization's quality level. Yet the companies outsourcing their software development work depend on these certifications and ratings to select a vendor. The volume of outsourcing in software development is at an all-time high, running into billions of dollars worldwide, and there simply are too many instances of organizations not delivering adequate quality. No objective quality data is disclosed to the public, and no one accepts liability. These are the reasons why a new paradigm for software quality is urgently needed.

The Proposed Paradigm

I propose a paradigm modeled after the paradigm for QA in financial matters. The salient points in the financial assurance paradigm for public corporations (those that raise money from public) are as follows:

1. There must be internal controls.
2. There must be one external auditor who is qualified to audit the accounting books of corporations.
3. The external auditor conducts five audits per year (one every quarter and one at the end of the fiscal year).
4. Financial statements are not accepted as authentic by any statutory agency unless authenticated by the external auditor.
5. Each quarterly audit takes a minimum of two weeks to complete, and a yearly audit takes anywhere between two and six weeks to complete.
6. Corporations are mandated to make their financial results public and to make them available to the public on demand.

Software development needs a similar paradigm, albeit not as rigorous, for software QA. The new paradigm would be applicable to the following types of software development organizations:

1. Organizations that develop and maintain software predominantly for others
2. Organizations that develop and maintain a software product that is sold to the public as a commercial off-the-shelf product or on request
3. Organizations that develop and maintain a software product that is sold to other organizations
4. Organizations that develop and maintain a commercial off-the-shelf software product that is sold along with computer hardware to the public or other organizations

The new paradigm would shift the focus away from the certificate of compliance (or capability rating) to certification and disclosure of past performance. Just as a financial audit demands, this new paradigm would require organizations to disclose their quality metrics. Based on these metrics, prospective customers can draw their own inferences as to the quality of the organization's deliverables.

Organizations that develop and maintain a software product purely for their internal use need not adopt this new paradigm.

Salient Features of the Proposed Paradigm

The salient features of the new paradigm for software QA are as follows:

1. The software development organization would make its objective quality data public as well as make it available to concerned persons on demand. The data would include sigma level, residual defect density, defect injection rate, productivity, customer feedback including complaints and commendations, details of its quality model, success rate of projects, project sizes (minimum and maximum) handled, and any other data relevant to software quality.
2. The software development organization would select and define a quality model which would ensure that its quality level is a minimum of 4-sigma level on 6-sigma philosophy, meaning 3 defects in 10,000 opportunities.
3. The quality model would include the following:
   a. The quality objectives for the organizational deliverables
   b. The minimum set of QA activities that would be carried out in the organization

    c. The measures and metrics that would be collated in the organization, which would determine its quality level

    d. Agencies responsible for carrying out various QA activities

    e. Alignment of organizational quality standards with the standards of a professional body such as the IEEE, an industry association, or a government agency

4. The software development organization would maintain mandatory internal controls. That is, the organization would have an internal QA department, staffed with an adequate number of qualified persons so that the department can ensure that all necessary QA activities are performed in the organization.

5. The QA department would be headed by a quality professional who is equal in rank with the person responsible for delivering software to the organization's clients (delivery head). The head of the QA department would report to the same person to whom the delivery head reports.

6. The software development organization would appoint an external QA professional or organization to audit its QA activities.

7. The external quality auditor would audit the implementation of the organization's QA activities in a rigorous manner, similar to a financial assurance auditor, and issue a certificate of due diligence in QA to the organization.

8. The external quality auditor would audit the following aspects of QA activities:

    a. The adequacy of the QA model selected by the organization vis-à-vis the software development being carried out by the organization. Any modifications to the selected model made during the audit period also would be assessed to see if they have any negative impact on organizational quality.

    b. The quality control activities carried out during the audit period vis-à-vis the development activities carried out in the organization, to ensure the level of quality control is adequate and is in conformance with the organization's selected quality model.

    c. The position of the QA department in the organization, to assess its influence on organizational activities.

    d. The process of compiling and resolving customer feedback and analysis of such feedback.

    e. The data utilized to derive various quality metrics that would determine the quality levels of the organization, to ensure that the metrics reflect the reality in the organization.

9. The external auditor would provide a certificate, in the same way an external financial auditor would. The certificate would indicate that the organization conformed to its defined quality model and complied with all the requirements during the audit period. This would not be any indicator of future performance, just as it is not in the case of financial audit certificates.
10. The external quality auditor's certificate would indicate various quality metrics and measures, just as a financial audit certificate would, which would help prospective customers to draw their own independent inferences about the quality capability of the organization.
11. The external audit would be carried out at least once a year.

Audit and Certification Agencies

All certification agencies prescribe qualifications that include attending a training program or passing an exam as the prime criterion for being eligible to conduct audits or appraisals and to provide certificates or ratings. They do not insist on hands-on experience. Under the proposed paradigm, the emphasis would be on hands-on experience and professional competence. The suggested eligibility criteria are as follows:

★ A minimum of five years of experience in software development or software QA in organizations that employ a minimum of 150 persons.

★ Membership in such professional organizations as the Computer Society of IEEE, the British Computer Society, the Australian Computer Society, the Irish Computer Society, the Computer Society of India, the American Society for Quality, or an equivalent society. The professional organization should meet the following requirements:

  ☆ The organization should be a national-level, not-for-profit society engaged in promoting computer science in general. Its interest should not be limited to one branch of computer science.

  ☆ Membership should be granted to an individual based on his or her qualifications and experience.

  ☆ The organization should be run on democratic principles.

  ☆ The organization should be funded either by membership fees or government grants. It should not be funded by corporations.

  ☆ Associations of companies engaged in software development should not be eligible to audit and certify under this quality paradigm.

★ Full-level membership. That is, student, graduate, affiliate, associate, etc. membership is not construed as membership.
   ☆ The duration of full membership should be a minimum of two years.
   ☆ Membership should be granted on an individual basis. That is, acting as the representative of a corporate member does not constitute membership.
★ The person should not be a full-time or part-time employee of a software development organization. The person may be a freelance consultant or employed by a consultancy firm that offers only software quality consultancy.
★ The same firm cannot offer both software quality consultancy and certification of quality, even if two separate departments perform these two activities.
★ The experience and professional society membership criteria should not be waived, even if the person is employed by a firm that offers only software quality consultancy.

Consequential Liability

The certification process falls under the jurisdiction of consumer protection acts, so that the individuals or organizations granting certification can be held liable if they are found to have been negligent in ensuring the accuracy of the quality data of an organization, just as external financial auditors are liable in such situations. The person conducting an audit and granting a certificate must agree to assume consequential liability in either of the following scenarios:

1. The quality auditor is found to have been negligent in ensuring the accuracy of the quality data provided by the organization being certified.
2. The organization certified by the quality auditor turns out to be fraudulent in matters of quality.

The Certificate

The quality audit certificate should be similar to the certificate provided by an external financial auditor, and it should be signed by both the external auditor and the head of the organization's QA department. The certificate should contain an affirmation from the auditor that he or she has examined the quality records of the organization and is satisfied with the implementation of quality practices that are conducive to achieving quality in the company's deliverables.

It should disclose the quality data of the organization. It also should contain the standards against which the organization is assessed and the date on which the assessment is made, as well as the validity period of the certificate. The certificate should become part of the organization's annual report, just as a financial auditor's certificate would.

FINAL WORDS

There are plenty of models that accord a certificate or a maturity rating to software development organizations. Although these models do not explicitly address software quality issues, their certificates or ratings are relied upon by many organizations—including the defense departments of the United States and many other countries, among other important organizations—as indicators of organizational quality when selecting a suitable organization as a source of software development work.

As discussed in this chapter, certificates and ratings do not provide any objective data to help a company select the right organization to which to outsource its software development work. Clearly, the present models fall far too short of requirements and expectations. There is an urgent need for a new paradigm in view of the large amount of outsourcing that is taking place in the world today. This chapter presents a new paradigm that would provide objective data on an organization's quality capabilities, in which the auditor would take ownership for such data and accept liability should the data contain any errors.

APPENDIX A: AUDIT PROCESS

PURPOSE

This document defines a sample process for conducting audits in the organization. It covers both periodic audits and phase-end audits.

SCOPE

This process is applicable for all software projects executed in the organization.

ENTRY CRITERIA

The entry criterion for periodic audits is approval of yearly audit plans. The entry criterion for phase-end audits is completion of a software development phase.

EXIT CRITERIA

The audit is conducted, all nonconformance reports are closed, nonconformance reports are analyzed, findings are presented to management, and the results of the nonconformance report analysis are tracked until improvement is effected in the organizational process.

PROCESS DESCRIPTION

The organization conducts two types of audits: periodic audits and phase-end audits. This section describes the audit process for each type of audit.

Periodic Audits

Agency Responsible for Conducting Audits

The quality assurance (QA) department is the coordinating agency that plans and arranges audits, and it is the repository for nonconformance reports generated during the audits, tracking them to their resolution. In addition, the QA department consolidates audit findings at the end of every periodic audit, presents them to management, and, in coordination with the software engineering process group, effects the necessary improvements in the organizational process.

Audit Planning

The QA department prepares the annual audit plan for periodic audits. Normally, these audits are conducted once every quarter. The plan is reviewed by the software engineering process group and approved by the head of the QA department before the start of the new fiscal year. In each cycle of audits, 25% of the projects in the state of execution are covered, and all service departments (human resources, administration, network and systems administration, technical heads, and QA) are audited. The types of audit conducted in periodic audits are conformance audits and vertical audits. Figure A.1 depicts yearly audit planning.

Audit Schedule for Each Audit

The actual schedule for each cycle of the audit is prepared one week in advance of the audit cycle dates. This schedule consists of the projects to be audited, assignment of auditors to projects and service departments, and date and time of the audit. It is prepared as agreed to by the auditors included in the schedule and by their supervisors, as well as by the head of the technical department. The schedule is circulated to all auditors and auditees included in the audit schedule.

Auditors

The QA department arranges for periodic training of selected candidates in the precepts and practices of conducting internal audits and maintains a list of

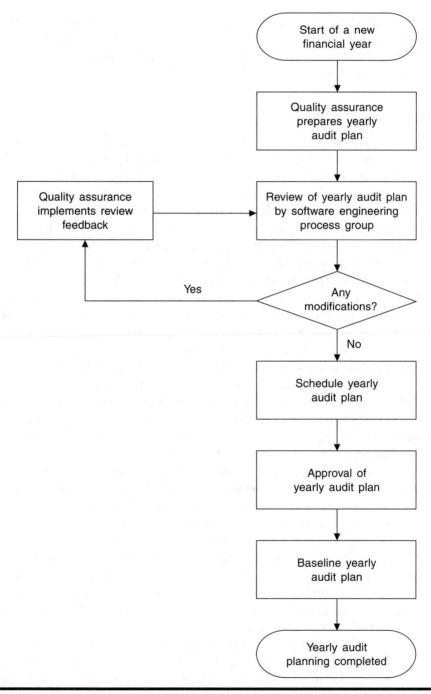

Figure A.1. Yearly audit planning

internal auditors who can be assigned to carry out the scheduled audits. Auditors are selected mainly from the technical, QA, and other service departments. Internal audit training is conducted by a lead auditor qualified to conduct certification audits for the ISO 9001 series of standards.

Periodic Audit Process

The scheduled audit begins with an opening meeting among the auditors, auditees, and management representative. The head of the QA department presents the audit objectives and schedule, resolving any issues in the schedule as well as seeking cooperation from all involved to conclude the audit successfully.

The auditor reaches the auditee's location five minutes in advance of the scheduled start time. The auditee is present to receive the auditor. The auditee submits all requested records and data to the auditor, including evidence of the action taken on previous nonconformance reports. When asked to produce a document, the auditee must do so in three minutes or less.

The auditor examines the records of the project or department and compares them with the corresponding organizational process to uncover nonconformances. Using a nonconformance report form, the auditor records any nonconformances uncovered during the audit as well as observations on any best practice or worst practice implemented in the project or department. These nonconformances and observations are discussed with the auditee, and the auditee's explanations are taken into consideration before the auditor finalizes the nonconformance report. The auditor might also record any recommendations that he or she believes to be fit and proper. The nonconformances are classified as either major or minor by the auditor. If the auditee disagrees with the auditor about the appropriateness or classification of a nonconformance, the matter can be escalated to the head of the QA department, whose decision on the matter is final and binding on both parties. The auditor has the nonconformance report reviewed by the head of the QA department and hands it over to the auditee; the QA department also retains a copy.

The auditee resolves all nonconformances in two calendar weeks or less and arranges for closure of the nonconformance report by the auditor. The auditor cooperates with the auditee in closing the nonconformance report. The closed nonconformance report is signed off by both the auditor and the auditee and is made part of the QA department's audit records.

The head of the QA department arranges for consolidation of the audit findings. All auditees and auditors are informed of these findings in the audit closure meeting that is conducted once all the scheduled audits have been concluded and all nonconformance reports have been received.

Depending on the nature of nonconformances uncovered during the audits, the head of QA coordinates with the software engineering process group to effect any necessary improvements in the organizational process. The periodic audit process is depicted in Figure A.2.

Phase-End Audits

Phase-end audits are conducted for every project at the end of the project initiation, requirements analysis, software design, construction, testing, and project closure phases.

Audit Plans

Phase-end audits are planned on a monthly basis. By the 25th of every month, all software project managers inform the head of the QA department of the likely completion dates for the project phases that are scheduled to be completed in the following month. The head of QA consolidates the requirements and prepares a phase-end audit plan, which includes the projects, probable completion dates, and the auditor assigned to each project, ensuring that dates and projects for periodic audits and phase-end audits do not clash. The plan is circulated to all software project managers and auditors.

Auditors

Phase-end audits are conducted by executives of the QA department. If no QA executive is available, then a trained internal auditor conducts the audit.

Phase-End Audit Process

Software project managers inform the QA department at least one business day in advance that a phase-end audit is needed, which allows QA to locate a suitable auditor. The selected auditor arrives at the location of the auditee at the agreed-upon time and conducts the audit. The auditee has all necessary artifacts ready and provides them to the auditor as requested. The auditor conducts the audit and records any nonconformances uncovered after considering any prior explanations from the auditee. The auditor then prepares the nonconformance report and obtains approval from the head of the QA department. The auditor submits the nonconformance report to the software project manager for the project. The software project manager arranges resolution of the nonconformance report and requests the auditor to verify the resolution of nonconformances and close

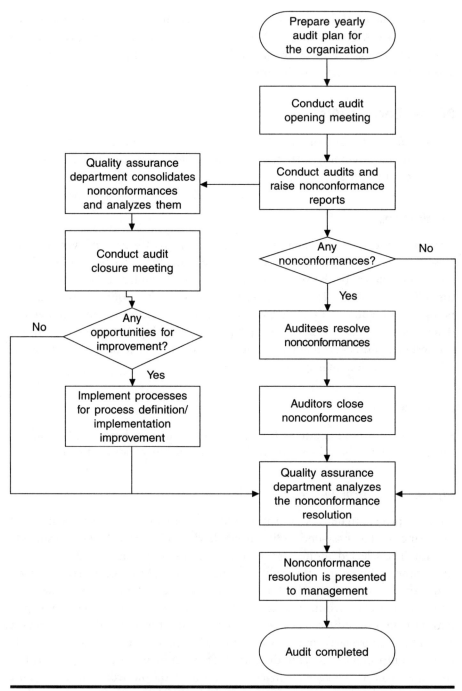

Figure A.2. Periodic audit process

the nonconformance report. The auditor verifies the resolution and informs the software project manager if it is not satisfactory. When all the nonconformances are satisfactorily resolved, the auditor closes the nonconformance report and hands it over to the software project manager for inclusion in the project records, which concludes the requested phase-end audit. The phase-end audit process is depicted in Figure A.3.

A checklist to ensure comprehensiveness of audits is provided in Table A.1. The format in Table A.2 should be used for planning annual audits.

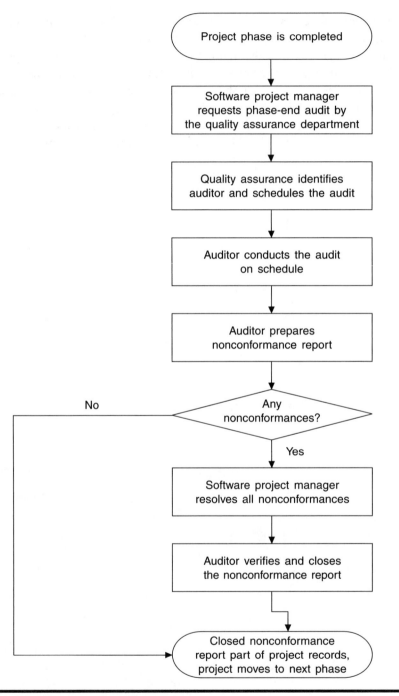

Figure A.3. Phase-end audit process

Table A.1. Checklist for auditing projects

Aspect	Checkpoint	Yes/No
Project plans	Is the project management plan available?	
	Is the configuration management plan available?	
	Is the quality management plan available?	
	Are review records for all project plans available?	
	Are all project plans duly approved?	
	If any changes were effected in the project plans, did they undergo the due quality process?	
	Is there any mix-up between current plans and archived plans?	
Configuration management	Is the information management in accordance with the configuration management plan?	
	Is the code management in accordance with the configuration management plan?	
	Is the change register being maintained properly?	
	Does the configuration register contain all configurable items, and do their versions match the actual artifacts?	
	Is baselining of items in conformance with the configuration management plan?	
	Is the change approval process in accordance with the configuration management plan?	
Quality management	Are all QA activities being conducted in accordance with the quality management plan?	
	Are review records of all artifacts available?	
	Are test plans and test logs available as mentioned in the quality management plan?	
	Were any waivers granted for the project? Are the waivers available in the project records?	
Client	Is there negative feedback from the client? If so, has a causal analysis been conducted?	
	Were any defects reported by the client?	
	Is the acceptance letter or e-mail available for deliveries made?	
	Were there any client complaints? If so, were they tracked to closure?	
	Were there any commendations from the client?	

Table A.1. Checklist for auditing projects (continued)

Aspect	Checkpoint	Yes/No
Metrics	Is the schedule variance metric beyond acceptable limits?	
	Is the defect injection rate above the organizational level?	
	Is project productivity in line with organizational norms?	
Quality awareness	Is the project team's awareness of organizational processes adequate?	
Nonconformance reports from past audits	Were all nonconformances from past audits closed?	
Project tracking and monitoring	Are weekly status reports being prepared regularly?	
	Are weekly status reports being sent to all stakeholders regularly?	
	Are weekly team meetings for project progress monitoring being conducted regularly?	
	Are progress-monitoring meetings with stakeholders being conducted regularly?	
	Are minutes of all progress-monitoring meetings (with the project team as well as other stakeholders) available?	
	Are all action items recorded in the minutes of the meeting tracked to closure?	
Human resources	Are all appraisals filled in as and when required?	
	Are induction training records available for each team member?	
	Is any project-specific training being conducted, and if so, are the records available?	
Other project records	Is the project initiation note available in the project records?	
	Do actual resource allocations match the existing project resources?	
	Are there any confidentiality agreements with the client? If so, is there evidence of a breach of the confidentiality agreements?	

Table A.2. Annual audit plan format

Audit cycle	Functions to be audited (projects/support)	Scheduled date	Auditor	Auditee	Remarks
1					
2					
3					
4					

APPENDIX B: DEFECT RESOLUTION METHODOLOGY

Quality assurance (QA) activities uncover defects in software artifacts during project execution. These defects need to be resolved. With a properly defined methodology, defect resolution facilitates analysis of the nature of defects, which leads to effecting improvements that will eliminate a recurrence of defects. The defect resolution process must facilitate not only the efficient resolution of defects but also capturing data that can be subjected to analysis.

DEFECT REPORTING

Defects can be uncovered during QA activities through the various verifications and validations carried out on the software artifacts, including information artifacts and code artifacts. Defects generally are detailed in a report or directly entered into a defect register software tool. It is better to maintain a single defect resolution register for the entire project, as doing so facilitates the grouping of data and makes the data amenable to statistical analysis. Figure B.1 depicts a suggested defect resolution register format. The entries in the defect resolution register are as follows:

1. **Defect ID**—Needed only if a manual register is maintained. The defect ID is used to enter the effort spent from the time sheets. The ID can be either numeric or alphanumeric, whichever the organization prefers.

Project ID:	
	Defect ID
	Defect description
	Reported by
	Report date
	Development phase
	QA activity
	Component affected
	Component type
	Component size
	Analyzed by
	Analysis start date
	Analysis end date
	Fixed by
	Fix start date
	Fix end date
	Reviewed by
	Review start date
	Review end date
	Regression tested by
	Regression testing start date
	Regression testing end date
	Status
	Defect category
	Defect origin
	Acceptance tested on
	Delivered on

Figure B.1. Defect resolution register format for a project

2. **Defect description**—A detailed description of the defect.

3. **Reported by**—The name of the person who uncovered the defect.

4. **Report date**—The date on which the defect is reported.

5. **Development phase**—The phase in which the defect is uncovered. The development phases include requirements analysis, software design, construction, test planning, project planning, build preparation, etc. The phases standardized within the organization are the ones used.

6. **QA activity**—The QA activity that uncovered the defect, which could be a peer review, unit testing, integration testing, system testing, positive testing, negative testing, etc.

7. **Component affected**—The name of the component in which the defect is uncovered. The component can be either a document artifact or a code artifact.

8. **Component type**—The type of component, which could be a screen, a report, a requirements document, an architecture document, a detailed design document, a stored procedure, etc.

9. **Component size**—The size of the component. The size of a document can be expressed as number of pages. The size of a program unit can be expressed as number of lines of code. The size of screens and reports can be expressed using a software size measure such as function points, object points, or software size units, where lines of code would not be accurate enough to indicate the size of the component. (Items 1 to 9 are filled in at the time of reporting the defect.)

10. **Analyzed by**—The name of the person who analyzed the defect.

11. **Analysis start date**—The date on which the defect analysis was started.

12. **Analysis end date**—The date on which the defect analysis was completed.

13. **Fixed by**—The name of the person who fixed the defect.

14. **Fix start date**—The date on which fixing the defect was started.

15. **Fix end date**—The date on which fixing the defect was completed.

16. **Reviewed by**—The name of the person who carried out the peer review. Defect fixing does not normally need to pass through a group review. However, when it does, the names of all persons who conducted the review are entered.

17. **Review start date**—The date on which the review of the fixed defect was started.

18. **Review end date**—The date on which the review of the fixed defect was completed.

19. **Regression tested by**—The name of the person who conducted the regression testing on the fixed defect. In some cases, there may not be any regression testing, as in the case for defects reported on information artifacts. In such cases, the columns that pertain to regression testing may be left blank or may be filled in with NA (not applicable).

20. **Regression testing start date**—The date on which the regression testing of the fixed defect was started.

21. **Regression testing end date**—The date on which the regression testing of the fixed defect was completed. (Items 10 to 21 are filled in as the activities are performed.)

22. **Status**—The status can be "open" or "closed." The status starts with "open" and is closed only when the defect is fixed, reviewed, and regression tested. Status is originally filled in at the time of reporting the defect. It is changed to "closed" when the defect is resolved and the rectified code is delivered back to the concerned party.

23. **Defect category**—The category of the defect. A suggested list of defect categories is given in Table B.1. However, the organization's standard defect categories can be used. The defect category is filled in after the defect analysis is completed.

24. **Defect origin**—The stage at which the defect originated, which could be the requirements, software design, software detailed design, construction, etc. stages. The defect origin is filled in after the defect analysis is completed.

25. **Acceptance tested on**—The date on which the acceptance testing is conducted with the customer. This column might not be applicable for defects uncovered before acceptance testing.

26. **Delivered on**—The date on which the fixed defect is delivered to the customer or the next software development stage.

DEFECT RESOLUTION PROCEDURE

Defect resolution consists of the following steps:

1. A defect is uncovered during a QA activity being carried out on a software artifact.
2. The person who uncovered the defect reports it in accordance with the organizational procedure for reporting defects. Normally, all

Table B.1. Suggested defect categories

Defect category	Defect origin	Defect severity
Accessed or stored data incorrectly	coding	major
Add new capability	requirements	major
Ambiguous statement	coding	minor
Applicable standards not met	design	critical
Change in program requirements	requirements	major
Checking wrong variable	coding	major
Computational problem	coding	major
Conflicting item	design	major
Confusing item	design	minor
Data handling problem	coding	critical
Data problem	coding	minor
Data referenced out of bounds	coding	major
Dimensioned data incorrectly	coding	minor
Documentation problem	coding	minor
Document quality problem	documentation	minor
Duplicate logic	coding	minor
Embedded data in tables incorrect or missing	coding	critical
Enhancement	design	major
Equation insufficient or incorrect	coding	critical
External data incorrect or missing	coding	major
Extreme conditions neglected	coding	critical
Failure caused by a previous fix	coding	critical
Flag or index set incorrectly	coding	major
Forgotten cases or steps	coding	critical
Illogical item	design	major
Implement editorial changes	documentation	minor
Improve code efficiency	coding	major
Improve comments	documentation	minor
Improve usability	design	major
Incomplete item	coding	major
Incomplete statement	coding	critical
Inconsistencies	coding	critical
Inconsistent subroutine arguments	coding	major
Incorrect item	coding	critical
Incorrectly located subroutine called	coding	major
Initialized data incorrectly	coding	major
Input data incorrect or missing	coding	critical
Input or output timing incorrect	coding	critical
Interface or timing problem	coding	critical
Interrupts handled incorrectly	coding	critical
Iterating loop incorrectly	coding	major
Logic problem	coding	critical

Table B.1. Suggested defect categories (continued)

Defect category	Defect origin	Defect severity
Misinterpretation	coding	major
Missing computation	coding	critical
Missing condition test	coding	critical
Missing item	design	critical
Mixed modes	coding	major
No identification	coding	minor
Nonexistent subroutine called	coding	critical
Nonverifiable item	design	major
Not a defect	reporting	minor
Not current	coding	major
Not traceable	requirements	critical
Operand in equation incorrect	coding	major
Operator data incorrect or missing	coding	critical
Operator in equation incorrect	coding	major
Other enhancement	coding	major
Other problem (could not classify)	requirements	major
Output data incorrect or missing	coding	critical
Packed or unpacked data incorrectly	coding	major
Parenthesis used incorrectly	coding	critical
Precision loss	coding	minor
Redundant item	design	minor
Referenced wrong data variable	coding	minor
Remove unnecessary capability	design	minor
Rounding or truncation fault	coding	minor
Scaling or units of data incorrect	coding	minor
Scope of data incorrect	coding	major
Sensor data incorrect or missing	coding	critical
Sign convention fault	coding	major
Software fix or a hardware problem	coding	major
Subroutine or module mismatch	coding	critical
Subscripted variable incorrectly	coding	minor
Timing fault causes data loss	coding	critical
Unachievable item	design	critical
Unnecessary function	coding	minor
Update current capability	design	major
Variable type incorrect	coding	minor
Wrong subroutine called	coding	major

defects uncovered during a QA activity are consolidated and reported at the end of that QA activity, either in a report or by direct entry into the project defect resolution register.

3. The defect is allocated for analysis. Defect analysis involves the following steps:

   a. Replicate the defect to ensure it is indeed a defect. If the defect cannot be replicated, the analyzer contacts the person who reported it to verify that the defect is in fact a true defect. If it turns out that the reported defect is not a true defect, the defect is closed.

   b. The analyzer analyzes the defect, determines its category and origin, and records this information in the defect resolution register.

   c. The analyzer estimates the impact of the defect on effort, schedule, and cost of the project. If the defect resolution can be charged to the customer, the analyzer obtains customer approval for the estimates.

   d. The analyzer reports the defect analysis with the estimate information for resolution back to the software project manager.

   e. Analysis completion details are recorded in the defect resolution register.

4. The defect is then allocated for fixing, preferably to the original author. If the original author is unavailable, fixing the defect is assigned to another suitable person.

5. The person allocated makes the necessary correction in the artifact, resolves the defect, and reports the completion details back to the software project manager.

6. The defect resolution register is updated with the details of fixing the defect, and the defect is allocated for review.

7. The person allocated conducts a peer review to ensure all standards and guidelines are followed and that the resolution is appropriate for the defect. If any defects are uncovered, the artifact is returned to the person who fixed the defect for further correction.

8. Once the review is completed and defects uncovered in the review, if any, are closed, the defect resolution register is updated. If the component affected by the defect was an information artifact, it would not go through testing but would be delivered for the next stage. The defect is allocated for regression testing.

9. The person allocated conducts regression testing to ensure that the defect is properly fixed. If any defects are uncovered, the artifact is returned to the person who fixed the defect for further correction.

10. Once regression testing is completed and any defects uncovered during regression testing are closed, the defect resolution register is updated with the regression testing details.

11. If the defect was uncovered during the development stage, the artifact is released for the next stage of software development.

12. If the defect was uncovered during the acceptance testing stage or later, acceptance testing is conducted with the customer for acceptance of the artifact.

13. Once acceptance testing is completed and the artifact is accepted by the customer, the artifact is delivered to the customer.

14. The defect status in the defect resolution register is then changed to "closed."

15. The defect resolution process is now complete.

The defect resolution process is depicted in Figure B.2. Table B.1 lists suggested defect categories and defect severities for use in the defect analysis activity.

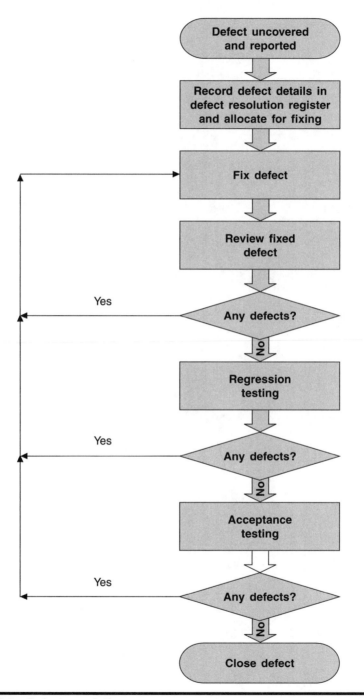

Figure B.2. Defect resolution process

APPENDIX C: GUIDELINES FOR ERROR GUESSING

Error guessing has two purposes: to ascertain the efficiency of quality assurance (QA) activities and to try to locate as many errors as possible in a software product.

ERROR GUESSING TO ASCERTAIN THE EFFICIENCY OF QUALITY ASSURANCE ACTIVITIES

The efficiency of a QA activity is the ratio of the number of defects uncovered in a software artifact during a specific QA activity to the total number of defects present in the software artifact, expressed as a percentage. The formula is

$$\frac{\text{Number of defects uncovered}}{\text{Total number of defects}} \times 100$$

The number of defects uncovered is available in the defect report for the QA activity of the software artifact. Defects uncovered in all the QA activities preceding the present QA activity need to be considered and subtracted from the total defects.

The total number of defects is the sum of all the defects uncovered in the software artifact in all the QA activities performed on the artifact. The total number of defects uncovered includes those uncovered during the following QA activities:

1. Peer review
2. Unit testing
3. Integration testing
4. System testing
5. Acceptance testing
6. Any other testing
7. Report from the field or customer site

The following examples are provided to make this computation clearer.

Example 1

A peer review of a software unit has uncovered 15 defects. This was the first QA activity conducted on the software unit. The total number of defects that could be lurking in the software is estimated to be 45. Therefore:

$$\text{Efficiency of QA peer review} = \frac{15}{45} \times 100 = 33.33\%$$

Example 2

Unit testing of the software unit in Example 1 was conducted after the peer review was completed and 20 defects were uncovered. Therefore:

$$\text{New total number of defects} = \text{Total defects} - \text{Defects uncovered in the preceding QA activities}$$

$$= 45 - 15$$

$$= 30$$

$$\text{Efficiency of QA unit testing} = \frac{20}{30} \times 100 = 66.66\%$$

Example 3

All planned QA activities for the software unit in Examples 1 and 2 have been completed, and a total of 40 defects were uncovered in all the QA activities. Therefore:

$$\text{Efficiency of all QA activities} = \frac{40}{45} \times 100 = 88.89\%$$

One thing that needs to be made clear here is how the total number of defects in a software unit is estimated. After all the QA activities are completed, only the number of uncovered defects is known. This is why the term "guessing" is used here.

The defect injection rate is used for guessing the total number of defects. Appendix G illustrates how to compute the defect injection rate, which is expressed as defects per unit of size. It is computed at the organizational level for each attribute of a software artifact and is maintained in the organizational knowledge repository or by the QA department. The appropriate defect injection rate can be obtained from this source.

Take, for example, a software artifact size of 15 function points with a corresponding defect injection rate of 1.25 defects per function point. The total number of defects in this software artifact is

$$\text{Total number of defects} = \text{Software size} \times \text{Defect injection rate}$$

$$= 15 \times 1.25$$

$$= 18.75 \text{ defects or 19 defects}$$

This method can be used to estimate the total number of defects in an artifact.

Computing this figure gives the number of defects that ought to be uncovered in the present QA activity in addition to the efficiency with which the present QA activity is carried out.

ERROR GUESSING AS AN AID TO DESIGN TEST CASES AND CONDUCT TESTING

Software development has existed for many years, and a few areas are now recognized for the occurrence of common errors. These areas are documented in Table C.1 for convenient reference and use in designing test cases or conducting the software testing. The table offers guidelines for error guessing so that test cases can be designed to ensure that software is defect-free and also lists some rules which are sometimes forgotten.

Table C.1. Guidelines for error guessing

Error case	Description of example test cases	Remarks
Programming shortfalls	Programmer oversights, such as not handling all possible data validations.	Use negative testing guidelines to detect these errors.
Wrong sequence of operations	1. For example, in a warehouse application, material should be received before it can be issued. 2. The employee's age must be in the "employable" range when a new hire joins the organization. 3. In a production management application, fabrication must be completed before it can be inspected. 4. In a time sheet application, entering data for a future date should not be allowed.	Design test cases to ensure that operations are permitted in the proper sequence only.
Integrity issues	1. After an invoice is submitted to a customer, modification of it should not be allowed. 2. After a purchase order has been issued, modification of it should not be allowed. 3. After time sheet data is submitted to payroll or billed to the customer, changes to include more data should not be permitted. 4. After a balance sheet has been produced, modification to the data for that period should not be allowed.	Design test cases to ensure integrity of data.
Consistency issues—key values should not be deleted after some transactions have taken place	1. In a time sheet application, project information should not be deleted after data against a project has been entered. 2. In a warehouse application, reducing the quantity of receipts should not be allowed after that quantity has been issued. 3. In a finance application, an account should not be deleted or modified after income or an expenditure has been booked against it.	Design test cases to ensure data consistency.

Consistency of information presented—often information is retrieved and displayed either on a screen or in a report; in all instances, the information must be the same	1. In a warehouse application, stock information for an item is obtained from multiple places, such as before issue of the item, in the stock report, in the stock inquiry by the production team, etc., and the value must be the same in all places. 2. In an enterprise resource planning application, the value of production from the finance, production, or marketing module can be obtained, and the value must be same. 3. In a customer relationship management application, a request for proposal is a prerequisite for a proposal and a proposal is a prerequisite for an order. 4. When a report is generated after processing a number of records, the sum of the records included in the report and excluded from the report must equal the number of records that are in the database.	Design test cases to ensure that the application presents consistent information irrespective of the source from which it is obtained.
Computational issues	1. When maximum values are input for performing multiplication, the receiving variable might not have adequate size to accommodate the result. 2. When the denominator in a division operation becomes zero, the "division by zero" error often is not handled in the software.	Design test cases to ensure that results given by computations are properly stored.
Loops	1. Loops often go into infinite iterations. 2. Often, the file or table record reading in a loop may not read all records until the end-of-file condition is reached.	Design test cases to ensure that loops iterate for all the designed iterations and that they terminate.
Control structures	1. It is common to forget to include the "else" part of "if" statements. 2. It is common to forget the "default" case in "switch-case" statements.	Design test cases to ensure all paths of a control structure.

APPENDIX D:
GUIDELINES FOR
GRAPHICAL USER INTERFACE
QUALITY CONFORMANCE

Conformance of quality for a graphical user interface (GUI) is very important because of its ability to move the cursor directly to any location through use of the mouse. In the earlier days of character user interface, the programmer could set the order of movement and prevent the user from moving to a certain location on a screen. The mouse interface and GUI freed the user from the programmed restriction of movement to data items. GUI controls provide a number of methods for programming, and the behavior of these methods is uncertain, especially if they are left to their default behavior.

It is possible to open multiple windows in an application, and users can easily resize or reposition a window if this option is not specifically restricted by the programmer.

In each window and control, a large number of events are possible. Some of these events are handled by the programmer, and the rest are handled by the operating system or the browser. In these days of multiple browsers and multiple versions of operating systems, how these events are handled is unpredictable, given their random behavior.

Because of the freedom the mouse interface allows the user in terms of movement to any control on a screen, it cannot be assumed that sequential movement is the only manner of moving from one control to another. One of the frequent causes of errors is the assumption that the event of "lost focus" (or "out of focus") is activated before another control activates the event of "got focus." If code is written in the "lost focus" event, the event might never be activated at all. GUI makes the sequence of events completely immaterial.

These specific capabilities of a GUI make it necessary to ensure the quality of the GUI separately, in addition to normal review and testing. Table D.1 lists the aspects that need to be inspected to ensure the quality of the GUI. Table D.2 lists test cases to ensure the quality of the GUI.

Table D.1. Suggested cases for inspection of the GUI

Aspect	Description	Expected result
Spelling accuracy	Check all spellings for accuracy with the set spelling. Use *Merriam-Webster's* dictionary as the setting for American spelling and the *Oxford English Dictionary* as the setting for British spelling.	All spellings are correct.
Spelling accuracy	Check capitalization of words against capitalization guidelines. Check for consistency in capitalization of words.	Capitalization rules follow a set guideline, be it organizational or from another source.
Label positioning	Check all labels for their proximity to the controls for which they provide explanation.	All labels are close to the controls, with a uniform gap between the last character and the edge of the control.
Label positioning	Check that labels are positioned either on the left or at the top of the control.	1. All labels are positioned either to the left or at the top of the control. 2. If the label is above the control, it is either aligned with the left corner or centered. 3. If a label is aligned to the right of the control or is below the control, there must be a valid reason.
Font color	For readability, check that the contrast of the font color is appropriate for the background. Inspect all screens to ensure that all characters are clearly legible.	All characters on all screens are legible.

Table D.1. Suggested cases for inspection of the GUI (continued)

Aspect	Description	Expected result
Font color	Red color text indicates danger and therefore must be reserved for warnings and error messages. It should not be used for other purposes. Check and ensure that red color is used appropriately on the screen.	1. Red color font is not used for titles, headers, or normal text. 2. Warnings and error messages are in red color font.
Font color	Blue color text is usually difficult to read and should be avoided.	If blue color text is present, it is clearly legible.
Font color	A dark-colored font is easier to read. A light-colored font on a dark-colored background is difficult to read.	The font color is a darker shade than the background color.
Font type	The font selected must be of the type that is right for the screen. Fonts selected also must be uniform across the application.	All characters on a screen are in the same font. If not, there is a valid reason, and the different font is appropriate for the screen and for its purpose.
Font size	The size of fonts must be consistent for normal text, titles, headers, warnings, etc.	1. All titles are in the same font size. 2. All headers are in the same font size. 3. All normal text is in the same font size. 4. All warnings are in the same font size. 5. The sizes of titles, headers, warnings, and normal text can differ from one another, to make each clearly distinct from the others.

Color scheme	The color scheme should be consistent throughout the application on all screens. Consistency means that the background, menu items, fonts, pictures, and messages all have a consistent color scheme.	All screens use a consistent color scheme
Color scheme	Color schemes must differentiate between different classes of information on a screen. Menus should have a different color scheme than normal text, titles and headers should have a different color scheme than normal text, etc. This assists users in differentiating between levels of information.	The color scheme differs for different classes of information on a screen.
Color scheme	Information such as special offers, discounts, and warning notices (for example, expiration of membership) must have a color scheme that attracts the attention of users.	All special information on a screen has a color scheme that differs from the rest of the screen, and the color scheme is able to attract immediate attention.
Color scheme	Different colors connote different meanings to people. These connotations can differ for people from different countries, but common color connotations include the following: 1. Red—danger, stop, hot, financial loss 2. Green—okay, go 3. Yellow—warning, approaching stop sign or danger 4. Blue—cool 5. Black—financial profit 6. Gray—dull 7. Orange—energy 8. White—purity	Color schemes are consistent with their implicit meanings. Preferably, there is no wrong usage of color, especially for special information.

Table D.1. Suggested cases for inspection of the GUI (continued)

Aspect	Description	Expected result
Graphics	Graphics should show a clear purpose. Check that graphics convey their intended meaning.	Graphics match the purpose for which they are intended.
Graphics	Web site graphics should not be offensive to different cultures. For example, displaying a middle finger or fore-finger is offensive in many cultures. Ensure that graphics do not offend religious or other sentiments.	Only standard or culture-neutral graphics are used.
Graphics	Sometimes graphics are not automatically displayed. In such cases, alternate text is displayed. Therefore, en-sure that every graphic has alternate text.	Every graphic has alternate text.
Icons	Icons should reflect their functionality. Also, every icon should have a tool tip.	All icons reflect their functionality and display tool tips that explain their functions.
Icons	Each icon should have a keyboard shortcut so that its function can be accessed using the keyboard.	Each clickable icon can be accessed by an alternate mechanism using the keyboard.

Table D.2. Suggested test cases for validation of GUI

Aspect	Description	Expected result
Multiple instances	If the product allows execution of multiple instances, then start two or more instances.	Does not fail.
Multiple instances	If the product should not allow execution of multiple instances, then start a second instance.	Second instance is not allowed. The message that another instance is already running is displayed. The first instance continues to run.
Window resizing	If window resizing is allowed in the product, then resize, minimize, and maximize the windows.	The windows allow resizing, minimizing, and maximizing.
Enable and disable	Buttons can be enabled and disabled, depending on the need of the application. The Delete button in particular might need to be disabled when nothing is selected for deletion or in similar situations.	Buttons can be enabled and disabled as necessary.
Enable and disable	Menu items should be enabled and disabled based on the security settings of the application. Run the application with different security authorizations.	Menu items not appropriate to the security authorization are disabled, and menu items appropriate to the security authorization are enabled.
Modal dialogs	When a modal dialog is displayed, the parent window or form should not be accessible. Display a modal dialog and see if the parent window is accessible.	The parent window is not accessible.
Modeless dialogs	Modeless dialogs should be tied to the parent window. Display a modeless dialog, and then try to minimize and maximize the parent window or form.	The modeless dialog minimizes and maximizes along with the parent window or form.

Table D.2. Suggested test cases for validation of GUI (continued)

Aspect	Description	Expected result
Cursor focus	When the screen freshly loads, the cursor needs to be focused on the default field. Sometimes there is no default field.	There is a default field for every screen and the cursor sets focus to that field when freshly loaded.
Cursor focus	When focus is shifted to a field control that contains data, all data must be selected. This prevents additions to the data already present in the field control. Enter data in a field control and shift focus to that field control.	All data is selected.
Messages	After an error message is displayed and closed, the focus should shift to the error field. Sometimes the cursor does not focus on any field.	The cursor focuses on the error field.
Messages	After a message is displayed and closed, the cursor should return the focus to the field where it was before the message was displayed. Sometimes the focus is simply not set.	The cursor sets the focus to the field where it was prior to the display of the message.
Screen refresh	It is necessary to reload the screen after operations like "save" and "delete." While the screen is reloading, it is essential to blank out fields that might be left blank during usage. It is also necessary to load values in the selectable fields, such as the combo box, list box, list view, etc. Perform a "save" or "delete" operation, and observe the screen as it refreshes.	The screen refreshes correctly.

Click events	Areas where a click is not expected should not activate an action. For example, frames, labels, and empty lists should not activate any action when clicked. Click and double-click on such areas and observe the response.	There is no response.
Navigation	Navigation using the Tab key must be from left to right and top to bottom. Tab from one control to another control.	The focus shifts from the left control to the right and then to the next row of controls. When tabbed from the last control on the screen, the focus returns to the first control.
Navigation	Personal disabilities—especially visual—might necessitate keyboard use in addition to mouse use.	All functionalities are accessible through keyboard usage.
Navigation	Having to scroll the screen in both the horizontal and vertical directions is laborious.	There is no need to scroll the screen in both directions, unless there is a valid reason.
Defaults	The default button should be clicked when loaded in a panel of radio buttons.	One radio button is clicked when loaded.
Defaults	The check box should be checked or not checked, depending on the default value.	The check box is checked or not checked, depending on the default value when freshly loaded.
Defaults	One command button should be the default for the screen.	1. One command button is activated by default when the Enter key is hit. 2. The default command button is normally the positive button—that is, the "save" or "OK" button. Negative buttons such as "delete" or "cancel" are not default buttons. 3. There is a valid reason if negative buttons are default buttons.

Table D.2. Suggested test cases for validation of GUI (continued)

Aspect	Description	Expected result
Action responses	The "save" action should indicate that a record is saved.	Confirmation for the "save" action is shown by a progress bar, a change in cursor shape, a confirmation message, or some other means. The "save" action is not left without any confirmatory action.
Consistency	There should be consistency between toolbar buttons and menu list items. Initiate action for each option first from the toolbar and then from the menu (the reverse order is also acceptable).	The same action is activated when initiated from the toolbar button or the menu list item.
Toolbar	Each toolbar button should have a corresponding menu item.	Each toolbar button has a corresponding menu item.
Toolbar	Each toolbar button should have a tool tip that describes the action that will be activated by the button. Ensure that each toolbar button has tool tip text by hovering the mouse over each button.	Each button on the toolbar has tool tip text.
Tab order	All input controls should be accessible using the Tab key. Their order should be from left to right and top to bottom.	The cursor moves from input control to input control with the Tab key, from left to right and from top to bottom.

APPENDIX E: GUIDELINES FOR STRESS TESTING

Applications most often fail not because there is a deficiency in the program logic but due to stress caused by the environment (system configuration) in which an application is functioning. To ensure that an application runs properly or to record the known defects, stress testing needs to be conducted. Stress testing involves making the expected resources unavailable to the application.

Stress testing is a form of software testing that is conducted to determine the reliability of a software product working under stress. The main objective of stress testing is to subject a software product to stress by denying it the expected resources (network connectivity, data files or tables, shared library, etc.). The idea is to stress a system to the breaking point in order to uncover defects that could be present in the software product. Stress testing can be carried out after positive testing is completed and during the system testing stage.

STRESS TESTING GUIDELINES

The tables in this section specify the suggested tests to be carried out for each type of stress to which a software product can be subjected:

Table E.1   Suggested test cases to cause printer-related stress
Table E.2   Suggested test cases to cause network-related stress
Table E.3   Suggested test cases to assess the impact of improper handling of the keyboard

Table E.1. Printer stress testing

Test case	Expected result
Initiate printing from the application and then turn the printer off.	Appropriate error message should be displayed with a facility to retry and return to another functionality.
Initiate printing from the application and then switch the printer to offline status.	Appropriate error message should be displayed with a facility to retry and return to another functionality.
Initiate printing from the application to a printer without paper.	Appropriate error message should be displayed with a facility to retry and return to another functionality.
Initiate printing from the application without connecting a printer to the system.	Appropriate error message should be displayed with a facility to retry and return to another functionality.

Table E.2. Network stress testing

Test case	Expected result
Unplug the network cable from the database server while the application is running.	Appropriate error message should be displayed with a facility to retry and return to another functionality (no data should be lost).
Remove the network connection from a local workstation while the application is running.	Appropriate error message should be displayed with a facility to retry and return to another functionality.
Remove the network connection between the application server and the client while the application is running.	Appropriate error message should be displayed with a facility to retry and return to another functionality.
Remove the network connection between the application server and the database server while the application is running.	Appropriate error message should be displayed with a facility to retry and return to another functionality (no data should be lost).
Shut down one application server while clients are running the application.	Appropriate error message should be displayed with a facility to retry and return to another functionality.

Table E.3. Keyboard stress testing

Test case	Expected result
Press all function keys one by one.	Application should not abort, and where designed, appropriate action should be initiated.
Press any key in combination with various function keys.	Application should not abort.
Press any key in combination with the Alt key.	Application should not abort.
Press any key in combination with the Ctrl key, especially with the characters C, Z, and D.	Application should not abort.
Press any key in combination with the Shift, Ctrl, and Alt keys.	Application should not abort.
Press multiple keys simultaneously.	Application should not abort.
Press both palms on the keyboard.	Application should not abort.

Table E.4. Power outage stress testing

Test case	Expected result
Switch off the power to the system (server) when the application is running.	Data should not be corrupted.
Switch off the power at the source for the server while the application is running.	Data should not be corrupted.
Switch off the power at the source for a client machine while the application is running.	Data should not be corrupted and the session should end for the client.

Table E.5. Data-related stress testing

Test case	Expected result
Corrupt some data in a couple of records.	Appropriate error message should be displayed.
Delete a table or any other database object (such as stored procedure, trigger, view, etc.) from the database.	Appropriate error message should be displayed.
Place one unexpected (undefined) parameter in the parameter file.	Appropriate error message should be displayed.
Put a huge volume of data in a file or table that is used as input for a process when the application expects the file to contain only a small number of records.	Some indication that processing is underway should be displayed, and an appropriate error message should be displayed.
Rename the database.	The application should not hang, and an appropriate error message should be displayed.

Table E.6. System configuration change stress testing

Test case	Expected result
Load the application on a different version of the operating system and test it.	If it is a compatible operating system, the application should function properly or display an appropriate error message, and the application should not hang.
Load a different version of the database and test the application.	The application should function properly or display an appropriate error message.
Use a different browser or a different version of the browser.	The application should function properly or display an appropriate error message.

Table E.7. Reduced availability of RAM stress testing

Test case	Expected result
Load and run memory-resident utilities until the available RAM is reduced to slightly below the minimum required for the application to run, and then run the application.	The application should run, but perhaps with a slower response time.

Table E.8. Reduced disk space availability stress testing

Test case	Expected result
Reduce the disk space on the C drive (or the volume on which the operating system is loaded) to a barely acceptable value by loading data or applications.	The application should run or display an appropriate error message.

Table E.9. Inadequate database size stress testing

Test case	Expected result
Reduce the maximum size of the database to the present size of the database, then run the application, and try to input records; this tests the condition when the database reaches its maximum permissible size.	An appropriate error message should be displayed.

Table E.10. Antivirus software stress testing

Test case	Expected result
Uninstall the current antivirus software, install other antivirus software, and then run the application.	The application should function properly or display an appropriate error message, and the application should not hang.
Load more than one antivirus software on the system and run the application.	The application should function properly or display an appropriate error message.
Uninstall all antivirus software from the system and run the application.	The application should function properly or display an appropriate error message.

APPENDIX F: GUIDELINES FOR NEGATIVE TESTING

Negative testing is carried out with the specific intention of failing the software or, in other words, to find out if there is any possibility that the application could fail. Testers use their intuition to run the application in a way they expect a person intent on proving it will fail would. They perform operations the application is not expected to perform. The only exception in negative testing is that the system is not subjected to physical damage.

Negative testing mostly deals with the user interface. Either wrong input or no input is given to the system to see if the software responds appropriately. The software should reject wrong input and display an appropriate error message. When no input is given to the system, the software must respond with a message that asks for input.

The tables in this section provide test cases to assist in conducting negative testing on software:

Table F.1. Negative testing guidelines for screens

Type of entry	Test case description	Remarks
Numeric values	1. Should not allow entry of nonnumeric characters.	Try to enter nonnumeric values.
	2. Where only positive numbers are expected, a minus sign should not be allowed.	Enter numbers with a minus sign.
	3. Where decimal numbers are expected, two decimal points should not be allowed.	Try to enter a number with two decimal points.
	4. Where whole numbers are expected, decimal points and fractions should not be permitted.	Enter fractional numbers where integers are expected.
	5. Because data types allow numbers up to their maximum capacity, the software should check the size of the value entered and prevent a user from entering a number that is larger than the maximum expected.	Enter a higher number of digits or very large numbers.
	6. Check that when a field is left blank, the software stores zero in the database or has routines to handle null.	Leave fields blank and try to save the data.
	7. Boundary values for ranges are likely to be in error.	Enter values just above and below the boundaries.
	8. Values are not initialized for the second iteration onward, especially after "save" operations. Always perform a second iteration for "save" operations with a different set of values.	Check for proper default values when the screen is refreshed.
	9. Most common errors are in the results of computation operations.	Check computation results manually.

10. Check that the division operation returns an error condition when the denominator becomes zero or when both the numerator and the denominator become zero.

Try to make the denominator zero.

| Alphanumeric values | | |

1. The software should check the size and limit it to a permitted value.

Enter longer data than is permissible.

2. Where names of persons are expected, the software should ensure that numeric values are not entered.

Enter some numeric characters in name fields.

3. These fields should not allow special characters, such as combinations with the Ctrl or Alt keys. Check if these combinations cause any issues.

Enter some special characters in alphanumeric fields.

Date values

1. Check the consistency between the month and the date. For example, February can have either 28 or 29 days, March can have 31 days, April can have 30 days, etc. Sometimes programmers do not allow the appropriate number of days in months.

Enter inconsistent or invalid dates.

2. If months are allowed to be entered as numerals, a numeral greater than 12 as the month number should be rejected.

Enter invalid month numbers.

3. If there is a "from date" and a "to date" on a screen, the "to date" should be later than the "from date."

Enter higher "from date" than "to date."

4. Check the validity of the year. For example, year "9999" should be rejected. Depending on the application, enter some invalid year values and see if the application rejects them.

Try to enter 9999 as the year value.

Table F.1. Negative testing guidelines for screens (continued)

Type of entry	Test case description	Remarks
File and table operations	1. Most of the time, empty table conditions are not handled by programmers of master table transactions.	Empty the master table of all data and try to use the application.
	2. Another error commonly committed by programmers is leaving tables or files open. This can cause failures if the same table or file is opened again.	Try to run the same data entry screen in sequence and check if the data is being saved properly and that the application does not abort.
"Save" and "submit" events	Sometimes programmers check for data validation in the "lost focus" event of the controls such as the text box and combo box. This can be checked by keeping the focus in the control but clicking the Save or Submit button to verify if data validation happens.	After entering wrong data in a field, click the Save button. The validation should still be applied.
Labels	Labels should not be clickable unless they are links to a Web page.	Click all labels and see if any action results.
Delete buttons	1. Whenever a "delete" action is initiated, the system should seek confirmation for deletion by displaying an appropriate message.	Try to delete some values and ensure that the confirmation message is displayed.
	2. A "delete" action should not be allowed when no item is selected for deletion. The system should either display an error message or prevent initiation of the "delete" action.	Set focus to blank data and click the Delete button.

Category	Description	Action
Save and Submit buttons	1. When any of the mandatory fields is blank, the system should return an error message.	Leave some mandatory fields blank and click the Save button.
	2. When any field has a longer field width than permitted, the system should return an error message.	Enter longer than permissible values in some fields and click the Save button.
Lists	When a list is empty, the system should not respond or should not go into an error condition if the list is clicked or double-clicked.	Click and double-click on empty lists.
Click or double-click	When areas that are not supposed to be clicked are clicked on, the system should not take any action or fail.	Try to click randomly on areas of the screen not expected to be clicked, and check if anything happens or if the application fails.
Multiple screens	When applications allow multiple screens to be opened, open a few screens and check if it causes a failure.	Open multiple screens and switch between them.
Wrong key usage	1. Press keys in combination with the Ctrl and Alt keys, and check if it causes any problems.	Press C, Z, and D in combination with the Ctrl key and some keys with the Alt key.
	2. Press multiple keys at the same time and check if it causes any problems.	Press multiple keys at the same time.

Table F.2. Negative testing guidelines for reports

Aspect of report	Test case description	Remarks
Report parameters	1. In many cases, generation of a report requires entry of parameters such as dates, names, codes, etc. In cases where the parameters are blank, the system should respond with an error message or present a blank report, but should not fail.	Try to generate reports without giving the required parameters.
	2. In cases where parameters are wrong, the system should respond with an error message or present a blank report, but should not fail.	Try to generate reports by giving wrong parameters.
	3. In cases where parameters are illogical, such as a "from date" later than the "to date" or a nonexistent value, the system should respond with an error message, but should not fail.	Try to generate reports by giving illogical parameters.
Alignment	1. The data in the columns and the column headings must be aligned properly. Ensure that alphanumeric items are left aligned and numeric values are right aligned.	Check consistency of data and headings for every column of the report.
	2. Headings, date of the report, page number, etc. may be clipped due to lack of sufficient space allowed for them.	Check if the page headings, report headings, dates, page numbers, etc. are clipped.
Comprehensive processing	In large-volume reports, check if all the records are included in the processing. These reports normally give control statistics such as the number of records considered and the number actually included in the report.	Check if the report has control statistics. Check if all records are processed and all relevant records are included in the report.

Table F.3. Negative testing guidelines for Web pages

Aspect	Test case description	Remarks
Navigation	1. Click all links on the page and ensure that they navigate to the correct Web pages. Also check that no links are broken.	Check all navigation links.
	2. Check that links that navigate to other Web sites open in another window.	Click on links pointing to other Web sites.
	3. Using the Back button after logging out of a site should not allow functionality to be accessible. The system should respond with an error message which says the user needs to be logged in.	Log out of the application, and then click the Back button.
Wrong data input	When wrong data is input, an appropriate error message should be displayed either immediately after input or after the Submit button is clicked.	Enter wrong data in some fields to see if it is rejected.

APPENDIX G:
MEASUREMENT OF QUALITY

Measurement allows us to quantify something. Quantification facilitates comparison of that something with other things that are similar and allows us to draw inferences as to whether the entity we measured is equal to, worse than, or better than the entities similar to it. But can we measure quality?

Software is a special type of product in the sense that it has no moving parts, and therefore it does not deteriorate with usage or aging, as do physical products, which deteriorate in the form of wear and tear over time.

In the case of physical products, it is *sine qua non* that a product performs its intended functions without defects before it reaches the customer. However, it is possible that software products with defects lurking inside could reach customers, and it has more or less come to be accepted that the delivered software has some defects. Physical products (except use-and-throwaway products) are expected to undergo periodic maintenance, either to maintain their performance level (for example, changing the oil in a car), to prevent a breakdown (for example, periodically servicing a car), or to recover from a breakdown.

The reliability of physical products is measured in mean time between failures (MTBF) and mean time to repair (MTTR). The longer the MTBF, the better the reliability of the product. Conversely, the shorter the MTTR, the better the quality of the product. MTBF and MTTR normally are measured in running hours. Automakers, however, give the MTBF in miles, such as 100,000 miles of trouble-free operation, a measurement the general public understands. Automakers and other manufacturers give an MTBF and an MTTR for their products. These measures are not usable for software products because of the absence of physical parts that deteriorate with use or age. Some metrics that are useful for measurement of software quality are discussed in this appendix.

SOFTWARE PRODUCT QUALITY METRIC

This metric was discussed in detail in Chapter 3 on software product quality. However, there are two other metrics that are often mentioned in the literature on software quality measurement:

1. McCabe's metric or cyclomatic complexity
2. Halstead's metric

These two metrics measure quality at the program level.

Cyclomatic Complexity

This measure is designed to limit the complexity of a module, thereby promoting understandability of the module. It is the number of independent paths in a program.

The formula for computing complexity is

$$C = E - N + 1$$

where C = complexity of the program, N = number of nodes (sequential groups of program statements), and E = number of edges (program flows between nodes).

For a typical program, 10 represents maximum ideal complexity. This is used in mainframe COBOL environments even today.

Halstead's Metric for Program Difficulty

This measure computes program difficulty by counting the "operators" and the "operands." The formula for program difficulty is

$$D = \left(\frac{n_1}{2} \right) \times \left(\frac{N_2}{n_2} \right)$$

where D = program difficulty, n_1 = number of distinct operators in the program, n_2 = number of distinct operands in the program, and N_2 = total number of occurrences of operands in the program.

In this context, the "operators" are the programming language's key words, which operate on data used in the program to produce results. The "operands" are the variables that are declared within the program on which the key words operate to produce results.

McCabe's and Halstead's metrics measure the complexity of software at the program level. Because today's software products have a large number of software units, measuring the complexity of every program is very tedious and time consuming. These two metrics were developed during the COBOL days of software development. COBOL programs and other third-generation programming languages were amenable to measuring these metrics with the help of software tools. However, with today's event-oriented programming languages, using tools to compute these metrics is not very easy.

I do not recommend using McCabe's or Halstead's metric in the case of event-oriented programming languages. These two metrics are mentioned here only to satisfy the purists who would insist that a discussion on software quality measurement would not be complete without them.

DEFECT ANALYSIS

Defect analysis is carried out at both the project and organizational levels to detect recurring defect patterns and eliminate them through corrective and preventive action. Defect patterns can be eliminated through better training of personnel and by improving the standards and guidelines of the organizational software development processes. Suggested defect categories are listed in Table B.1 in Appendix B, and defect origins are listed here in Table G.1.

Defect Category Analysis

In defect category analysis, all the defects uncovered in the organization are collated into various categories to see how they are distributed among these

Table G.1. Suggested defect origins

Defect origin	Remarks
Coding	The defect was caused in the software construction stage.
Requirements analysis	The defect cropped up due to a mistake in the requirements analysis stage.
Software design	The defect cropped up due to a mistake in the software design stage.
Documentation	The defect cropped up due to a mistake in the document preparation.

categories. If the defects are distributed equally among all categories, it can be inferred that the errors are due to random causes. More defects found in certain categories than in others shows that the programmers exhibit a pattern of weakness in the areas that have more defects. This knowledge creates an opportunity to eliminate such special causes by providing better training, checklists, or tools.

Collating defects uncovered in various quality assurance (QA) activities into appropriate defect categories, as depicted in Table B.1, allows insight into the pattern of defects being injected into the software. Once the patterns are known, means to reduce these defect injections can be devised, and over a period of time the organization can move toward the goal of *right first time*. Ways to reduce the number of defects include devising a suitable training program or preparing checklists to alert the personnel concerned to the probable error situation.

Collation of uncovered defects into various categories can be carried out periodically. Monthly collation affords this activity a regularity and seriousness. However, it can be carried out quarterly as well.

Defect Origin Analysis

Defect origin analysis is similar to defect category analysis except that it is at a higher level with fewer categories. If the defects are evenly distributed, it can be inferred that they are due to random causes. If the defects cluster around one or two origins, then it can be concluded that the software engineers show a weakness in those areas. This information allows remedies to be devised that will eliminate those weaknesses and thus improve the quality of the software. Table G.1 depicts suggested defect origins.

ABC Analysis

ABC in this context stands for "always better control." ABC analysis is based on the Pareto principle of "the significant few and insignificant many." Pareto analysis divides the data into two classes: 80% (insignificant many) and 20% (significant few). ABC analysis divides the data into three classes. Typically, defect analyzers try to determine if (1) 70% of the defects fall under 10% of the categories (class A), (2) 10% of the defects fall under 70% of the categories (class C), and (3) 20% of the defects fall under 20% of the categories (class B). This analysis is carried out for both defect categories and defect origins. Defect analyzers try to determine if the majority of the defects are caused by only a few reasons. Class A defects indicate that there are weaknesses in the organization or project, resulting in a higher number of defects. Organizations try to eliminate or minimize class A defects through training or by improving standards, checklists, and guidelines. Analysis allows an organization to identify its major weaknesses and to improve on them.

Defect Removal Efficiency for Each Quality Assurance Activity

Defect removal efficiency (DRE) is performed for each QA activity carried out in a project as well as in the organization to derive the efficiency of each QA activity. Normally, DRE is computed for the most commonly performed QA activities (peer reviews, unit testing, integration testing, and system testing). QA activities rarely performed in the organization are not usually included in the computation, as calculating their efficiency and trying to improve them does not produce cost-effective benefits.

DRE is expressed as a percentage. The formula for the DRE for a QA activity is

$$\text{DRE for a QA activity} = \frac{\text{Defects uncovered in the activity}}{\substack{\text{All defects uncovered in this activity} \\ \text{and all subsequent activities}}}$$

To illustrate computation of the DRE, Table G.2 shows hypothetical data for defects uncovered in various QA activities for a software module.

Table G.2. Defect data for a software module

QA activity	Number of defects uncovered
Peer review	100
Unit testing	25
Integration testing	15
System testing	5
Acceptance testing	2
Total number of defects uncovered in all QA activities	147
DRE for peer review (100/147)	68.03%
DRE for unit testing (25/47)	53.19%
DRE for integration testing (15/22)	68.18%
DRE for system testing (5/7)	71.43%

DRE is computed both periodically as well as for a project. At an organizational level, DRE is computed every month or every quarter and takes into consideration the total number of defects (total defects uncovered plus the defects reported from client organizations or from the field) and the total number of defects uncovered by the QA activities.

At a project level, DRE is computed at the closure phase of the project. However, at that time, reports from the field about the residual defects uncovered during the operation of the software might not yet be available. It is customary to compute the DRE either at the completion of the warranty period or once every six months after the project is delivered, when software maintenance is also entrusted to the organization that developed the software.

Defect Injection Rate

Whereas defect category analysis and defect origin analysis reveal where defects are occurring and the DRE reveals how efficient the organization's QA activities are, the defect injection rate (DIR) reveals the quality capability of the organization's working, especially the first time an activity is accomplished. If the DIR is high, it is obvious that more time and effort are being spent on uncovering and removing those defects. Also, if the DIR is on the high side, the effort wasted on rework to fix those defects is also high. That means effort is being wasted on an activity that should not have been performed at all. Rework frustrates personnel and affects their motivation. A higher DIR also indicates that either the software development process, including standards, guidelines, and checklists, is not efficient enough to guide the software engineers in producing an error-free product or that the development environment, including training, development tools, supervision, instructions, etc., is not conducive to producing a defect-free product. A higher DIR indicates that the organization has weaknesses that need immediate attention if it wants to deliver quality deliverables to its clients and earn a reputation for quality. Therefore, the DIR is the most important measure of software quality.

The DIR is the rate at which defects are injected into a software product. It is expressed as defects per unit size of the software. Size can be expressed in any software size measure, such as function points (FP), software size units, object points, use case points, or lines of code (LOC).

To compute the DIR, the defects uncovered in all the QA activities performed in-house on the software must be included, as well as the defects reported from the field (from customer sites). For example, assume a size of 100 FP for a software module and 147 defects uncovered in all QA activities. The DIR is computed as follows:

$$DIR = \frac{147}{100}$$

$$= 1.47 \text{ defects per FP}$$

It is also common to use LOC when expressing DIR. Assume the software size is 155,000 LOC and there are 25 defects in that code. Now the DIR can be computed as follows:

$$DIR = \frac{25}{155,000}$$

$$= 1 \text{ defect for every 6,200 LOC}$$

The DIR is also computed by the origin of the defect or the software engineering activity that was at the root of the injected defect. Using the data in Table G.3, the DIR for defect origin can be computed as follows:

$$DIR \text{ due to requirements analysis} = \frac{28}{100} = 0.28 \text{ defects per FP}$$

$$DIR \text{ due to software design} = \frac{37}{100} = 0.37 \text{ defects per FP}$$

$$DIR \text{ due to construction} = \frac{82}{100} = 0.82 \text{ defects per FP}$$

These values reveal which software engineering activity is injecting the most errors. If the same pattern emerges at the organizational level, improvements to the specific software engineering activity can be made by either training the resources concerned or improving the process, including its standards and guidelines.

Table G.3. Defect data by origin of defect

Software engineering activity	Number of defects
Requirements analysis	28
Software design	37
Construction	82
Total	147

QA activities are designed to uncover and eliminate all defects from the software product and to prevent defective product from reaching the customer. Then why is the DIR important?

If the DIR is low, the amount of effort spent on QA activities can be minimized. To determine if the DIR is high or low, the Six Sigma philosophy (three defects per million opportunities) can be used.

When defects are uncovered, they need to be rectified, which means rework—rework to fix them, rework to review them, and rework to test them. An injected defect causes rework, and rework means loss of productive effort that could be profitably used for fresh development of another software artifact. In addition, rework is tedious and demotivating for the people who have to perform it.

The DIR helps in analyzing the causes that lead to defects being injected into the product and in drawing the proper conclusions; based on these conclusions, the causes of defect injection into the product can be eliminated. When the DIR is minimized, the effort spent on rework decreases, and consequently productivity increases. Another benefit of the DIR is that since rework is reduced, the team's motivation improves significantly. Proper use of the DIR promotes the concept of *right first time*, perhaps even making it a reality in most cases. The DIR reveals the capability and maturity of an organization's developers, and it facilitates objective performance appraisals by the human resources department.

The efficacy of QA activities is not based on uncovering defects themselves but rather finding and eliminating causes of defect injection. The DIR helps with precisely this, and that is the reason why the DIR is of utmost importance to organizations.

DEFECT DENSITY

Defect density refers to the number of defects per unit of software size. Alternatively, it also is expressed as the amount of software per one defect. Defect density normally is computed for delivered software products, which means after the product is delivered to the customer and the defects are detected at the customer location. This metric also is referred to as delivered defect density or residual defect density.

For the following sample calculation of DIR, assume that:

Product size = 100 FP
Number of defects reported by the customer = 3

Therefore:

$$\text{Defect density} = \frac{3}{100} = 0.03 \text{ defects per FP}$$

Alternatively:

$$\text{Defect density} = \frac{100}{3} = 33.3 \text{ FP per defect}$$

This normally is stated as 1 defect for every 33.3 FP (or 33.3 FP per defect). Either method of statement can be adopted.

Many practitioners measure the sigma level (from the Six Sigma philosophy) of an organization based on this delivered defect density. However, sigma level normally is computed using LOC as the software size measure.

For the following sample calculation of sigma level, assume that:

Product size = 10,000 LOC
Number of defects reported by the customer = 3 (that is, there are 3 defects per 10,000 opportunities for error)

Select from the following sigma levels where this information fits:

3 defects per 1,000,000 opportunities for error = 6 sigma
3 defects per 100,000 opportunities for error = 5 sigma
3 defects per 10,000 opportunities for error = 4 sigma
3 defects per 1,000 opportunities for error = 3 sigma
3 defects per 100 opportunities for error = 2 sigma

Based on the information in this example, the sigma level for the organization is 4 sigma. Compare this level with the ideal of a 6-sigma level of quality, which is 3 defects per 1 million opportunities for injecting errors.

INTERPRETATION OF DEFECT DENSITY AND DEFECT INJECTION RATE TOGETHER

Management is usually interested in the delivered defect density, which means the number of defects that reach the customer. If it is low, the organization receives fewer complaints from the customer and enjoys a better reputation in

Table G.4. Interpretation of defect density and defect injection rate

Defect density	DIR	Inference	Necessary action
High	High	Both software development and QA activities are inefficient.	Improve both QA and software development activities.
Low	Low	Both software development and QA activities are efficient.	Maintain the status quo. This is the ideal scenario.
High	Low	Software development activities are efficient. QA activities are not as efficient as development activities. The organization is not spending adequate effort on QA activities.	Improve QA activities or processes and other relevant aspects.
Low	High	The organization is spending more effort on QA activities. QA activities are more efficient than development activities. Software development activities are not efficient.	Improve software development process, activities, and other relevant aspects to reduce the DIR.

the market. Therefore, it is imperative that both delivered defect density and DIR be computed and their results be used in conjunction to improve organizational quality and productivity. Table G.4 details the interpretation of defect density and DIR.

EFFICIENCY OF QUALITY ASSURANCE ACTIVITIES

The efficiency of QA activities also can be computed. It is measured as the percentage of defects that the QA activities are able to uncover and then arrange for rectification. The formula is as follows:

$$\text{Efficiency of QA activities for a project} = \frac{A}{(A + B + C)}$$

where A = the total number of defects uncovered within the organization up to acceptance testing, B = the number of defects uncovered in acceptance testing, and C = the number of defects reported by the customer after delivery.

Using the data from the previous example:

Number of defects uncovered up to acceptance testing = 145
Number of defects uncovered in acceptance testing = 2
Number of defects reported by the customer after delivery = 3

Now the efficiency of QA activities can be computed as follows:

$$\text{Efficiency of QA activities} \; = \; \frac{145}{(145 \; + \; 2 \; + \; 3)}$$

$$= \quad 0.9667 \text{ or } 96.67\%$$

Only one question needs to be answered now: How long should the organization wait for the customer to report defects after delivery? One school of thought is that the organization should take into consideration all the defects reported up to the end of the warranty period. This way, there is a finite waiting period before the delivered defect density and efficiency of QA activities can be computed. However, since all defects are not included, the metrics might not reflect reality accurately.

The other school of thought is that the organization should wait until the completion of the warranty period before computing the delivered defect density and efficiency of QA activities initially. However, these metrics have to be updated every time a new defect is reported by the customer. Using this method, the organization has both the initial metrics and the final metric that reflects reality.

AVERAGE DEFECT TARDINESS

Average defect tardiness is the length of time a defect is waiting for resolution or the turnaround time for a defect from the time it is reported to the time it is resolved and delivered back to the customer. This metric is usually computed in the case of customer-reported defects, especially during the warranty period or during software maintenance, where this metric gives maximum benefit. By using this metric, targets can be set for reducing the turnaround time for defect resolution. Normally, calendar days are used to indicate the amount of time a defect is waiting for resolution, but in the case of urgent defects, clock-hours also can be used.

Table G.5 shows an example of turnaround times for defect resolution. The total number of defects is 5, and total turnaround time is 13 days. Therefore:

Table G.5. Defect resolution turnaround time

Defect ID	Reported on	Delivered on	Number of days
Defect 1	1-Aug-10	5-Aug-10	4
Defect 2	6-Aug-10	9-Aug-10	3
Defect 3	8-Aug-10	10-Aug-10	2
Defect 4	14-Aug-10	17-Aug-10	3
Defect 5	22-Aug-10	23-Aug-10	1

$$\text{Average turnaround time} \; = \; \frac{13}{5} \; = \; 2.6 \; \text{days}$$

The statistical mode also can used for this metric. In this example, the modal turnaround time is 3 days. This metric is also referred to as *defect tardiness.*

Using this metric, improvement can be effected in the turnaround time for defect resolution by reducing the number of defects. However, some organizations exclude minor defects and the corresponding effort from this metric, as minor defects take much less time to resolve and are low in importance and priority.

TREND ANALYSIS

Trend analysis is carried out to monitor the efficiency and effectiveness of QA activities in the organization. One precaution is important in carrying out trend analysis: data needs to be depicted in its chronological sequence of occurrence. Otherwise, results can be erroneous. The different types of trend analysis are discussed in the following sections.

Quality Assurance Effort Analysis

This metric computes the effort spent on QA activities as a percentage of the total effort spent on project activities. For example, assume that 25 person-hours of effort is spent on QA activities for a project where the total effort spent is 100 person-hours. The percentage of effort spent on QA activities is computed to be 25% of the total effort.

This metric is monitored for trends—either increasing or decreasing. An organization should aim to reduce the percentage over a period of time. There

Table G.6. Effort spent on QA activities

Project	Total effort in person-hours	QA effort in person-hours	QA percentage
Project A	3,600	580	16.11%
Project B	3,200	525	16.41%
Project C	3,750	545	14.53%
Project D	3,325	475	14.29%
Project E	4,575	620	13.55%
Project F	4,250	445	10.47%
Project G	4,300	540	12.56%

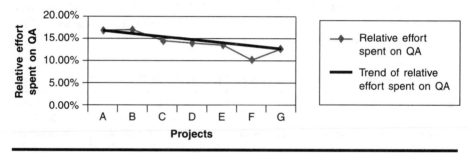

Figure G.1. Trend graph of relative effort spent on QA activities in the organization

is no hard-and-fast rule for how much effort can be spent on QA activities in a project. It varies with the number of tests conducted and the number of defects uncovered.

The data in Table G.6 can be used to carry out a trend analysis for effort spent on QA activities. Using this data, a graph can be plotted using Microsoft Excel or some other graphing tool. Figure G.1 represents the graph depicting this information. As seen in the graph, the overall trend is decreasing, even though the last project veers slightly against the trend. This indicates that project G needs to be looked at more critically to find out what caused its reverse trend, so that preventive action can be taken to curb the trend in future projects.

Defect-Fixing Effort Analysis

This metric computes the effort spent on fixing defects as a percentage of the total effort spent on project activities. For example, assume that 15 person-hours of effort is spent on fixing defects for a project where the total effort spent is

100 person-hours. The percentage of effort spent on fixing defects is 15% of the total effort.

This metric also is monitored for increasing and decreasing trends. An organization should aim to reduce the percentage over a period of time. The ideal is to achieve 0%—meaning no defects are uncovered in the QA activities and everything is done right the first time. Over a period of time, this metric should tend toward zero.

Table G.7 provides project data to demonstrate this analysis and plot the trend graph. Using this data, a graph that shows a trend line can be plotted using Microsoft Excel or a similar graphing tool. The trend graph is shown in Figure G.2. While the values of individual projects are moving up and down, the graph shows a declining trend. It also shows a saw-toothed line, indicating either a lack of control or a deficient process within the organization. This calls for critical examination of the necessity for defect fixing.

Table G.7. Relative effort spent on fixing defects in the organization

Project	Total effort in person-hours	QA effort in person-hours	Effort in defect-fixing in person-hours	Defect-fixing effort percentage
Project A	3,600	580	132	3.67%
Project B	3,200	525	152	4.75%
Project C	3,750	545	128	3.41%
Project D	3,325	475	145	4.36%
Project E	4,575	620	138	3.02%
Project F	4,250	445	165	3.88%
Project G	4,300	540	125	2.91%
Project H	5,400	624	176	3.26%

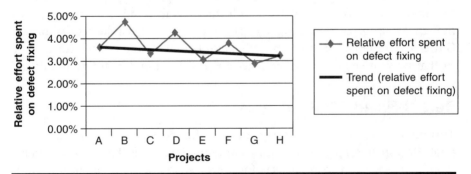

Figure G.2. Trend graph of relative effort spent on fixing defects in the organization

Deject Injection Rate Trend Analysis

The importance of the DIR and how to compute it were discussed earlier. It is also very important to carry out trend analysis for the DIR in the organization. This analysis will reveal if the DIR is remaining constant or if it is increasing or decreasing. Ideally, the DIR should be decreasing.

Table G.8 provides DIR data to demonstrate this analysis and plot the trend graph. Using this data, a graph showing a trend line can be plotted using Microsoft Excel or a similar graphing tool. The trend graph is shown in Figure G.3. As the graph shows, there is an increasing trend in the DIR. This calls for closer examination of the defects, which can be achieved by defect analysis (defect category analysis and defect origin analysis), so that the reasons behind the defects can be uncovered and preventive actions taken so that the defects do not recur, which would cause the DIR to decrease.

Table G.8. Defect injection rate data for projects

Project	Size in FP	Defects	DIR (FP per defect)
Project A	1,250	67	18.66
Project B	1,500	76	19.74
Project C	2,200	111	19.82
Project D	3,100	156	19.87
Project E	1,100	57	19.30
Project F	4,200	211	19.91
Project G	5,200	256	20.31

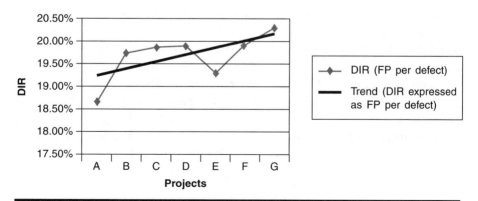

Figure G.3. Trend analysis for defect injection rate

DATA REQUIRED FOR THESE QUALITY METRICS

The following data is necessary for computing the metrics discussed in this appendix:

1. Defects, categorized and classified properly, are the primary data for these metrics. The necessary data is obtained from the defect reports generated at the conclusion of any QA activity. It is easy to collate information from these reports. When a defect-tracking software tool is used, these metrics are readily provided by the tool itself.

2. Defects reported from client reports need to be collated. If a collaborative Web-based defect-reporting tool is being used for this purpose, these data items can be obtained from the tool itself. Alternatively, these data items are available in the status reports of the personnel who attend to client requests for support. Some organizations have a help desk to attend to customer support requests, and this data can be obtained from that source as well.

3. An organizational guideline is needed for categorizing defects and assigning the origin of defects. Process-driven organizations have such guidelines, and the personnel who carry out the QA activities have the necessary skills and training to properly categorize and assign the origin of defects. This information also normally is part of the defect reports.

4. Effort spent on QA activities and on fixing defects can be obtained from a well-designed time sheet or a tool such as PMPal, which provides this data automatically.

To carry out measurement and analysis, an organizational entity responsible for this purpose is necessary. Normally, the QA department carries out this activity. In the absence of a QA department, a process-driven organization has a metrics group to carry out measurement and analysis. In some organizations, a project management office can carry out this activity.

Clearly, extra money does not need to be spent to carry out measurement and analysis of metrics. All that is required is the will of management to detect the real quality level of the organization's operations and the determination to continually improve quality and sustain the drive toward excellence.

FINAL WORDS ON MEASUREMENT OF QUALITY

Measurement for determining quality has to be simple to implement and easy to interpret. In addition, in these days of stiff competition and dwindling margins, spending extra money for any activity that does not either contribute to revenue or result in tangible and perceptible savings is difficult for any management team to accept. There are quite a few measures in addition to the ones discussed here, many of which are not easy to implement in terms of data collection, computation, and interpretation, and at the end of the day, their contribution is not very tangible or certain.

Quality measures that are easy to implement, easy to compute, and easy to interpret are presented in this appendix; they result in tangible and perceptible savings through measurable improvements in software product quality and the quality of organizational deliverables. To learn about all methods of measurement, I recommend that you study the Institute of Electrical and Electronics Engineers Standard 982 titled "IEEE Standard Dictionary of Measures to Produce Reliable Software."

APPENDIX H:
QUALITY ASSURANCE
OF DATABASES

Data is the heart of any computer-based application. In fact, a computer itself is defined as "a data-processing tool." In most modern applications, the database management system (DBMS) is at the back end, storing data and making it available to applications for processing. Therefore, it is imperative that the database has quality built into it and that it is *confirmed* to have built-in quality.

The primary responsibility of a DBMS is to protect the integrity of the data that it stores. The following aspects define data quality in DBMS systems:

1. **Data consistency**—It is possible that the same data item can be stored in many tables. Examples are key values such as employee ID in a payroll application, material code in a material management application, and customer ID in a marketing application. Such values can be found in multiple tables across the database. They should all be defined in the same manner in all the tables, wherever they are defined. This is called data consistency.

2. **Data integrity**—Data stored inside a DBMS must be protected against corruption. Data corruption can introduce a wrong value into the database. Examples include storing a nonexistent employee ID in a human resources application, a nonexistent material code in a material management application, and a nonexistent customer ID in a marketing application. When such data is introduced, it either causes the application to fail or it can present the user with wrong results or information.

3. **Data redundancy**—It is inevitable that some redundancy will occur when storing data across multiple tables. What must be achieved, however, is controlled redundancy. When too much data is repeated in too many tables, the data can lose consistency and integrity. Redundancy must be controlled so as to allow only the key values to be repeated for the purpose of cross-linking data across tables.

The following scenarios can cause issues with data in databases:

1. **Data type**—A data item that is used in multiple tables must be defined with the same data type. The following are some examples:
   ★ A numeric data item that is not to be used in computations can be defined as a numeric data type or a character data type. In order to allow leading zeros, sometimes these values are defined as character data types. Key values such as employee ID, material code, and customer ID can fall under this category. If data is defined as numeric in the main table, all other tables must follow this definition.
   ★ A character- (alphanumeric-) type data item also must be consistently defined across all tables. It can be defined as a fixed-length data item or a variable-length data item, but it is important to use the same definition across all tables in the database.
   ★ A numeric-type data item also must be defined consistently. There are many numeric data types, such as:
      ☆ Short integer (2 bytes long)
      ☆ Long integer (4 bytes long)
      ☆ Floating point, single precision (8 bytes long)
      ☆ Floating point, double precision (16 bytes long)
      ☆ Currency (8 bytes with 2 digits after the decimal point)
      ☆ Real (allows imaginary numbers)
   ★ There are many instances in applications where "yes" or "no" type data is used. These are called flags (also referred to as Boolean data). Flags can be either numeric (1 or 0) or characters (Y or N, yes or no). They must be defined consistently across the database.
   ★ Date-type data items can cause confusion. Dates can be used in computations as well as in comparisons. Computations permitted on date-type data include finding the difference between two dates or adding a number of days to a date to arrive at a new date. If

a date is defined at multiple places, it is necessary to define the data type consistently. Dates can be defined as:

☆ Short date

☆ Long date

☆ Alphanumeric

★ Null-type data—This is a special data type, and most databases treat null in a special way. The records with null attributes can be ignored during table joins. It is possible to enter null into a numeric data type definition. Computations and comparisons throw up errors when they encounter null values. Therefore, careful consideration must be given to whether the default value in a table field should be null, zero, or a blank character.

2. **Data item size**—This is one of the most common errors encountered in software application failures. If a data item is used in multiple tables, the size—in addition to data type—must be the same. In numeric data items, the type defines the size, but the length of alphanumeric data must be consistent across all tables. For example, if employee ID is defined as having six characters, it cannot have five characters in one table and eight characters in another table. It must be defined as six characters in all tables.

3. **Data deletion**—Data items might have to be deleted on occasion. For example, an employee may leave the organization or a customer may cancel an order. In such cases, deletion of the main record must be followed by deletion of all dependent records all across the table. Otherwise, the application might not be able to find connecting information and might throw up errors or fail.

TECHNIQUES FOR QUALITY ASSURANCE OF DATABASES

The tools used for quality assurance of databases are the same tools used for software development: verification and validation.

Database Verification

Definition of database schema (that is, definition of table structures, selection of data types, respective lengths, etc.) is subject to peer review. It is better to use a group review for verification of database schema, as there are three viewpoints from which verification is needed:

1. **Domain expert point of view**—The field definitions can hold the data efficiently.
2. **Database expert point of view**—Data redundancy is controlled, and the schema is optimized for effective and efficient data manipulation (data entry and retrieval) and fosters data consistency and integrity.
3. **Software development point of view**—The data types defined in the database match the data types of the programming language being used, and that database schema is appropriate for table joins to retrieve data from multiple tables.

Because the database schema should be evaluated from these three viewpoints, a group review is suggested. It also would be better to arrange for a guided group review, as it facilitates discussion of different viewpoints, resulting in these three types of experts coming to a common understanding.

Database design needs to be understood as a strategic activity in software development, as the rest of software development revolves around manipulation and processing of data that is stored inside the database. Therefore, verification using a guided group review that includes experts from the domain, database, and programming fields to the assure quality of database schema is recommended.

Database Validation

Most databases allow the writing of programs for data processing at the database level. These programs are called by various names, such as stored procedures, triggers, macros, etc. Database testing involves validating these programs as well as testing the backup, recovery procedures, and database application programming interfaces, if any. All software code (stored procedures, triggers, macros, etc.) needs to be subjected to software testing. Since each of these programs is a single unit and is accessed by the software independently, unit testing is the right type of testing for these programs, and they should undergo testing as detailed in Chapter 6.

APPENDIX I:
CODING GUIDELINES

SOME QUOTABLE QUOTES ON CODING

If debugging is the process of removing the bugs, then programming must be the process of putting them in.
—Edsger Dijkstra

Everything should be made as simple as possible, but not simpler.
—Albert Einstein

Writing compact source files that make full use of C's shortcut operators has been a test of manhood for many C programmers. Many C hackers and even some authors of C books will tell you that you have to use all of C's features and write compact but unreadable source files. This is not true: Writing obscure, tricky programs is good for a hacker's ego, but unnecessary and dangerous in serious programming projects.
—William Hunt

I like to think the whole program through at a design level before I sit down and write any of the code....The really great programs I've written have all been the ones that I have thought about for a huge amount of time before I ever wrote them....Part of our strategy is getting the programmers to think everything through before they go to the coding phase. Writing the design document is crucial....The worst programs are the ones where the programmers doing the work don't lay a solid foundation....I really hate it when I watch some people program and I don't see them thinking.
—Bill Gates

A great programmer loves to look at his or her own code and go through it....Greatness is the notion of always wanting to simplify, always thinking you can make it better, and really loving to look at your own code....There are some people who, once a thing works, won't go back and look at it— that's a crummy programmer.

—Bill Gates

INTRODUCTION

It is a common occurrence for programmers to leave a project or organization in the middle of a project; they do so for a variety of personal or professional reasons. When operating under such conditions, it is imperative that an organization have an established set of simple coding guidelines for each programming language so that the next programmer can continue the code where the first programmer left off. Without a set of coding guidelines, an organization would have to throw away the code written by a programmer who left the project.

The benefits of establishing a set of coding guidelines include the following:

★ It becomes feasible for a different programmer to enhance the code developed earlier.

★ The code written by programmers for one project can be reused by other programmers in a different project.

★ Software maintenance, which is inevitable, is much easier on code that has been developed using a set of guidelines than it is on code that was developed without adhering to any guidelines.

★ An organization needs to use multiple programmers in a software project, and coding guidelines assist the organization to achieve uniformity in the code produced by all its programmers.

★ Code that is written in adherence with coding guidelines can be used for training new programmers in writing maintainable and reusable code.

★ Coding guidelines ensure a minimum set of quality imperatives, including defect prevention and efficiency of execution inside the code.

SCOPE OF THE GUIDELINES

The coding guidelines in this appendix are general in nature and can be tailored to suit any programming language. In addition, the principles offered here are useful for any programming language. These guidelines can be used as an overall coding guidelines document, and all other documents on coding guidelines would contain only the exceptions to this document specific to a programming language. Unless stated otherwise in a specific programming guidelines document, an organization should follow the guidelines specified in this appendix.

CODE CONSISTENCY GUIDELINES

Naming Conventions

Naming conventions enable the person reading the code to distinguish among program-defined variables, table fields, file fields, constants, flags, counters, file names, etc. quickly and to effect necessary enhancements or fix defects.

Currently, most modern programming languages permit long variable names so that variables can be named meaningfully to reflect their function. However, long variables increase the statement length and reduce programmer productivity, as it takes more time to type longer names than it does shorter names. A balance needs to be struck between meaningfulness and brevity. The guideline is that a name must not be shorter than 5 characters and longer than 25 characters.

A three-character prefix is used to denote the type and origin of a name. It is suggested that a name be preceded by two or three prefixes. These prefixes are separated by an underscore character. If an underscore character is not permitted by the programming language, then the first character of each name segment should be a capital letter.

The following diagram illustrates the naming convention:

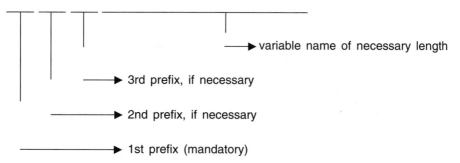

Table I.1. Sample of suggested prefixes

Code	Control	Code	Control
AVR	Alphanumeric variable	FLG	Flag
CHK	Check box	LBX	List box
CLS	Class module	LVW	List view
CMB	Combo box	MSG	Message box/dialog box
CMD	Command button	MTD	Method
CNS	Constant	NVR	Numeric variable
CTR	Counter	RBT	Radio button
CXN	Connection	RPT	Report
DGR	Data grid	SBR	Subroutine/subprogram
ERM	Error message	SCR	Screen
FGR	Flexi grid	TBL	Table
FLD	Table or data file field	TXT	Text box

Table I.1 lists some suggested prefixes and their meaning. These suggested prefixes do not cover the entire spectrum, and more prefixes can be added, depending on requirements.

It often might be necessary to abbreviate names in programs. In such cases, it is suggested that three characters be used when abbreviating names, as shown in Table I.2. Some examples of variable names are listed in Table I.3.

Table I.2. Sample of suggested name abbreviations

CUS	Customer	PWD	Password
EMP	Employee	SAL	Salary
ID	Identification	WST	Workstation
LOC	Location	QTY	Quantity
MAT	Material	AMT	Amount
PRJ	Project		

Table I.3. Sample variable names

Variable name	Explanation
txt_userid	Text box to receive user ID
cmb_prjname	Combo box to contain project names
lvw_matcodes	List view to contain material codes
tbl_projects	Database table containing project information
fld_prj_prjid	Table field in projects table with project ID
nvr_qty_stock	Numeric variable of quantity in stock
flg_arrayfull	Flag to check if the array is full
ctr_items	Counter to count number of items

If a project needs a different set of naming conventions or if the customer has specified a naming convention, the names should be recorded in the configuration management plan for the project and then used.

Formatting Source Code

Formatting source code improves readability and ease of understanding. Guidelines for formatting the code are as follows.

Identify the Main Statements and the Subordinate Statements

Whenever there are nested control flows (if, while, case, for, etc.), the subordinate statements are indented by moving the left margin of each subordinate statement one tab character length. The left margin of each subordinate level is moved to the right one tab. This is illustrated in the following example:

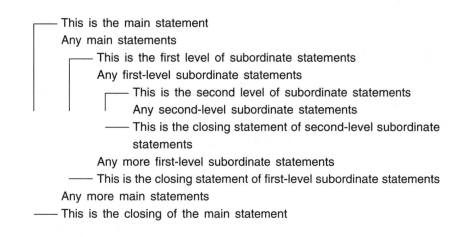

This helps programmers to correctly understand the program logic, the order of execution, and the control flow of the program.

Limit the Length of the Line Such That It Becomes Easily Readable

Modern programming languages permit longer line lengths—up to 255 characters per line. Similarly, modern visual display units also permit longer lines. The length of a programming line must be limited to the length of a line permitted by the screen. It should not be necessary to scroll horizontally to read the program. If longer lines are required, they can be broken down into multiple lines using the statement continue convention permitted by the programming language. However, the continuation lines must be treated as subordinate statements, as described previously, and their left margin must be offset one tab character length.

Separate Segments of the Code

Separating the code segments using separators makes it easy to understand the functionality of the program. The separator should be a commented statement. The following are some examples, using /* and */ as the beginning and ending commenting character sets:

```
/* Begin the case statement to select the appropriate category of the ticket */
/* End the case statement to select the appropriate category of the ticket */
/* Begin the loop for reading all the records in the table */
/* End the loop for reading all the records in the table */
```

INLINE DOCUMENTATION AND COMMENTING

The logic for each code segment needs to be explained using the commenting feature of the programming language, so that the people who will maintain the software later do not have a problem understanding the logic of the program. Every program should have the following inline documentation:

★ Each program should have a header. The header should contain the following:
  ☆ The name of the program
  ☆ The name of the organization that developed the program
  ☆ The date the coding began on the program
  ☆ The functionality achieved by the program
  ☆ References to calling programs and the programs called from this program, if any
  ☆ The revision history of the program, including the following:
    ★ The date of modification
    ★ The name of the programmer who made the modification
    ★ A description of the modification
★ Each control statement should have an explanation of its purpose and the expected results.

★ Each loop, especially those used for reading all the records from tables, should have an explanation at the beginning and at the end of the loop.

★ Each subroutine and subprogram should have an explanation of its purpose and of the parameters required by it. The expected parameters that are to be received as well as the values returned by them, if any, also should be explained.

Commenting Style

★ As far as possible, comment and code should not be mixed in the same line. The comment should precede the statement.

★ Keep the length of the commenting line to the length permitted by the screen. There should be no need to scroll the screen horizontally to read the comments.

★ As far as possible, do not spread the comment across multiple lines. Each commenting line should be self-contained. If more than one comment line is required, the # character should be used at the end of the previous line to indicate that the comment is continued on the next line. The following is an example of a two-line commenting statement:

```
/* Copyright = Company Name           # */
/* New York                  */
```

Program Header Example

```
/* Name of the organization                    */
/* Program ID/Name                             */
/* Original author = software development organization    */
/* Original creation date                      */
/* Parameter list                              */
/* Program explanation                         */
/* IPR rights belong to                        */
```

Example of Revision History Documentation

```
/* Revision history              */
/***************************************************************************/
```

```
/* Programmer    Date     Description of modification              */
/**********************************************************************/


/**********************************************************************/
```

Example of Loop Control Documentation

```
/* Purpose =          */
/* Entry condition =       */
/* Exit condition =        */
```

Special Inline Documentation

Whenever there is complexity in the code, especially when writing long computational statements or a procedure for complex decision making or mathematical processing, suitable inline documentation can be included.

Declaration Statements

Declaration statements are used to declare variables and other objects as necessary. The following are guidelines for these types of statements:

1. Declare only one variable or object for each line.
2. Code all declaration statements at the beginning of the program.
3. It is preferable not to mix declarations. Code declarations in groups in the following order:
   a. All integer-type numeric variables
   b. All single-precision floating point numeric variables
   c. All double-precision floating point variables
   d. All date type variables
   e. All alphanumeric variables
   f. All numeric arrays
   g. All alphanumeric arrays
   h. All database objects including connections and tables

DEFECT PREVENTION GUIDELINES

The way programs are written can leave loopholes that allow defects to creep in. The following are some guidelines that can plug loopholes and prevent defects from creeping in.

Control Statements

Computational statements are one source of defect injection. When control structures are not used with diligent care, the program execution might not go through the path the programmers assume it will, leading to erroneous results or failures. The following guidelines help to ensure that control structures are properly coded to prevent defects:

1. Using the right control structure will go a long way in preventing defects. Some guidelines for selecting the right control structure are as follows:

   ★ Use a "case" structure when multiple courses of action are available based on the result of one condition that results in multiple outcomes.

   ★ Use an "if" control statement when a set of statements has to be executed only once, depending on one or more conditions.

   ★ Use a "for" loop when the maximum number of iterations expected for the loop is finite.

   ★ Use a "while" loop when the maximum number of iterations for the loop is not known beforehand and is dependent on a condition. There are two kinds of "while" loops; one type checks the condition at the start of the loop, and the other type checks the condition at the end of the loop. It is preferable to use the loop that checks the condition at the start of the loop.

   ★ Avoid using the "goto" structure as much as possible for the following reasons:

      ☆ It leads to free-fall execution of the program, and it is difficult to predict the course of execution.

      ☆ If it results in the program closing, the programmer might not be able to control the cleanup activities before smoothly closing the program.

   ★ Ensure that a program has only one entry and one exit only. It is preferable that the same code segment has the entry point and exit point. The program execution control is exercised from this segment to other segments and finally exits from this segment.

2. When using "if" statements, the following precautions are necessary:

   ★ Always code the "else" part of the statement. We may not be able to see the possibility of program execution traversing the "else" part, but it can. The conditions in the field are always beyond our comprehension, and the unthinkable can always happen. Therefore, coding the "else" part of an "if" statement helps to prevent defects.

★ It might become necessary to nest several "if" statements in the program (that is, inserting another "if" statement within an "if" statement). In such cases, limit the number of subordinate "if" statements to a maximum of three levels: one main "if" statement and two subordinate "if" statements, totaling a maximum of three "if" statements in one nest. If it becomes necessary to have more levels, use a "case" structure, break up the program, or look at the program design again.

3. When using a "while" loop, ensure that the condition has a probability of becoming true (or false, as the case may be) so that there is an exit point for the loop. It is very easy to enter an infinite loop when using a "while" structure. This "while" loop is the one that is used to read the records from a file or table until the end-of-file condition is reached. It is easy to forget to move the record pointer forward in each iteration, which leaves the loop processing only one record infinitely.

4. When nesting the "while" loops, again limit the nesting to a maximum of three levels. It is preferable to call a subroutine for each nesting of a "while" loop than to code all the statements together at one place. By doing so, the code segment that contains the "while" loops would be easier to read and maintain.

5. When using the "case" structure, always code the "default" option (that is, when none of the values mentioned in the "case" structure is valid). This prevents free-fall execution of the program.

Computational Statements

Computational statements are used to resolve mathematical formulas. Long computational statements in particular are likely to inject defects in the program execution. One of the reasons is that the order of processing the arithmetical operators is difficult to perceive. Second, the results from the computation also are difficult to predict.

The following guidelines will help to prevent defects that arise from improper coding of computational statements:

1. One of the danger signs is if the denominator in a division operation becomes zero. This will lead to program failure. Worse still is if both

the numerator and the denominator become zero. When there is a division operator in an equation, check if the denominator is zero before performing the division. It is better to perform division on a stand-alone statement.

2. A problem with precision occurs when multiplying two or more quantities; check that the variable receiving the result is large enough to hold it. This issue can be prevented at the design stage by identifying the largest possible values that can be used in multiplication and providing variables of appropriate size both in the program as well as in the database for storage.

3. Writing long computational statements is conducive to injecting defects in the program. Use the following guidelines:

   ★ Limit the number of sets of parentheses to a maximum of three (that is, three opening parentheses and three corresponding closing parentheses).

   ★ Limit the length of each computational statement so that it is visible without having to scroll the screen horizontally. Instead of coding a long computational statement, break it down into multiple computational statements.

   ★ Code "arithmetic division operations" in separate statements as much as possible, and write a preceding statement that checks if the denominator is zero.

4. When mixing addition, subtraction, multiplication, and division arithmetic operators, do not assume operator precedence of the software. Use parentheses liberally. More importantly, place the addition and subtraction operations inside parentheses if the mixing of operators is imperative.

5. Division and sometimes multiplication operations that use floating point variables cause rounding problems. In such cases, two possibilities exist for prevention of defects:

   ★ Always round off to one or two more digits of precision than required, and before either presenting the result or storing it, round off to the required precision.

   ★ Carry out the operation using whole numbers, and convert these numbers to decimals by dividing by 100 (or 10, 1,000, 10,000, etc.) for presentation or storage purposes.

6. Duplication of routines is another common cause of errors injected into code. When the same operations are to be performed in multiple programs, some programmers code or duplicate the routine. It is

always better to code one routine and use it in all places by passing appropriate parameters to it. This protects the integrity of processing and prevents defects from creeping in.

7. As far as possible, do not use table or data file fields in computational statements, especially to receive results of a computation. Always copy the value of the table or data file field into a variable and then use it in computations. Similarly, receive the value of the computation into a variable and then move it to a table or data file field just before writing it.

8. When rounding off a value, code the statement on a separate line, just for rounding off the variable. Do not use the rounding function in combination with a computational statement.

EFFICIENCY GUIDELINES

The following efficiency guidelines help to ensure the efficiency of execution as well as economize use of computer resources, especially the RAM:

1. Do not declare any variables or constants that do not have a purpose. It is common practice among programmers to declare a number of variables, believing that they might be necessary in the program. Avoid the temptation to declare too many variables; even though the stringency on resource usage is now a thing of the past, occupying too much RAM is likely to slow down program execution.

2. As far as possible, declare variables as local to the program and use parameters to pass values to other programs or subprograms. When variables are declared as local variables, their RAM is released on exit from the routine. If variables are declared as global variables, they would hold onto the RAM until execution of the entire set of programs is stopped.

3. Open files (or database tables) only when required (that is, just before the file operation statements begin) and close them as soon as the file operation statements end. Opening a file or database table occupies a chunk of memory, and it takes the central processing unit time to keep checking the file status and condition. It also can prevent other users from concurrently accessing the files or tables.

4. Limit the number of objects that can be kept open concurrently, as they use large chunks of RAM, which slows down program execution.

5. Do not pack too many controls onto one screen. Instead, divide the screen into multiple screens. This reduces the burden on RAM usage.

6. As much as possible, do not print directly from the program. Program-controlled printing is not very efficient. When printing directly from the program, the printer functionality needs to be controlled to trap errors, such as "out of paper," "out of ink/toner," "out of power," etc. Otherwise, the printer might cause program failure. Unless printing a receipt or ticket that is needed immediately for a waiting customer, create print files that can be printed using the operating system's print utility, which is much more efficient.

EFFECTIVENESS GUIDELINES

The following guidelines help programmers to ensure that users use the software effectively:

1. In the case of bulk data processing applications, appropriate control statistics (such as number of records processed, records included in the report, control totals, etc.) should be generated on suitable media and delivered to the user.

2. When coding screens for user input and query, the background and foreground contrast must be significant to ensure easy readability.

3. Unless the client requests otherwise, the cursor on input screens should not move from field to field automatically, and when the end-of-field condition is reached, an audio signal can be generated to alert the user to the end-of-field condition.

4. Try to use more statements rather than a fewer number of statements so that the program is easily understood during software maintenance. Whether you code a complex single line or simple multiple lines, ultimately both will translate to machine instructions, and the number of machine instructions in both cases will almost be the same.

TAILORING THE GUIDELINES

These guidelines were prepared as a starting point for you to develop your own coding guidelines best suited for your organization. You can use these guidelines as they are given here, add to them, modify them, or remove some of them as it suits your purpose. I suggest that you have guidelines for code consistency, defect prevention, and efficiency and effectiveness aspects of writing programs as well as efficiency and effectiveness aspects during program execution.

APPENDIX J: SAMPLE REVIEW PROCESS

PURPOSE

This document defines the review process for implementation during execution of projects.

PROCESS DESCRIPTION

The following sections describe the review process.

TYPES OF REVIEWS

Two types of reviews are conducted in the organization:

1. Managerial review
2. Peer review

Managerial Review

A managerial review is conducted by the person who directly supervises the author of the software artifact. It is conducted prior to approving the artifact for use in the next stage.

Peer Review

A peer or a group of identified peers perform this review. The following persons are considered to be peers in terms of reviewing each other's work:

★ Team members
★ Software project manager and project leader
★ Group leader and program manager

The peers may or may not be drawn from the same project team as the author of the software artifact.

The following persons are not considered to be peers:

★ Software project manager and project leader for team members
★ Group leader and program managers for software project manager and project leader
★ Approving authority for any artifact
★ Direct supervisor for any person

This review methodology is used to uncover the defects and shortcomings in the software artifact.

CANDIDATES FOR REVIEW PROCESS

The possible candidates for the review process are listed in Table J.1.

MODE OF CONDUCTING A REVIEW

Two modes of conducting a review are approved for the organization: meeting review and postal review. These are described in the following sections.

Meeting Review

A meeting review is conducted in a meeting, where all the reviewers come together and conduct the review. The meeting is convened by the requestor of the review. The reviewers are identified by the author of the artifact in consultation with the software project manager or his or her supervisor. Selection of

Table J.1. Candidates for review

Software artifact	Type of review	Responsibility for arranging review
Proposal	Peer review	Marketing
Software estimation	Peer review	Marketing
Contract	Peer review	Marketing
User requirements specification	Peer review	Software project manager
Software requirements specification	Peer review and managerial review	Software project manager
Software design description	Peer review and managerial review	Software project manager
Project plans	Peer review	Software project manager
Induction training plan	Managerial review	Software project manager
Source code	Peer review	Software project manager
Project schedule	Managerial review	Software project manager
Work breakdown structure	Peer review	Software project manager
Unit test plan	Peer review	Software project manager
Integration and system test plan	Peer review and managerial review	Software project manager
Acceptance test plan	Peer review and managerial review	Software project manager
Corporate training plan	Managerial review	Head of human resources department
Standards and guidelines	Peer review and managerial review	Head of quality assurance department
Client-supplied documents	Managerial review	Software project manager

the reviewers is based on their suitability, availability, and convenience. This review can be a guided review in which the author presents the artifact and the reviewers give their feedback. Alternatively, the reviewers can discuss the artifact and give their feedback. The software project manager, in advance of the meeting, provides the identified reviewers with the following:

1. A copy of the software artifact so that the reviewers can come to the review prepared
2. The date, time, and venue for the meeting
3. An agenda for the meeting

The identified reviewers meet on the appointed date and time at the selected venue. Normally one of the reviewers is nominated to coordinate the collation of review feedback and to close the review report. The review coordinator collates the feedback given by the reviewers at the end of the review meeting and provides the review report to the author of the artifact. The author implements the feedback into the artifact, presents the implementation to the review coordinator, and arranges for closing the review report. The completed review report becomes part of the project records.

Postal Review

A postal review is conducted by the reviewers at their respective locations. This review can be conducted by one reviewer or by multiple reviewers. The author of the software artifact provides the identified reviewer(s) with a copy of the software artifact.

When a single reviewer is used, the reviewer provides the feedback in the form of a review report to the author of the artifact. The author implements the feedback and presents the artifact to the reviewer again. The reviewer verifies the resolution of the review feedback and closes the review report.

When there are multiple reviewers, a review coordinator is nominated by the software project manager to collate the review feedback and to close the review report. The reviewers submit their review feedback to the review coordinator. The review coordinator collates the feedback from the reviewers and provides the review report to the author of the artifact. The author implements the feedback into the artifact, presents the artifact to the review coordinator again, and arranges for closing the review report. The completed review report becomes part of the project records.

MEASUREMENT OF REVIEW PROCESS PERFORMANCE

The following measurements are carried out to assess the review process performance:

1. Defect removal efficiency of the review process
2. Relative effort spent on performing the review process for the project as well as the organization as a percentage of the total effort spent on software engineering activities
3. Cost for each defect uncovered in the review process in number of person-hours spent per defect

TAILORING GUIDELINES

Table J.2 lists the guidelines for tailoring this procedure to projects. Other review checklists are provided in Tables J.3 through J.7.

Table J.2. Guidelines for tailoring the review process

Topic	Tailoring guidelines
Fast-track projects	Will be executed as per the project management process
Software development projects	Nil
Software maintenance projects	Nil

Table J.3. Checklist for reviewing user requirements specification

Item no.	Item	Yes/No
1	Are the requirements in compliance with the contract?	
2	Have all the requirements been listed?	
3	Are there any ambiguous requirements?	
4	Is each requirement described completely?	
5	Have the requirements been specified consistently throughout the document?	
6	Can the requirements be verified?	
7	Has any additional functionality been included beyond the scope of the contract?	
8	Are project management requirements included in the requirements?	
9	Is the rationale for any derived requirements satisfactory?	
10	Are the specified external interfaces compatible?	
11	Are the user interface requirements complete?	
12	Can the requirements be tested? Can the requirements be used directly for validation during acceptance testing?	
13	Are the performance requirements adequate and feasible?	
14	Have the security requirements been determined?	
15	Do any requirements conflict with or duplicate other requirements?	
16	Is each requirement written in clear, concise, unambiguous language?	
17	Is each requirement free of content and grammatical errors?	
18	Are the time-critical functions identified, and are the timing criteria for them specified?	
19	Have internationalization issues been adequately addressed?	
20	Is the format in conformance with the format in the organizational process?	
21	Are all internal cross-references to other requirements correct?	
22	Do the requirements provide an adequate basis for software requirement specification?	
23	Have algorithms intrinsic to the functional requirements been defined?	
24	Is each requirement in scope for the project?	
25	Are all security and safety considerations properly specified?	

Table J.4. **Checklist for reviewing software requirements specification**

Item no.	Item	Yes/No
1	Does the software requirements specification follow the standards and guidelines stated in the project plan?	
2	Is the software architecture optimal for the platform used for implementation?	
3	In the case of products, have the following been specified:	
	a. System portability to other machines?	
	b. Interface with existing documents?	
	c. Interface with existing software and hardware?	
4	Does the design of the file or database take into account the following (wherever applicable):	
	a. Volume and organization?	
	b. Access methods (for flat file system)?	
	c. If indexed, is the index (unique/alternate/secondary)?	
	d. Record layouts?	
	e. Integrity checks?	
	f. Data domain (type, size, range)?	
	g. Security?	
	h. Normalization?	
5	Does the document identify components such as the following:	
	a. Reports?	
	b. Screens?	
	c. Programs and code components?	
6	Do command line procedures and job control procedures exist?	
7	Does the document give a complete and accurate description of external dependencies?	
8	Has the design been made flexible to meet future requirements?	
9	Is the design of the interface and coupling between modules complete? Is the coupling data based or process based?	
10	In the case of screen design, have the following been verified:	
	a. Are all input fields included in the screen layout?	
	b. Are derived data being captured on the screen?	
	c. Is the layout compatible with the input documents?	

Table J.4. Checklist for reviewing software requirements specification (continued)

Item no.	Item	Yes/No
	d. Are the field attributes specified for the screen consistent with the corresponding field type and length specified in the tables and files?	
	e. Is there any usage of special features of the screen design software?	
	f. Is the help facility context sensitive?	
	g. Does the screen design incorporate data validation for input fields?	
	h. Does screen navigation follow the organizational graphical user interface standards?	
11	Have all the validations specified in the user requirements been included?	
12	Are the error messages, warnings, and information messages adequate?	
13	Does the software requirements specification include the design selection rationale?	
14	Are the standard operating environments mentioned?	
15	Are the software operational procedures or references to them included?	
16	Does the software requirements specification include assumptions made?	
17	Does software requirements specification include risks factors?	
18	For reports, have the following been included:	
	a. Do the fields specified in the report exist in the database, or can they be computed?	
	b. Is the functionality specified in the user requirements specification covered in the report?	
	c. Are the report parameters specified?	
	d. Is the report sort order specified?	
	e. Are control statistics designed?	
19	Does the software requirements specification include procedures for security?	
20	Does it include procedures for audit?	
21	Does it include procedures for fallback?	
22	Does it include procedures for backup?	

Table J.4. Checklist for reviewing software requirements specification (continued)

Item no.	Item	Yes/No
23	Does it include procedures for data restore from backups?	
24	Does it include necessary manual procedures?	
25	Does it include archival policies?	
26	Have periodic processing procedures (for example, daily, monthly) been included?	
27	Have all interfaces between components been identified?	
28	Are the interfaces provided easy to use and consistent in format?	
29	Have all external user interfaces been identified?	
30	Would this document be adequate to be able to proceed with software design description?	
31	Has any additional functionality been included (exceeding the scope of the contract)?	
32	Are all requirements in the user requirements specification included in this document?	
33	Is any necessary information missing from a requirement? If so, is it identified as TBD?	
34	Is the expected behavior documented for all anticipated error conditions?	

Table J.5. Checklist for reviewing software design description

Item no.	Item	Yes/No
1	Do the programming specifications fulfill the program objectives?	
2	Have the common and shared functions been defined?	
3	Has each module of the software requirements specification been included?	
4	Have all the exception conditions been handled?	
5	Does the design conform to structured methodologies?	
6	Are there safeguards against data overflow?	
7	Can the program specification be easily coded?	
8	Have the loop termination conditions been properly taken care of?	
9	Do the nesting conditions conform to standards?	
10	Are the modules independent and self-sufficient?	
11	Are the test plans developed?	

Table J.5. Checklist for reviewing software design description (continued)

Item no.	Item	Yes/No
12	Are the screen layouts, report layouts, and table and file usage in the program specifications identical to those specified in the software requirements specification?	
13	Have the error messages been defined?	
14	Are the program specifications consistent with the software requirements specification process logic?	

Database Design Review: This section provides checks for the design of the database to ensure that the database design conforms to the standards.

15	Was each entity transformed into a table?	
16	Has each attribute been mapped to a field in the database table of the entity?	
17	Has each key field been mapped to an index?	
18	Have all foreign keys been specified NOT NULL (if applicable)?	
19	Are there any data integrity rules that violate the referential integrity rules of the relational database management system?	
20	Have the triggers, events, objects such as stored procedures and functions, and actions been defined where the relational database management system supports them?	
21	Do all the views have a valid purpose?	
22	Have the views that can be updated been correctly designed?	
23	Have the free space parameters been set depending on table size and table use? Has enough free space been specified?	
24	Have stored procedures been designed for frequently executed transactions?	
25	Have all the queries been analyzed to determine the most frequently used columns in the DISTINCT, GROUP BY, ORDER BY, and WHERE clauses?	
26	Have all the indexes created been used?	
27	Have the bottlenecks in meeting performance requirements been identified?	
28	Does the database implicitly provide for locking?	
29	Have time-outs for locks and sessions been optimized?	
30	Have the roles and schemas been adequately defined to address the security issues?	
31	Have privileges and authorities, data access control, etc. been implemented?	

Table J.6. Checklist for code review

Item no.	Item	Yes/No
1	Has the coding guideline specified in the project plan been adhered to?	
2	Is inline documentation adequate?	
3	Do naming conventions conform to the configuration management plan?	
4	Has code been properly formatted?	
5	Has a common set of routines been written without duplicating these routines in different programs?	
6	Is there any redundant or trash code?	
7	Has any label not been referenced?	
8	Have pointers been set to NULL if necessary?	
9	Does pointer arithmetic result in pointing to memory that is out of range?	
10	Are all the array indices within bounds?	
11	Are all the array indices correctly initialized?	
12	Are all the branch conditions correct?	
13	Do all loops terminate?	
14	Is the condition for terminating a loop realistic?	
15	Have the denominators in division operations been checked for zero before performing the division?	
16	Can any statements placed inside a loop be placed outside the loop?	
17	Are there any portions in the code that the thread of execution never reaches?	
18	Are "if" statements nested to more than three levels?	
19	Do the actual and formal interface parameters match?	
20	Are there any unused variables declared?	
21	Has the memory been correctly initialized?	
22	Has dynamic memory that has been allocated on entry been released at all exit points?	
23	Do queries on tables enforce the use of indices?	
24	Is error status checked after each structured query language statement?	

Table J.6. Checklist for code review (continued)

Item no.	Item	Yes/No
25	Is locking performed prior to updates where necessary?	
26	Have the following conditions been checked in expressions:	
	a. Rounding off?	
	b. Possibility of division by zero?	
27	Will the requirements of response time be met?	
28	Is there a better alternative for improving the response times?	
29	Have the following checks been performed:	
	a. Checks for empty table and file?	
	b. Checks for IO error?	
30	Are the error messages clear? Are the error messages adequate?	
31	Have all error conditions been trapped and handled?	
32	In arithmetic expressions, have the following been addressed:	
	a. Is the order of processing unambiguous?	
	b. Is there any need for horizontal scrolling to read the entire expression?	
	c. Are all parentheses properly closed? Do they ensure proper order of processing?	
	d. Is rounding off performed along with the expression?	
	e. Is division joined with another expression?	
	f. Does any expression use table fields or file fields directly in the expression?	
33	In relational expressions, have the following been addressed:	
	a. Are comparisons between the same types of data?	
	b. Is it possible to have more than two outcomes for any expression?	
	c. Does the expression serve the purpose for which it is used?	
	d. Is there any need for horizontal scrolling to read the entire expression?	
34	In logical expressions, have the following been addressed:	
	a. Does the logical expression serve the purpose for which it is used?	

Table J.6. Checklist for code review (continued)

Item no.	Item	Yes/No
	b. Does each relational expression used result in a true or false outcome?	
	c. Is each relational expression inside a set of parentheses?	
	d. At any given time, are only two relational expressions compared?	
	e. Is there any need for horizontal scrolling to read the entire expression?	
35	In file and table operations, have the following been addressed:	
	a. Are any files or tables opened much sooner than they are required?	
	b. Are any files or tables left open when the operations are completed?	
36	In variable declarations, have the following been addressed:	
	a. Do all the variables declared as global or static really need to be global or static?	
	b. Are there any declarations of unnecessary variables?	
	c. Would any variable name conflict with the key word of the programming language being used?	
	d. Is there any hard coding inside the code?	

Table J.7. Checklist for test plans and test cases

Item no.	Item	Yes/No
Test Plan Checklist		
1	Does the plan reflect the requirements?	
2	Have the acceptance criteria for acceptance test plans been specified?	
3	Is the test strategy adequate to uncover all defects?	
4	Is a test description available? Does the test description include the following:	
	a. Test objectives?	
	b. Test inputs?	
	c. Test outputs?	
	d. Test procedures?	
	e. Test sequence?	
5	Does each test plan list all test requirements, such as test schedule and resources for testing?	
Test Cases		
1	Does each test case specify the test condition, test procedure, and expected results?	
2	Have the results been recorded in adequate detail?	
3	Do test cases for field validations, record validations, and database updates include the following:	
	a. Valid conditions?	
	b. Invalid conditions?	
	c. Unexpected or unusual conditions?	
	d. Boundary conditions?	
4	Do the test cases for reports include the test data along with the expected output?	
5	Have all the business functions been included?	
6	Are business functions listed consistent with the description of equivalent functions in the software requirements specification?	
7	Have the criteria for each structural function been stated?	
8	Are all requirements traceable to test cases?	

APPENDIX K: SOFTWARE QUALITY ASSURANCE PLAN

The software quality assurance plan is one of the most important plans that should be prepared before embarking on a software development project. It is the project's charter for achieving quality in the project deliverables.

The following details are recorded in the software quality assurance plan:

1. **Standards**—Include coding guidelines, design guidelines, testing guidelines, etc. selected for use in the project. These standards ensure a minimum level of quality in software development as well as uniformity of output from the project resources.
2. **Quality control activities**—Proposed activities for the project include code walkthrough, requirements and design review, and tests (unit testing, integration testing, functional testing, negative testing, end-to-end testing, system testing, acceptance testing, etc.). Quality control activities ensure the necessary conformance to quality requirements in the project, especially to the three dimensions of quality: specifications (requirements), software design, and construction.
3. **Software metrics**—Metrics collected for the project define the desired level of quality for the artifacts developed for the project.
4. **Procedures and events that trigger causal analysis**—Include failures, defects, and successes.
5. **Audits**—To analyze the exceptions in the project so that necessary corrective and preventive actions are taken to ensure the exceptions do not recur in the project.

6. **Institute of Electrical and Electronics Engineers Standard 730**—Gives details on how to prepare a quality assurance plan, including a suggested template.

Each of these aspects is covered in greater detail below.

Details of the following standards should be included in the software quality assurance plan to guide project personnel in carrying out their assignments effectively and with the desired levels of productivity and quality:

★ Coding standards for the programming languages used in the project
★ Database design standards
★ Graphical user interface design standards
★ Test case design standards
★ Testing standards
★ Review standards
★ Organizational process reference

The following specifications of quality levels (quality metrics) for the project should be stated in the software quality assurance plan:

★ Defect injection rate
★ Defect density
★ Defect removal efficiency for various quality assurance activities
★ Productivity for various artifacts of the project
★ Schedule variances

The following quality control activities proposed to be implemented in the project should be included in the software quality assurance plan:

★ Code walkthrough
★ Peer review
★ Formal review
★ Various types of software tests that would be carried out during project execution, which at a minimum should include the following:
   ☆ Unit testing
   ☆ Integration testing
   ☆ System testing
   ☆ Acceptance testing

The software quality assurance plan should contain measurements for the defined quality levels, including their periodicity and trigger events. It also should include the vehicle for conveying to the stakeholders concerned the measurements taken, along with the baselines set for the project. Normally this would be the weekly status report for the project.

The plan should include the causal analysis that will be carried out for both positive and negative variances, as well as the schedule for the causal analysis. The methodology for causal analysis should be described in the plan or a reference to the organizational causal analysis procedure should be included in it.

It also should contain the schedules for the following audits proposed for the project:

★   Periodic conformance audits
★   Phase-end audits
★   Investigative audits (and criteria)
★   Delivery audits

The software quality assurance plan should state the proposed process improvement activities along with the trigger events or periodicity for such process improvement activities. It also should include the procedure for progress reporting to all concerned parties about the status of quality assurance activities implemented in the project. Figure K.1 presents a software quality assurance plan template.

Software Quality Assurance Plan
for Sample Project

Name of the Client

Revision History

Version no.	Date	Description of changes	Prepared by	Approved by
Draft		Initial draft	XYZ	ABC
1.0		First release	XYZ	ABC

Table of Contents

Figure K.1. Suggested software quality assurance plan template (page 1 of 5)

1. Introduction

1.1. Scope
Briefly describe the scope of the plan, the areas of the project addressed by the plan, etc.

1.2. Objectives
Describe the objectives of the plan.

1.3. Overview
Provide a brief overview of the project and the product.

2. References

Reference	Origin	Comments
	Client/project team/ organizational process/ IEEE standard/etc.	

3. Definitions and Acronyms
Describe any definitions and acronyms that are unique to the project.

Term/acronym	Definition/full form

4. Roles and Responsibilities
Describe the roles and responsibilities of the people who will perform quality assurance activities for the project and indicate approval authorities.

Figure K.1. Suggested software quality assurance plan template (page 2 of 5)

5. Standards and Guidelines

List all the standards and guidelines proposed to be used in the project.

Project area	Reference to applicable standard or guideline

6. Quality Assurance Activities

List all the quality assurance activities proposed for the project.

6.1. Proposed Reviews for the Project

List all the reviews proposed for the project for each type of artifact.

Project artifact	Type of review	No. and type of reviewers
Requirements documents	Guided walkthrough/postal review/ meeting review/managerial review	
Design documents		
Source code		
Project plans		
Test plans		
Test cases		
Test results		
Table scripts		
User documentation		
Operations documentation		
Other		

6.2. Proposed Testing Strategy for the Project

Describe the test strategy proposed for the project. Include aspects such as selection of testers, test environment, pass/fail criteria, testing completion criteria, regression testing strategy, usage of testing tools, test case design strategy, intuitive testing, etc.

Figure K.1. Suggested software quality assurance plan template (page 3 of 5)

6.3. Proposed Tests for the Project
List all the proposed tests for the project for each test unit.

Project test unit	Type of tests proposed	Test environment	Who will conduct the test	Pass/fail criteria
Program unit	Unit test/ integration test/system test/functional test/negative test/load test/ stress test/ acceptance test/other	Development/ environment/ test environ- ment/target environment/ other	Peer/project leader/software project manager/ testing team/ client/other	
Submodule				
Module				
Product				
Each customer release				
Product				

7. Metrics Proposed to Be Collected for the Project

List all the metrics proposed to be collected, with norms and permitted variance.

Metrics	Norm for the project	Permitted variance	Periodicity of reporting
Productivity		Percentage or absolute value	Weekly/monthly
Quality			
Schedule variance			
Effort variance			
Change			
Other			

Figure K.1. Suggested software quality assurance plan template (page 4 of 5)

8. Tools, Techniques, and Methodologies
Describe the testing tools, testing techniques, and methodologies adopted in the project for carrying out the quality assurance activities. If automated testing tools are to be used, then provide a reference to the user guides for the proposed tools. Methodologies for work allocation, progress reporting, test result evaluation, and completion of testing also can be described here.

9. Causal Analysis Proposed
Describe the causal analysis and defect analysis to be performed for defects unearthed during quality assurance activities. Also describe the events and threshold levels that trigger causal analysis.

10. Quality Assurance of Subcontracted/Client-Supplied Product
Describe the methodology to carry out quality assurance activities for the parts of the software that are to be subcontracted, if any, including the activities and tests to be carried out. Describe the activities to be carried out on client-supplied product, if any.

11. Training
Describe the training necessary for carrying out the quality assurance activities described above and the plan to carry out the quality assurance activities. If these topics are included in the introduction training program, provide a reference to that document.

Figure K.1. Suggested software quality assurance plan template (page 5 of 5)

APPENDIX L: ABBREVIATIONS

CD	Compact disk
CEO	Chief executive officer
CMM®	Capability Maturity Model
CMMI®	Capability Maturity Model Integration
CNC	Computer numerical control
COTS	Commercial off-the-shelf
CPQR	Composite product quality rating
DBMS	Database management system
DIR	Defect injection rate
DRE	Defect removal efficiency
EQAR	Effectiveness of organizational quality assurance activities rating
ETR	Exhaustiveness of testing rating
FP	Function point
GUI	Graphical user interface
IDE	Interactive development environment
IEEE	Institute of Electrical and Electronics Engineers
ISO	International Organization for Standardization
LOC	Lines of code
MTBF	Mean time between failures
MTTR	Mean time to repair
NC	Nonconformance
NCR	Nonconformance report
OER	Organizational environment rating

PL	Project leader
PRCR	Peer review coverage rating
QA	Quality assurance
RAM	Random access memory
RDBMS	Relational database management system
SCAMPI®	Standard CMMI Appraisal Method for Process Improvement
SEI	Software Engineering Institute of Carnegie Mellon University
SPM	Software project manager
TBD	To be determined
TPM	Total productive maintenance
TQM	Total quality management
UAT	User acceptance testing
UTCR	Unit testing coverage rating
Y2K	Year 2000

INDEX

A

Abbreviations for names, 312
ABC analysis, 290–291
Acceptance plan, 107
Acceptance testing, 72, 120, 147, 178, 291, 296–297
  readiness inspection, 107–108, 125
Aesthetics guidelines, 38, 39
Algorithms, 48, 87, 137
Alphanumeric data, 306
Alpha testing, 177
Ancillary functionality, 35, 36–38, 170
  verification of, 88
Antivirus software, 7, 176, 278
Appraisers, liability of, 225–226
Arithmetic statements, 48
Atarimae hinshitsu, 17
Auditors, 110, 122, 123, 236, 238
  auditing, 227
Audit process, 235–245
Audit report, 116–118, 214
Audits, 18, 34, 68, 69, 70, 71, 75, 86, 89, 110–124, 214, see also specific types
  best practices in, 123–124
  conformance vs. investigative, 113, 126
  internal vs. external, 122–123
  NCR, 110–112
  periodic vs. phase-end, 113, 115–121, 126
  process for, 125
  vertical vs. horizontal, 113
Automation, 11
  of testing, 183–186
Automobile industry, 8, 287–288
Average defect tardiness, 297–298

B

Bandwidth, 105, 169
Batch manufacturing, 8
Batch processing systems, 135–136, 138
Benchmarking, 31, 33, 34, 36, 64, 177
Best testing, 177, 183
Black box testing, 72, 136, 139–141, 165, 168, 180
Bottom-up approach to process definition, 201, 202, 204
Boundary value analysis, 154–155
Brainstorming, 27, 29, 38, 133
British Standards Institution Standard BS7925-1, 133
Browsers, 164–165, 167–168
Bug, 42
Build-and-improve prototypes, 132
Business analysts, 27

C

Capability Maturity Model (CMM®), 198, 220, 221, 226
Capability Maturity Model Integration (CMMI®), 10, 16, 49, 70, 73, 213, 215, 216, 219, 220, 221, 222, 224, 225, 226
  definition of institutionalization, 78
  definition of validation, 130
  definition of verification, 86
  QA department and, 18–19
Capacity specification, 26, 27
Central processing unit, 40
Certificate of compliance, 205, 213, 216
Certification, 23, 70, 122, 213, 215–216
  criticisms of maturity models, 221–227